Brit

In the new millennium Britain is changing rapidly. Global influences have created a more open but also more complex society, with a high degree of cultural diversity. At the same time the arts have become more central to everyday life, with both specialists and the general public joining the debate over their meaning and merit.

Exploring a wide range of areas including literature, film, television, magazines, sport and popular music, David P. Christopher observes and investigates key movements and issues, placing them in a clear, historical context. This creates a comprehensive introduction which allows students of British society to understand, study and enjoy a fascinating range of unique cultural materials.

This second edition of David P. Christopher's book offers a wider range of topics, and gives special emphasis to outstanding artists and developments in the field. The new edition features:

- fully revised and updated chapters
- new chapters on sport, newspapers and magazines
- authentic extracts from novels, plays and television series
- discussion of recent developments such as the greater commercialisation of cultural life and wider public participation through increased exposure in the mass media
- follow-up activities and suggestions for further reading to strengthen study skills.

This book is an engaging study of contemporary life and arts, and is essential reading for every student of modern Britain.

David P. Christopher is Subject Leader in English at the European Business School – London.

British Culture

An Introduction
Second Edition

David P. Christopher

Routledge
Taylor & Francis Group

LONDON AND NEW YORK

First published 1999
by Routledge
2 Park Square, Milton Park, Abingdon, Oxon OX14 4RN

Simultaneously published in the USA and Canada
by Routledge
270 Madison Ave, New York, NY 10016

Second edition published 2006

Routledge is an imprint of the Taylor & Francis Group, an informa business

© 1999, 2006 David P. Christopher

Typeset in Sabon and Frutiger by
Florence Production Ltd, Stoodleigh, Devon
Printed and bound in Great Britain by
Antony Rowe Ltd, Chippenham, Wiltshire

British Library Cataloguing in Publication Data
A catalogue record for this book is available from the
British Library

Library of Congress Cataloging in Publication Data
Christopher, David, date
    British culture : an introduction/David P. Christopher. – 2nd ed.
        p. cm.
    Includes bibliographical references and index.
    1. Great Britain – Civilization – 20th century.   2. Great Britain –
    Civilization – 21st century.   3. Popular culture – Great Britain –
    History – 20th century.   4. Popular culture – Great Britain –
    History – 21st century.   I. Title.
    DA566.4.C46 2006
    941.082–dc22   2005034722

ISBN10: 0–415–35396–3 (hbk)
ISBN10: 0–415–35397–1 (pbk)
ISBN10: 0–203–00016–1 (ebk)

ISBN13: 978–0–415–35396–0 (hbk)
ISBN13: 978–0–415–35397–7 (pbk)
ISBN13: 978–0–203–00016–8 (ebk)

Contents

Illustrations

Acknowledgements

This book describes some of the most significant features of cultural and artistic life in modern Britain. Such a work is indebted to a wide variety of descriptive and analytic texts, and some of those used in its compilation can be found in the sections on further reading.

A large number of people have made this second edition possible in different ways, and I would like to thank Ruth Cherrington, Chris Bishop and Dietmar Boehnke, who all provided useful comments and criticisms. I am also extremely grateful to all at Routledge for their commitment to the book, to Kristina Wischenkämper for her sharp eye and especially to Dr Eve Setch for her assistance, patience and enthusiasm beyond the call of duty. Finally, I would like to express my special gratitude to Nargis, who helped all along the way.

Photo credits

Photo illustrations are courtesy of:
Reuters/CORBIS (4.1), Thomas Barker (5.1), EON PRODUCTIONS/ Ronald Grant Archive (6.1), Ronald Grant Archive (6.2), Reuters/CORBIS (8.1), CARDINALE STEPHANE/CORBIS SYGMA (8.2), Bettmann/ CORBIS (9.1), The Tate, London 2005/The David Hockney Trust (10.1), David P. Christopher (10.2), Lamplight, Wakefield (10.3), Thomas Barker (10.4).
Every effort has been made to obtain permission to reproduce copyright material. If any proper acknowledgement has not been made, I would invite copyright holders to inform me of the oversight.

Introduction

For the student of British Studies, British Culture and Civilisation, English Philology, English, or merely the interested reader, there are many textbooks, journals and articles which analyse and comment on different aspects of cultural life: for example, the feminist novel, ethnicity in television soap opera, or the standing of BritArt. However, it is often difficult to acquire the basic knowledge on which the debates are founded without carrying out extensive research in books and articles which assume background knowledge, and which are mostly written for British-based specialists.

This book aims to meet that need by introducing the reader to the latest debates and developments in society and the arts, and linking them to selected texts and authors that have shaped British culture and society in the late twentieth and early twenty-first century. Thus, developments in language, journalism, literature, theatre, music, film, television, sport, art and architecture are presented together, in order to show how they have often mirrored social trends, and sometimes have contrasted with them in surprising and unexpected ways. In this respect the book presents a contextual history, which illustrates how different texts and practices from the UK connect to the broader patterns of social and cultural life.

To overseas students, the question of differences between 'English' and 'British' and the UK may be confusing. England, Scotland and Wales together constitute the island of Great Britain. The United Kingdom refers to Great Britain and Northern Ireland. 'British' is the nationality of people from the United Kingdom, and 'English' is the language predominantly spoken there.

A related matter is the question of what is meant by 'English', when referring to a particular subject area, for example, literature. Although textbooks on the topic refer primarily to the literature of England, they frequently extend their coverage to literature written in English from other home countries, for example, Scotland. They may also include literature written in English from Commonwealth countries, such as South Africa. The term 'English' is therefore used flexibly, but for the purposes of this book, the main focus is on texts and practices created by people in England, Scotland, Wales and Northern Ireland.

A similar question may arise over what constitutes a 'British' film. In order to receive government or lottery funding, there has to be 'substantial British involvement' in the sense of using British actors, crew and locations. But many other films considered to be quintessentially British are financed jointly between US and UK companies, for example the James Bond films are financed by MGM, Warner pays for Harry Potter, while the production company Working Title (which made *Love Actually*, *Bridget Jones* and *Billy Elliot*) is financed by Universal. As with literature, the main focus of the chapter on cinema is on films created in and about people in the UK, even though some or all the finance may be from elsewhere.

A separate issue is that any text about 'British culture' must immediately recognise the problematic nature of a concept containing numerous differences as well as similarities. Since the 1950s the expression and experience of cultural life in Britain has become fragmented and reshaped by the influences of gender, ethnicity and region. Moreover, early in the third millennium, with the gradual devolution of power to Scotland, Wales and Northern Ireland, it seems likely that regional cultural identities will be expressed more distinctively. This will inevitably lead to greater investment in regional arts and a stronger expression of locality in cultural life.

Precise definitions of the terms 'culture' and 'arts' have always been elusive and frequently elitist. However, current trends point towards a more inclusive notion of culture that embraces a broad range of texts and practices. This is reflected in public administration, with the government's own Department of Culture, Media and Sport, headed by its own Culture Secretary, as well as in arts criticism, with comment and reviews within the British media frequently appearing under the heading of 'culture'.

Furthermore, selection of material for this book does not recognise the misleading and dated distinction between 'high' and 'low' culture. The popular culture of the twentieth century produced an enormous number of highly talented writers, performers, directors, musicians and designers with a creative energy that made traditional forms seem staid and conservative. Thus, the old distinctions are less and less relevant to what is going on. Moreover, 'good' and 'bad' examples exist within all categories of arts, and while some examples are more easily accessible than others, this does not imply their inferiority.

The choice of material is obviously bound by a degree of subjectivity. Although there are important works and writers who have not been given the attention they might deserve, the choice here is not significantly out of step with the main trends of the period. Similarly, trends do not change simultaneously and any particular 'scene' is always plural and varied, with many earlier styles co-existing with more recent ones. But it is hoped that the reader will be aware of these inevitabilities and will consider the cited works, and read some of the suggested texts at the end of each chapter. In this way they can form their own opinions about different types of material, and their relevance to particular areas of critical and cultural interest.

Aims of the book

The main aim of this book is to provide readers with a map of the terrain: to offer signposts and co-ordinates to the people, places and events that make up substantial and evolving areas of cultural life, and from where they may go on to examine the broader, theoretical issues involved in their research.

A subsequent concern is the study of change. Many textbooks consider aspects of cultural life as if they were inert or static. But as the rhythms of social and cultural change continue to quicken, it is possible that, on entering the third millennium, we stand before a period of transition as fundamental as those of the late eighteenth and nineteenth centuries. This book reflects on the main changes that have taken place in the recent past and identifies the major developments taking place in Britain today.

Third, the book recognises the need to provide a historical context for its subject matter. This involves more than just a chapter on the cultural context created by recent social and political events. Such information is certainly necessary, given that students' knowledge of even relatively recent history may be limited. But it is also included because an important development in the recent study of culture has been the resurgence of historical analysis, which contributes to our understanding of society and the arts in the present. Therefore, the accounts and interpretations offered within most of the separate chapters are located within a historical framework.

A fourth aim is to give particular attention to changing expressions of ethnicity and gender in culture and the arts. The period under review has coincided with the break-up of the British Empire and an expansion in the Commonwealth, which have led to the immigration of people of numerous nationalities, languages, cultures and heritages, whose expression increasingly contributes to the themes and trends found in cultural and artistic life. Similarly, the second wave of the feminist movement, which started in the 1960s, has brought about fundamental changes in the position of women in society and their relations with men. This period has therefore witnessed the impact of social movements of race, ethnicity, multiculturalism and feminism, and their subsequent transition into the mainstream from the margins of cultural expression.

To the British reader, a fifth aim is to keep alive the increasingly short popular memory, to provide a 'defence against forgetting' where this is due to the regular inundation of images and news through the popular media, such as television, radio, newspapers and the internet. For readers outside Britain, the study of another culture may provide a useful comparison with one's own. It should be a liberating experience which improves understanding and imagination, and helps to provide new perspectives and thoughts.

The book is also intended to strengthen study skills, through follow-up activities and suggestions for further reading provided at the end of each chapter, for exploitation in pairs, small groups and individual research (see also 'Using this book' below).

Using this book

The book is designed to be flexible, for use either at home or in class, and can easily be adapted to the needs of particular courses. Chapters can be studied in a different order or omitted, as each one is written as an independent unit. However, the reader may find the first chapter on social and political change particularly relevant to an understanding of thematic chapters, since it provides a context for their study. A timeline, index and glossary are also provided to assist the reader.

For classroom use, it is suggested that teachers assemble their own archive of material to supplement the text, which can be developed and exploited according to the aims of the course, the level of the class, students' interests and so on. Material might include video recordings of films, plays and television programmes; audio recordings of music, radio news and reviews; as well as books, pictures and other visual aids. Photocopies of old newspapers also make interesting documents for exploitation in and out of class, and BBC television's Learning Zone offers another good audiovisual resource. Almost all the material mentioned in the text is available on video or sound recordings and is often broadcast on terrestrial and satellite television channels. Other material may be obtained from literary or pictorial sources (see below for more information), and sociology and media/cultural studies textbooks can also provide a rich source of contemporary material.

At the end of each chapter are various discussion topics and activities, which can be chosen and dealt with in class according to students' particular interests or needs. They may be used for subsequent projects or essays. Alternatively, it may be necessary to obtain more information before beginning a longer piece of work and some suggestions on further reading are provided in each relevant section.

Sources of information in British Studies

For the student beginning to explore a particular topic related to the study of Britain, there are a number of useful sources. Inevitably, the internet has become an essential tool which students and teachers can use to consult a variety of topics and terms. Major encyclopaedias, such as the *Encyclopaedia Britannica*, contain many relevant entries. Similarly, modern dictionaries, reference texts and online material provide useful sources, along with short lists of books and articles to guide further reading.

Students may wish to prepare a longer piece of work such as a dissertation, and for such research newspapers offer a wealth of information, especially the Sunday ones which contain many articles and reviews of cultural interest. The *Guardian, Independent, Observer, Telegraph* and *The Times* newspapers are the most important in this respect, and each produces an annual index of topics and names that have appeared in its pages that year. Newspapers from previous years are often held on microfilm or compact disc in many university and public libraries, and computers now allow rapid searches to be made. Students are always advised to read widely, as different newspapers may report the same stories in different ways.

With regard to other sources, such as books, films, plays and music, most if not all are easily obtainable from university or public libraries in Britain, or from larger bookshops. Films, television series and sound recordings are also available in video and compact disc format from many stockists, or on loan from the British Library (which incorporates the National Sound Archive), the British Film Institute, the BBC or the British Council. The scripts from many plays are also available from good bookshops.

Students should also become familiar with the main journals relevant to their field of interest. They usually appear three or four times a year, and the information and debates contained in them are usually more up to date than those in books, which take longer to write and publish. Although journal articles can be technical and difficult to understand for someone new to the field, many of the leading journals publish articles of general interest which are accessible to the reader with only a limited knowledge of the subject.

Finally, for selected statistical information on many aspects of cultural and social life in Britain, *Social Trends* and the *Annual Abstract of Statistics* are good starting points. They are both available from the government's publisher (HMSO) and appear every year.

Timeline

1939–45 Second World War

1944 The Butler Education Act greatly improves the opportunities for university education and social mobility among the post-war generation.

1945 Labour government elected. Churchill and Conservatives rejected.

1948 Labour introduces a new society based around a comprehensive welfare system, the nationalisation of key industries and free health care for all. The first immigrants arrive from the West Indies to help a growing economy.

1951 Conservative government elected. Festival of Britain takes place, the centenary of the Great Exhibition of 1851.

1953 The Coronation of Elizabeth II. *Panorama* current affairs programme starts on BBC.

1955 Tory government re-elected. Independent commercial television begins broadcasting. Rock and roll music comes to Britain in the film *The Blackboard Jungle*. Social realism predominant in literature, theatre and film.

1956 Egypt takes control of the Suez Canal, and Britain makes a politically embarassing withdrawal. Pop Art receives its first major exhibition, *This is Tomorrow*, at London's Whitechapel Gallery. John Osborne's *Look Back in Anger* opens at the Royal Court theatre in

London. 'Teddy Boys' increasingly reported in the press as a violent new youth culture.

1957 *The Uses of Literacy* by Richard Hoggart published, expressing anxiety over popular culture.

1958 Political dissent grows – the Campaign for Nuclear Disarmament founded. Race riots in Notting Hill.

1959 Tory government re-elected. Following a test case of the Obscene Publications Act, *Lady Chatterley's Lover* published in the UK, 30 years after D.H. Lawrence wrote it.

1960 National Service (military service) ended. The contraceptive pill introduced and made available from 1961. Gambling legalised. First episode of *Coronation Street* (ITV) broadcast.

1961 The UK applies for membership of the European Economic Community (now the EU). Political satire now well established in television and radio; *Private Eye*, a new satirical magazine, launched.

1962 The Commonwealth Immigration Act restricts immigration to the UK. The Beatles' first single *Love Me Do* released. Mick Jagger forms the Rolling Stones. The James Bond film *Dr No* released, starring Sean Connery.

1963 'Beatlemania' breaks out. The BBC ends its ban on mentioning politics, royalty, religion and sex in comedy programmes.

1964 Labour government elected with Harold Wilson as PM. 'Baby boom' peaks in the UK. The pirate radio station, Radio Caroline, begins broadcasting. Hysterical reports in tabloid press over youth subcultures Mods and Rockers. BBC2 begins broadcasting.

1965 Capital punishment suspended. The Who release *My Generation*. Rolling Stones' *(I Can't Get No) Satisfaction* Number 1 in USA. Cigarette advertising banned from British television. The Post Office Tower in London the tallest building in Britain. The Greater London Council established.

1966 England hosts and wins the soccer World Cup. Drama-documentary programme about homelessness *Cathy Come Home* shown on BBC and brings changes in the law. Student rebellion at the London School of Economics. First Notting Hill Carnival in London. Feminist movement gathers pace.

1967 The Abortion Law Reform Act allows legal terminations. Sexual Offences Act legalises homosexual acts between consenting adults over 21. First mass demonstration against the Vietnam war. Marine Broadcasting Act forces many pirate radio stations to close, while the BBC launches the new stations Radio 1, 2, 3 and 4. The Beatles release *Sergeant Pepper's Lonely Hearts Club Band*. *Rosencrantz and Guildenstern are Dead* by T. Stoppard. BBC starts transmitting in colour. The Purcell Room and the Queen Elizabeth Hall open at the South Bank arts complex. Celtic become the first British team to win the European Cup.

1968   Enoch Powell makes controversial 'rivers of blood' immigration speech. *Hair* musical opens in London. *Yellow Submarine* film opens; *2001: A Space Odyssey* (S. Kubrick). Theatres Act removes the need to license individual plays.

1969   Divorce Reform Act makes divorce easier to obtain. Capital punishment abolished. British troops patrol the streets of Northern Ireland. *Oh! Calcutta!* by K. Tynan. Gilbert and George begin as 'living sculptures'. Film *Kes* (K. Loach) released. Last public performance of the Beatles on the roof of the Apple Corps building in Saville Row, London.

1970   Tory government elected with Edward Heath as PM. *The Female Eunuch* by G. Greer published, to great acclaim by the movement for women's liberation, which holds a major conference at Oxford. Equal Pay Act introduced (not to take effect until 1975). The Beatles split up.

1971   The divorce rate remains low, with only 6 divorces per 1000 people. First women's liberation march. First Gay Pride march. *A Clockwork Orange* (S. Kubrick) released. *Jesus Christ Superstar* by T. Rice and A. Lloyd-Webber. *Bleak Moments* (M. Leigh). Metric 'decimal' currency replaces pounds, shillings and pence.

1972   *Cosmopolitan* magazine goes on sale in Britain. David Bowie releases *Ziggy Stardust* album to popular acclaim.

1973   UK joins European Economic Community (now the European Union). Ecology Party founded, and later becomes the Green Party. Glam rock at its peak. Skinheads youth subculture and football hooliganism. Independent local radio begins. *Not I* by S. Beckett. *Equus* by P. Schaffer. *Magnificence* by H. Brenton. *Freedom of the City* by B. Friel.

1974   Unemployment over 1 million, 16 per cent inflation. Coal-miners on strike. Three-day working week introduced to save electricity. Narrow election victory for Labour with Harold Wilson as PM. A repeat election held soon afterwards establishes Labour's majority. First summer solstice festival at Stonehenge.

1975   Economy in crisis with 1.25 million unemployed and inflation at 21 per cent. The Sex Discrimination Act and the Equal Pay Act introduced, aiming to end discrimination over offers of work and pay to men and women. *Pressure* (H. Ove). *No Man's Land* by Harold Pinter. *Love Thy Neighbour* (BBC). *The Sweeney* (ITV).

1976 Race Relations Act 1976 makes it unlawful to discriminate on grounds of race, colour, nationality or ethnic origins. Rock Against Racism movement. *Prostitution* exhibition opens at ICA. Independent Film-Makers Association formed. 'Punk rock' explodes on to the music scene.

1977 Queen Elizabeth II Silver Jubilee. Sex Pistols' *God Save the Queen* Number 1 in the charts. 55 per cent of women between 15 and 65 now in the UK labour force. Inflation down to 8.3 per cent

1978 Many strikes in public sector during winter, which the press call the 'winter of discontent' (after a line from the beginning of Shakespeare's play *Richard III*). The film *Jubilee* (Derek Jarman) released, a punk satire on the Queen's Silver Jubilee year.

1979 Margaret Thatcher elected Tory PM. Trade union membership peaks at 13.3 million. Privatisation programme begins with BP oil company. New, 'alternative' comedy shows appear. *Quadrophenia* (F. Roddam). Barbican Estate in London completed.

1980 John Lennon murdered in New York. *Inglan is a Bitch* and *Bass Culture* by L. Kwesi Johnson. *Romans in Britain* by H. Brenton. *Translations* by B. Friel. *Yes, Minister* (BBC) political satire.

1981 Around 3 million unemployed. Rioting in cities around Britain. Prince Charles and Diana marry. *Chariots of Fire* (H. Hudson). *Brideshead Revisited* (ITV). MTV launched. Salman Rushdie wins the Booker Prize for *Midnight's Children*. *Burning an Illusion* (M. Shabazz). *Maeve* (P. Murphy and J. Davies).

1982 War with Argentina over the Malvinas/Falkland Islands. *Boys from the Blackstuff* (BBC drama). *The Great Fire of London* by P. Ackroyd. New classification system for films introduced. *Gandhi* (R. Attenborough). *Pink Floyd – The Wall* (A. Parker). Channel 4 begins broadcasting. Annual WOMAD (World Of Music and Dance) festival begins.

1983 Tories win second election under Margaret Thatcher. *Waterland* by G. Swift. *The Last Testament of Oscar Wilde* by P. Ackroyd. *Educating Rita* (L. Gilbert). *The Ploughman's Lunch* (R. Eyre).

1984 Nationwide miners' strike in 1984–85. Turner Prize for contemporary art introduced. *Money* by M. Amis. *A Passage to India* (D. Lean). *Another Country* (M. Kanievska). *Territories* (I. Julien). *Spitting Image* (ITV).

1985   More rioting in cities around Britain. *Pravda: A Fleet Street Comedy* by D. Hare and H. Brenton. *A Room with a View* (J. Ivory). The screenplay of *My Beautiful Laundrette* by H. Kureishi is nominated for an Oscar. *A Room with a View* (J. Ivory). *EastEnders* (BBC). *Edge of Darkness* (BBC). Live Aid shows. Saatchi Gallery opens in London.

1986   London's Stock Exchange closes. Online trading begins. A three-year economic boom starts. The futuristic Lloyds Building completed (R. Rogers). *Einstein's Monsters* by M. Amis. *An Artist of the Floating World* by K. Ishiguro. *Insular Possession* by T. Mo. *Remembrance* (I. Julien). *Yes, Prime Minister* (BBC) political satire.

1987   *Serious Money* by C. Churchill. *Maurice* (J. Ivory). *The Belly of an Architect* (P. Greenaway). *Prick Up Your Ears* (S. Frears). *Sammy and Rosie Get Laid* (H. Kureishi and S. Frears). *Secret Society* (BBC/D. Campbell).

1988   Warehouse parties around Britain spread 'rave' music subculture. Warehouse show – 'Freeze' – in London's Docklands organised by Damien Hirst. *The Satanic Verses* by S. Rushdie leads to death threats against the author. *Inna Liverpool* by B. Zephaniah. *High Hopes* (M. Leigh).

1989   New satellite TV stations broadcasting to the UK. Acid House youth culture. *The Cloning of Joanna May* by F. Weldon. *The Remains of the Day* by K. Ishiguro.

1990   Thatcher resigns; John Major new Tory PM. Poll tax riots. An economic recession sets in until mid-1990s. *The Buddha of Suburbia* by H. Kureishi. *Racing Demon* by D. Hare. *Have I Got News for You* political satire panel game begins on BBC.

1991   First Gulf War. Canary Wharf Tower finished. *Murmuring Judges* by D. Hare. *Time's Arrow* by M. Amis. *The Famished Road* by B. Okri. *Life is Sweet* (M. Leigh). BBC World Service TV begins broadcasting. The 1991 Broadcasting Act exposes broadcasting to market forces.

1992   John Major leads the Tories to a third election victory. Department of National Heritage created. Church of England votes in favour of women's ordination. *Fever Pitch* by N. Hornby.

1993   *Trainspotting* by I. Welsh. *The Remains of the Day* (J. Ivory). Gaelic television begins broadcasting. Paul Ince is the first black footballer to captain England.

1994   Criminal Justice and Public Order Act is introduced to counter growing public disorder, despite strong opposition. The homosexual age of consent lowered from 21 to 18. *The Acid House* and *How*

Late it Was, How Late by I. Welsh. *High Fidelity* by N. Hornby. *Riff Raff* and *Raining Stones* (K. Loach). *Shallow Grave* (D. Boyle). *Bhaji on the Beach* (G. Chadha). Channel Tunnel rail link opens. National Lottery introduced, which contributes to arts and sport projects. Blur release *Parklife* and Oasis debut with *Definitely Maybe*.

1995 Disability Discrimination Act. *Michael Collins* (N. Jordan). *Land and Freedom* (K. Loach). *Braveheart* (M. Gibson). *The Madness of King George* (N. Hytner). *Trainspotting* (D. Boyle). D. Hirst wins Turner Prize for *Mother and Child Divided (1991)*.

1996 Euro '96 football tournament in England. Britpop reaches its zenith, with 2.5 million applications for Knebworth pop festival. *Out* first gay TV drama. *Propa Propaganda* by B. Zephaniah. *Jude* (M. Winterbottom). *Secrets and Lies* (M. Leigh). *Brassed Off* (M. Herman).

1997 Labour government elected, Tony Blair becomes PM. Princess Diana dies in car crash. Hong Kong returned to China. *The Full Monty* (P. Cattaneo). *About a Boy* by N. Hornby. *Bridget Jones's Diary* by H. Fielding. *Mrs Brown* (J. Madden). *Nil by Mouth* (G. Oldman). Success of the exhibition *Sensation* confirms high levels of interest in new British art. In television, Channel 5 begins broadcasting.

1998 Belfast ('Good Friday') Agreement in Northern Ireland results in Northern Ireland Assembly elections. *Angel of the North* sculpture (A. Gormley); *England, England* (J. Barnes); *My Name is Joe* (K. Loach); *My Son the Fanatic* (U. Prasad). Introduction of digital television. Media talk of 'Cool Britannia' following a wave of successful, distinctively English creative projects in mid-1990s.

1999 The first Scottish Parliament since 1707 elected. National Assembly for Wales and Northern Ireland Assembly assume devolved powers. House of Lords Act reduces number of hereditary peers entitled to sit in Parliament from over 750 to 92. A former High Court judge finds 'institutional racism' in the Metropolitan Police.

2000 Millennium Projects around Britain. In London, the Dome is the focal point. *Big Brother* 'reality show' launched. Ban on homosexuals in the armed forces lifted. The homosexual age of consent lowered to 16.

2001 Second election victory for the Labour Party under Tony Blair. Terrorist attack on the twin towers in New York, now known as 9/11. A new 'morning after' pill (a female contraceptive) made available in shops. The government takes military action in Afghanistan.

New comedy series *The Office* shown on BBC2 to popular acclaim. BBC Director General Greg Dyke describes the BBC as 'hideously white'.

2002 Immigration and Asylum Act. The House of Lords passes measures allowing gay couples to adopt children. Gurinder Chadha's low-budget film *Bend it Like Beckham* is a major commercial success. Commonwealth Games held in Manchester. Queen Elizabeth's Golden Jubilee celebrates a 50 year reign, with celebrations around the country. Princess Margaret (sister of Queen Elizabeth) and the Queen Mother both pass away after short illnesses.

2003 Invasion of Iraq. Anti-war march the largest ever, with some 2 million people on the streets. England wins Rugby Union World Cup. The M6 Toll Road is the first private motorway in the UK. Popular 'reality' television shows *I'm a Celebrity – Get me Out of Here!*, *Pop Idol*, and *Fame Academy* attract huge audiences.

2004 First citizenship ceremony in the UK – new citizens take the traditional oath of allegiance to the Queen and pledge to uphold UK democratic values. Gender Recognition Act 2004 gives transsexual people the right to seek legal recognition in their acquired gender. The Higher Education Act 2004 introduces variable tuition fees from 2006. *The Office* wins the award for the best comedy at the Golden Globes in America. Fiftieth anniversary of the publication of the first two parts of J.R.R. Tolkien's epic *Lord of the Rings* trilogy. UK première of *Harry Potter and the Prisoner of Azkaban*. Liverpool awarded UNESCO world heritage status.

2005 Labour Party wins historic third term under Tony Blair. Suicide bombers attack London in July. Freedom of Information Act brought into force establishing a public right of access to information held by public bodies. Civil partnerships approved for same-sex couples. Fox hunting made illegal. Prince Charles remarries.

1

The social and cultural context

Introduction

Since the 1950s, Britain has experienced a period of accelerated social and cultural change. This has coincided with the disintegration of the British Empire, the expansion of the Commonwealth, and the immigration of people of numerous nationalities, languages and cultures, producing a multi-ethnic country with a plurality of identities and heritages.

The social and cultural profile has been transformed not only by Britain's diverse ethnic communities, but also by the women's movement. The entry of women into the labour market and their increasing independence has brought about fundamental changes in their position in society, and their relations with men. Similarly, the emergence of youth as an identifiable group with a lifestyle different to that of members of an older generation has helped shape the characteristics of the country since the mid-twentieth century.

The impact of ethnicity, feminism and youth in Britain has been felt across the arts, as from 1948 successive governments provided funds through the Arts Council to encourage experimentation and even counter-cultural styles of expression. This continued until the election of the Conservative government in 1979, which marked an important turning point. 'Thatcherism' marked the greatest political, economic and cultural shift in Britain of the twentieth century. The consensus politics of the post-war era disappeared, and the country became politically polarised between the Tory Party and its free-market economics and the political left with its socialist ideals of nationalisation, high rates of taxation and attempts to redistribute wealth. State subsidies and benefits for the arts were replaced with a 'culture' of individualism, private enterprise and the values of the market place in almost every area of society, and government funding was reduced or disappeared. The arts were treated as any other business; plays, films and exhibitions were seen as products for consumption by consumers in a competitive market place, while it was left to a DIY culture of improvisation and home-brew to create challenging new works outside the mainstream.

By the mid-1990s the Conservative government was suffering from weak leadership, profound internal divisions and corruption among its leading members. There was enthusiasm for change, and the victory of the Labour Party in May 1997 provided the country and its cultural life with a new sense of self-confidence. In the years that followed there was a period of relative prosperity and stability, characterised by record levels of low unemployment, low inflation, rising living standards and investment in public services. However, the socialist ideology that had previously both characterised Labour Party policy and inspired some of the most challenging cultural works was abandoned, as the party redefined itself and adapted its manifesto to the needs of the late twentieth century.

The changes in society were mirrored in an increasing commercialisation of the arts. The spread of business values in their production and management became the norm, as practices once found only in the private sector came to be fully expressed in most areas of the economy. At the same time, the new cultural spaces created by black, Asian and feminist writers and artists, which were once considered marginal or even subversive, became absorbed into the mainstream as society became more tolerant, plural and diverse.

New society (1945–60)

Economy, politics and society

At the end of the twentieth century Britain bore little resemblance to the country in 1900, when for most of the people most of the time there had been terrible poverty and social inequality. Food was scarce for many years, and in 1926 there had been mass unemployment, a General Strike and hunger marches from the north-east to London. Most British houses had no bathroom or indoor toilet, people left school in their early teens, and there were no pensions, health service or social insurance. There was little government intervention until 1945, and most areas of the economy were left to private enterprise.

However, despite the distractions of wartime and perhaps because of them, there was a new aim to achieve equality and progress in key areas of the economy such as health, education, transport and housing, not with private enterprise, but with centralised planning by experts along rational, scientific lines.

2

Sir William Beveridge chaired a committee which reported back in 1942. In a key passage of the report Beveridge wrote: 'Want is one of only five giants on the road to reconstruction and in some ways it is the easiest to attack. The others are Disease, Ignorance, Squalor and Idleness.' Paradoxically, modern British politics are still concerned with finding solutions to similar problems, but in 1944 a new plan to reform education was introduced to wage war on 'ignorance'. The 1944 Butler Education Act made education free of charge in state-maintained grammar schools for children aged 11–18, as long as they passed the '11-plus' examination at age 11. This was a key measure in ensuring greater access to education and social mobility for children from poorer families, giving them the same opportunities to reach university as those from more privileged backgrounds.

The Beveridge Report became a manifesto for change in the country, and after the end of the war the people of Britain demanded it. After six years of fighting fascism, industry was in ruins, homes were destroyed and many people struggled to survive. The Tory government led by Winston Churchill was firmly rejected in favour of a Labour Party led by Clement Attlee, who introduced ambitious plans for a more equal and open society. Central to this was the promise to 'wage war on want', as the main parties agreed the state could and had to provide jobs, homes and decent living standards, in a way that it had never done before.

One of the first steps towards reform was the nationalisation of all key industries, such as coal, transport, iron and steel, to secure mass employment. Then in 1948 the 'welfare state' was set up, which provided social security and healthcare free of charge to all citizens. The measures were a brave attempt to build the 'new Jerusalem' and overcome the poverty of generations, in which people of all classes, incomes and colours would be cared for by the state 'from the cradle to the grave'.

Abroad, reform continued with the gradual dissolution of the British Empire, which had begun with the granting of independence to India in 1947. But despite the progress made on many fronts, it was still a time of austerity, with queues, shortages and inconveniences. The generation which had won the war also wanted fun and consumerism, both of which the government had conspicuously failed to deliver. Consequently, despite some of the most progressive social measures ever introduced in Britain, the Labour government was rejected in the election of 1951. The incoming Tory Party continued the tradition of post-war patrician government; it governed not only in the interests of landowners, factory owners and other business people, but in the interests of society as a whole. This way of managing society became known the 'post-war consensus', and characterised the way in which the country was governed by both main parties until the late 1970s.

In 1951 the Festival of Britain was organised to improve national morale. It marked the centenary of the Great Exhibition of 1851, held in London's Hyde Park to celebrate imperial achievements. It was a rare

3

moment of national self-expression, with parties, parades, speeches and optimism. It was a modest beginning to a decade in which crime rates fell, production rose and consumerism increased. Average industrial earnings rose by 34 per cent between 1955 and 1960, and with their new prosperity many ordinary people were able to discover cars, fashions and foreign holidays. Greeting this new wave of prosperity, Tory Prime Minister Harold Macmillan announced in 1957 that '[British] people have never had it so good' which was particularly true of the young, white working-class.

Immigration

Britain's economic growth created high levels of demand for manual labour in low-paid areas of work such as transport, health, and catering. There was a labour shortage, and the British municipal authorities began to offer jobs to Commonwealth citizens in the West Indies, India, Pakistan, Africa and Hong Kong. MPs from the two main parties went to the Caribbean territories on a recruitment exercise, and on 21 June 1948, the ship *Empire Windrush* docked at Tilbury, to the east of London, bringing 492 Commonwealth citizens to Britain. As the country attempted to rebuild its shattered economy, many found work in the newly nationalised essential industries, such as the health service and railways, as well as in important manufacturing sectors such as textiles and automobiles.

The initial motive for coming to Britain was often for the male head of the household to work and save money, before returning home to the country of origin. But economic realities meant that within a few years, the family and relatives were coming to Britain to join their menfolk. However, the process of immigration did not go smoothly. Britain was a strange, cold, alien country compared with the ones they had left behind, and large communities were established for support and friendship in poor, inner-city areas where housing was cheap. Many had to accept jobs for which they were overqualified; medical staff were cleaning hospitals, bus drivers were cleaning the streets. The presence of immigrant communities also disturbed the local population. Daily lives began to change, and as immigration increased, race became a source of social conflict. Prejudice and discrimination from employers, workmates and landlords became a regular feature of the immigrant experience, and several areas became the focal point for racial tensions, most infamously the Notting Hill area of London, where rioting broke out in 1958.

While immigration was mostly a working-class concern, middle-class worries centred on the increasing danger of nuclear war. Britain had successfully tested a nuclear bomb in Australia in 1953, but there was a strong feeling among the political left that the country would be safer without such weapons. A group of leading writers, musicians, artists and others formed the Campaign for Nuclear Disarmament, some of the

4

founder members including the philosopher Bertrand Russell, the composer Benjamin Britten, the sculptor Henry Moore, the historian A.J.P. Taylor, and the novelists E.M. Forster and Doris Lessing. At Easter in 1958, some 5,000 protesters marched from London to Aldermaston, the site of a nuclear research establishment. Bands and folk singers accompanied a mixture of pacifists, Christians, trade unionists, young parents and children. The movement captured the public imagination and became increasingly influential. The following year some 50,000 took part, and the march became not just an annual event, but marked the beginning of a trend towards popular, organised protest that has since become a common feature of the political landscape.

The debate about popular culture

The marches at Aldermaston were the tip of a much larger iceberg, in a decade which witnessed the disappearance of deference to authority among many young people. Among the middle classes this manifested itself as organised protest, but among the working classes as the more sinister spectre of rising criminality.

Due to the post-war 'baby boom', by the late 1950s the average age had dropped sharply, and by 1959 there were over 4 million single people aged between 13 and 25. Society was younger; it was also richer and more image-conscious. During the 1950s electronic goods such as televisions, small radios and record players had become cheap and widely available, and by 1960 most homes contained at least one. Cultural material was increasingly created for mass audiences in the form of television programmes, popular music and films. The sale of popular novels, women's magazines, sensational newspapers and comics also increased to meet demand for light entertainment. Moreover, with full employment, it was easy to achieve financial independence at an early age, and businesses began to market their products to teenagers who now had enough money to create a new world of their own, a 'youth culture'. Coffee bars and 'melody' (music) bars opened, providing meeting places for a generation with money to spend on leisure and pleasure. Record players and radios and clothes were essential equipment in this increasingly classless youth culture.

A young generation was emerging and they were avid consumers of the new commercial culture. One of the most visible signs of change could be seen around 1953 with the appearance of 'Teddy Boys', urban working-class gangs dressed in colourful suits. Their behaviour was said to be threatening and brutal, and there were frequent newspaper reports of violent confrontations. The mass media began to report incidents involving the 'Teds', and presented a shocking image which frightened people and succeeded in its aim of selling many newspapers.

Although unemployment was low, crimes by offenders under 21 rose from around 24,000 in 1955 to over 45,000 in 1959, prompting frequent

5

debates about the relationship between affluence and crime. The influence of television was often blamed, especially the content of the newly created commercial television, with its adverts, game shows and other cheap, populist programmes, as well as the negative influence of rock 'n' roll music with its suggestive rhythms and lyrics.

While politicians had generally ignored the new commercial culture, social commentators and academics were concerned about the mass consumption of films and music that had been created simply to make profits. They believed that if standards and quality in the arts fell, so would standards of education and behaviour in society. The study of crime had previously been concerned with individual pathology and levels of intelligence, as well as the notion that poverty could be a contributing factor. But the idea that *affluence* could contribute was difficult to appreciate. Like many earlier critics, such as Matthew Arnold and T.S. Eliot, F.R. Leavis argued that great works of art carried a moral, civilising message, which was educational, and served to improve the individual and society. But the mass-produced forms of music, art and popular entertainment did not and could not do this, and only encouraged individualism, hedonism, laziness and decadence.

In contrast, supporters of 'traditional' moral standards preferred to focus their attention on what they saw as the rapid decline and commercialisation of culture. They blamed rising rates of divorce and abortion on growing equality and law reforms, while increases in juvenile crime, violence and sexual promiscuity were blamed on a lack of discipline and the availability of the contraceptive pill. However, studies showed that the sexual behaviour of young people in fact changed very little, and that it was stories circulating in increasingly competitive and sensationalist newspapers which tried to frighten people and sell copies by suggesting otherwise.

Anxiety over the spread of popular culture produced several influential books which pontificated over the probable consequences. In *The Uses of Literacy* (1957), Richard Hoggart argued that the absence of moral content in popular literature and the arts made it more difficult for the ordinary person to become educated, wise and cultured. In *The Long Revolution* (1961) Raymond Williams considered the collective, social consequences, believing it would lead to an increase in materialism and self-interest, a reduction in the importance of the social services such as education and health, and a less radical, more individualist Labour Party. But he also believed that the negative effects could be combated with education and strong, left-wing government.

In spite of the worries about moral decay and cultural decline, by the end of the 1950s the consumer society had become firmly established, and society was about to be transformed. Its ethic of individualism and pleasure-seeking contrasted sharply with the collectivism and austerity which marked the beginning of the decade.

Progress and pop (1960–70)

Economy, politics and society

In spite of the material gains of the 1950s, by the mid-1960s there was a feeling of disappointment with a Conservative Party that had been in power for 13 years. The country had changed greatly, developing into a dynamic consumer society, but the old-fashioned speech, manners and dress of the figures of authority identified them with a much earlier age. The party had also begun to appear disorganised and out of touch with politics and people. In the mid-1950s there were stories of top civil servants defecting to Russia. In 1956 there was a major government failure in the handling of the Suez Canal crisis, which resulted in a brief war and an embarrassing retreat. Later in 1963 the Minister for War, John Profumo, resigned from government after admitting he had lied to Parliament about his affair with a prostitute. As a result, the public was beginning to lose respect for the government, its institutions and the ruling class.

In 1964 a Labour government won the election with Harold Wilson as its leader. With the rapid advances in science and industry, the Prime Minister famously spoke of 'the white heat of the technological revolution', and, with a television in nearly every home, the new revolution could be seen by all. There was a consumer boom and rising aspirations. Demand grew for secretarial, clerical and administrative skills, creating posts which were frequently taken by women. A commercial mass media, supermarkets, and tall, modernist apartment blocks all became part of everyday life.

But in spite of material improvements in the quality of life, dissent flourished. Numerous groups began to demand new freedoms – political, economic and personal – as rights. The government responded with a retreat from strict social controls and punishments, many of which had been introduced in the Victorian era. Capital punishment was suspended in 1965 and never returned, and criminal law was reformed in areas affecting private morality such as obscenity, homosexuality, abortion and gambling. In 1960 gambling was legalised, and many betting shops, bingo halls and clubs appeared. Homosexuality was legalised in 1967, and in 1969 eighteen-year-olds were given the right to vote, nine years after the abolition of compulsory military service.

But not everyone approved of the changes which the 1960s brought. The Church of England, other Protestant churches, and the Roman Catholic churches remained firmly traditional, but their influence gradually declined. Similarly, the political right opposed liberal reform, and when economic growth began to slow down around 1966 immigration was made a controversial issue, with the Conservative politician Enoch Powell encouraging anti-immigrant sentiments. With almost half a million West Indians in Britain, in a speech to the Conservative Party Conference in October 1968

Powell warned that integration was impossible. In another speech in Birmingham the same year, his inflammatory rhetoric used lines from an epic poem by Virgil, 'Like the Roman, I see the River Tiber foaming with much blood', a stance which was to be exploited by racist organisations such as the British National Front. Although he was sacked from the shadow cabinet by the party leader Edward Heath, it was a sharp warning of the increased polarisation of society that would characterise Britain in the 1970s.

But significant advance was achieved in the position of women. The style and ideology of the British women's movement was modelled on the movement in America, which in turn had modelled its style on the tactics of the American black liberation movement. Tactics included marches, sit-ins and strikes. But legislation was gradually introduced giving women the equality and rights for which they had fought. In 1967 the Abortion Act permitted legal terminations for social and health reasons. The same year, the Family Planning Act enabled women to obtain contraceptives through the National Health Service. These included the oral contraceptive known as 'the Pill', which became available free of charge from 1974. Before this time, women had had to rely on men with condoms, or simply trust their luck. Divorce was also made easier with the Divorce Reform Act of 1969, allowing women to break away from violent and abusive relationships.

Before the advances of the 1960s many women's lives were conditioned by their reproductive abilities. But on taking control of their fertility, they could begin to control their lives. They could decide if they wanted to become wives and mothers, or if they wanted to plan or postpone family life to fit in with their jobs. These measures helped to ensure that another 'baby boom' similar to that of the late 1940s would be unlikely.

As well as demands for more personal independence, the 1960s also witnessed demands for greater regional autonomy, as Scottish, Welsh and Irish nationalists all began to demand political freedom. In 1968 there were riots in Northern Ireland where the Civil Rights Association demanded equal treatment for Catholics and Protestants. In 1969 the British government sent troops there to keep order on the streets, where they remained into the twenty-first century.

Most people, however, regarded the changes as positive. Before the 1960s it was rarely possible to challenge the decisions taken by the police and magistrates. There was capital punishment. Theatre censorship was implemented by former military gentlemen with an office in St James's Palace. Gay men were often blackmailed, as homosexuality was a punishable offence. In schools there was beating and caning, and secret files were kept on students. The position of women was particularly unjust and often precarious as there were no equal rights in law. Divorce was difficult to obtain, and required witnesses to sexual misbehaviour. Contraception was not easily available, and there were dangerous illegal abortions that often went wrong. Single mothers and the children of the very poor were routinely separated from their parents, as were the blind and disabled. However, by the early 1970s all that had changed.

Anger and division (1970–79)

Economy, politics and society

In 1970 a Conservative Party was returned to power with Edward Heath as its leader. In contrast with the optimism and hedonism of the 1960s, it was the beginning of a dark decade marked by social division, strikes, high inflation, unemployment and political violence. The period was also marked by steep immigration: between 1968 and 1974 a final, major phase took place when over 70,000 Kenyan and Ugandan Asians arrived as refugees, and by 1974 there were over 1 million black and Asian immigrants in Britain. Racial tension increased in the major cities, where the National Front had begun openly to provoke black communities and their supporters. Conflict intensified following the 'Spaghetti House siege' in 1975, when three Afro-Caribbeans attempted a robbery and took hostages in a restaurant in the Brixton area of London.

The National Front was able to exploit the growing tension, and for a short time it became the third party in British politics, beating the Liberal Party in several contests. Then the Irish Republican Army (IRA) began a bombing campaign in several British cities, as not only Irish, but also Scottish and Welsh Nationalist parties began to make their demands felt.

Economists debated the reasons for persistent economic failure. The long-term decline of mining, shipbuilding, steel production and motor vehicle manufacture were all seen as significant. Heavy industries were no longer competitive in global markets. The resistance of the trade unions to industrial change, the tendency of management to think and plan only for the short term, as well as high rates of inflation and the oil crisis of the mid-1970s, were all blamed. In contrast, sociologists put forward the reasons for social disorder, crime and violence. Many concluded they were inevitable consequences of growing economic inequality, and would worsen without more extensive socialism, public ownership of the major industries and greater redistribution of wealth.

The Tory (Conservative) Prime Minister Edward Heath had been unable to steer the economy effectively through troubled waters, and in 1974 with inflation at 25 per cent and prolonged strikes by the mineworkers' union, the lights went out around the country in a series of national power cuts, which quickly forced an election. The result showed a narrow victory for the Labour Party with a minority government. Its leader Harold Wilson was able to settle the miners' strike, and in a second election the same year Labour won with a small majority. But high oil prices left the economy depressed. The trade unions were strong and well organised, and as the economic crisis worsened there were rumours of a communist plot to take

9

over the Labour Party. Political tension increased as International Marxists became more numerous, and various anarchist groups were visible, vocal and violent.

Towards the end of the decade social fragmentation across Britain was increasingly obvious, as nationalism, terrorism, strikes, violent crime and football hooliganism all indicated an end to an extraordinary, and unprecedented period of social solidarity and consensus that had characterised the UK since 1945. The tension was amplified by the popular press, as the *Sun*, the *Daily Mirror* and others carried sensational stories about racial violence, robbery, football hooliganism, pornography and rape. Punks appeared on streets around Britain, their shocking appearance reflecting a sense of disgust with a society which seemed to have abandoned its youth and its future. Amid a background of political polarisation at home and new international challenges abroad, it seemed no party could govern effectively. Confrontation appeared to be everywhere, and towards the end of the 1970s there was an acute sense of public desperation.

The end of consensus: Britain under the Tories (1979–97)

Economy, politics and society

Following their defeat in the 1974 election, Margaret Hilda Thatcher, a grocer's daughter from the market town of Grantham in Lincolnshire, became the leader of the Conservative (or Tory) Party. Her early publicity depicted her as a happily married suburban housewife, cheerfully washing up in her suburban semi-detached house. But at the same time she was developing economic ideas which were guided by the fashionable theories of monetarism. These involved reducing inflation with high interest rates, and submitting all aspects of the economy to free-market economics and the laws of supply and demand.

The late 1970s were times of strikes and confrontation, and many electors were attracted by her forceful personality and the simple certainties of her free-market ideology. It recalled a Victorian Britain when nation and Empire were at their height, but conveniently forgot the inequality, exploitation and suffering on which imperial success was based, and the need to police and control it with tough laws and punishments. Moreover, in a decade when political and economic achievements of feminism had been remarkable, she would be Britain's first woman prime minister. Yet Thatcher would do little to help the situation of women, and many argued she set back the movement by ten years.

Thatcher went on to lead the Conservatives to victory in the election of 1979, and the party remained in power until 1997. The period opened optimistically with Thatcher quoting St Francis of Assisi, a medieval saint who made a virtue of poverty:

Where there is discord, may we bring harmony,
Where there is error, may we bring truth,
Where there is doubt, may we bring faith,
Where there is despair, may we bring hope.

But in the early 1980s Britain's economic crisis worsened. Manufacturing declined and the shipbuilding, mining and steel industries practically disappeared. The regions of Scotland, the north of England, Wales and the West Midlands had traditionally depended on this kind of industry, and were economically devastated. Unemployment rose to over 13 per cent, and with more than 3 million people out of work the government became deeply unpopular. There was civil and industrial conflict in most areas, and in April 1981 rioting broke out in the streets of Brixton, south London, and in other cities around the country. It was spontaneous and anarchic, directed against the police and the local environment. The crisis seemed to deepen on 2 April 1982, when Thatcher led Britain into war with Argentina over the occupation of the Falklands Islands. However, when the British forces emerged victorious on 14 June, Thatcher was able to exploit the moment and distract attention from the economic crisis at home.

Next, the government forged a closer alliance with the USA to develop a Cold War strategy which involved holding nuclear weapons as a deterrent. A central element of policy was that of mutually assured destruction (MAD) of both parties in case of a strike by Soviet forces. The government's policies were supported by virtually all the daily newspapers except the *Guardian*, the *Daily Mirror*, and from August 1982 *The Voice*, a new weekly paper aimed at young black Britons. With the press on its side, in spite of record unemployment, riots and a war, the Conservatives emerged victorious in the general election of 1983, and the economic and political ideas which came to be known as Thatcherism began to be fully expressed and implemented. These included an even greater reduction of public spending, and measures to privatise industries in the public sector, such as gas, steel, transport and telecommunications. The measures were highly unpopular with the working class and unemployed, and resulted in more violent industrial disputes. They were also expensive to implement, being at great cost to the welfare state, but the discovery of oil in the North Sea in the 1970s helped to finance Thatcher's project.

To cement the government's authority, she next addressed those she called 'the enemy within'. These consisted of powerful trade unions, the miners, left-wing local governments, the IRA and its supporters, immigrants, the 'greens' and 'unreliable' members of her own party. The most notorious confrontation was the miners' strike of 1984–85, which Thatcher saw as part of her plan to break the power of the trade unions. She became known as the 'Iron Lady' and passed legislation to weaken the unions' power permanently.

Organised labour showed its opposition to Thatcher in its readiness to strike, while many middle-class protest groups also sprang up, notably the establishing of a women's 'peace camp' outside Greenham Common air base in 1981 against the stationing of nuclear weapons there. Other protest groups were more concerned about the environment, such as Greenpeace, the Ramblers Association, Friends of the Earth and Hunt Saboteurs Association, which all increased their memberships. Popular opposition was also to be found in the arts, which for many years had enjoyed support from the official body of the Arts Council despite the intention to criticise the government and politics of the time.

The Arts Council was created to support the arts in 1946 under the chairmanship of the economist John Maynard Keynes, and had never interfered with the work of artists and performers. Its ideology survived changes in government, and helped to support the wealth and variety of British theatre, music and the visual arts in its mission to bring a civilising influence to society. But in the 1980s its funding was sharply reduced, and the arts were treated as any other area of economic activity. The effects were widely felt. For the first time, many museums and galleries began to charge admission prices, while to attract subsidies, arts productions became less critical and adventurous and more populist and sentimental, for example by showing Shakespeare's plays in ways which removed their social content and stressed their sentimental aspects.

While the expression 'Thatcherite' was being applied (often pejoratively) from 1979, the term 'Thatcherism' only began to be heard after the British general election of 1983 following Thatcher's re-election. Her majority was large enough to reject the 'middle road' between the Conservatives and Labour which had characterised the consensus politics of the post-war period. It was argued that state regulation, subsidies, rights to education, health care and social security had made organisations inefficient, and people lazy and work-shy, a view which recalled the thought of early nineteenth-century economists. But implementing Thatcherism came at a high social cost. During 1985–86 there were more riots in cities around Britain. Burglary, car theft, violent crime and vandalism all increased. Football violence and hooliganism became a serious social problem, and relations between the police and public were tense. Commentators on the political left blamed high unemployment (almost 4 million), homelessness (around 1 million), and the loss of community, which an ethos of economic individualism had promoted. In contrast, those on the right blamed the permissive society of the 1960s, which had allowed the young to grow up with no respect for the police, teachers or authority.

Tory policies had the most severe consequences for the poorly educated and least skilled, who were unable to obtain manual work as they had done in previous generations. Some of the major casualties were immigrants and their families, and there were riots in many poor, racially mixed inner-city areas in 1979, 1981 and again in 1985. Many other social casualties were women, in particular those who transferred from manufacturing work to low-paid, part-time service industries in which there were no company pensions or union benefits. However, women on a different social level were beginning to occupy posts in traditional male-dominated areas such as business, law and banks. Many could enjoy the benefits of financial and personal freedom, and were postponing marriage and children until much later in life.

In the mid-1980s, after the government removed restrictions on money-lending and dealing in shares, the financial sector boomed. Credit was easy to obtain, and taxes were cut. Share prices rose quickly, especially those of newly privatised public industries such as British Airways, British Steel, and all the public utilities including gas, water and telecommunications, as Thatcher sought to promote a share-owning society. The dominant economic influences in Britain changed from heavy industry and manufacturing to financial services and North Sea oil revenues. By 1986 the economy was stronger, and house prices were rising sharply. There was an air of excitement and optimism as a new society emerged. Britain became more affluent and competitive; spending on restaurants, clothes, cars, homes and holidays reached record levels, fuelled by a new generation of aspirational, stylish and image-conscious consumers.

Advertising and publicity became fine arts. The Conservatives employed the services of the Saatchi and Saatchi advertising agency to promote the party, creating their logo of a flaming blue torch, a symbol closely associated with the Oscar-winning film *Chariots of Fire*. Meanwhile, Labour adopted a red rose as its logo, and hired the services of Hugh Hudson, the director of *Chariots*, to make a publicity film of the leader Neil Kinnock.

Following a third election victory in 1987 Thatcher claimed she had cured Britain of its strikes, low productivity, low investment and 'winters of discontent' forever. But the same year the economy began to stagnate again when share prices crashed. In a brief phase of recovery, house prices continued to rise dramatically, as did inflation. But government spending was further reduced, resulting in greater poverty and insecurity for the unemployed and sick. Homeless beggars appeared on the streets, the use of illegal drugs increased, the numbers of sufferers from AIDS and HIV grew alarmingly, and warnings about sexual behaviour were broadcast on television.

The spread of AIDS prompted more open, public discussion of gay lifestyles, but this was opposed by the Tory government, who in 1987 introduced the Local Government Act with its infamous Clause 28, which prohibited state schools from 'promoting homosexuality', in other words from teaching students that it is acceptable or normal. To counter this, groups promoting gay rights began campaigning for a better understanding of homosexuality with more widespread publicity, a high-profile annual Gay Pride march, and membership of pressure groups increased such as

Stonewall, Act Up and Outrage. Some tactics involved public exposure ('outing') of homosexuals and lesbians in politics and the media, which guaranteed high levels of public interest.

The government had ignored the gradual deterioration in many people's quality of life, and there had been little public debate about the need for more openness and tolerance and a more inclusive society; these were not part of the Thatcherite agenda. Yet the right-wing press at that time gave the impression that everything was going swimmingly; it was as if for several years Britain was living a kind of 'American dream'. Its dominant attitudes, values and beliefs were openly approved of by the majority, even if they were disadvantaged and excluded. But towards the end of the decade the public began to realise that what the politicians and papers said about Britain was very different from the reality of living in it.

By 1990 it was becoming increasingly difficult for Thatcher to keep her party united, particularly over the issue of closer political and economic integration with Europe, an issue which she had always opposed, and which would go on to divide the party into the next century. The same year, violent rioting broke out in London when the Tory government introduced the 'poll tax'. It was the combination of recession, her antipathy to Europe and the universally unpopular poll tax that dislodged Thatcher after 11 years in Downing Street, and one of the most controversial periods in British politics. To replace her, John Major was elected as the new leader of an increasingly divided party and a fractious nation. He managed briefly to reverse the Conservatives' fortunes with an unexpected victory in the 1992 election, bringing a record fourth consecutive Tory victory. But later that year the issue of 'Europe' resurfaced, and Major was humiliated when he faced rebellion from those in his party opposed to the Maastricht Treaty and closer monetary union with other European countries.

For much of the 1990s there was an overwhelming sense of public disillusionment. Studies repeatedly showed that public confidence in all the major institutions had fallen, especially in Parliament, the legal system and the press. And throughout the decade, the monarchy looked increasingly fragile and irrelevant, amid the devolution of power to Scotland, the plans of the Labour government to abolish the House of Lords and the increasing popularity of the pressure group 'Charter 88' with its demands for the introduction of a British republic.

By the middle of the 1990s there were more internal divisions in the Major government, over weak leadership an uncaring attitude towards weaker sections of the community, and doubts over closer European integration. In response, Major attempted to reintroduce elements of Thatcherism such as respect for authority and family values under the banner of 'Back to Basics'. But the press saw this as an opportunity to expose Tory hypocrisy with frequent allegations of 'sleaze' – financial and moral impropriety – within the party. As a result, several high-profile politicians such as Stephen Norris, Tim Yeo, Jonathan Aitken, Jeffrey Archer,

Neil Hamilton and David Mellor were forced to resign or arrested, amid high levels of public interest, incredulity and amusement. There seemed to be no end to the hypocrisy, as it later emerged that Major himself had departed from 'family values' when he began an affair with married MP Edwina Currie, who subsequently became a minister in his cabinet.

The decline in popularity of the Conservatives continued, and gave the Labour Party an opportunity to reorganise. Tony Blair was elected the new leader following the death of John Smith. Young and charismatic, he set about transforming the party, leaving behind the traditional socialist beliefs about stronger unions, nationalisation of the major industries and redistribution of wealth. Many of Labour's traditional supporters worried that the party was becoming too much like the Conservatives, but Blair repeated his message about party principles being futile without power.

Velvet Revolution: Britain under New Labour (1997–)

Economy, politics and society

As the Tory Party faltered in a storm of sleaze and incompetence, the opinion polls swung strongly in favour of Labour, and in May 1997 the party gained a historic electoral victory, with a majority of 179 MPs. Blair's youth and idealism and the general sense of public expectation made him appear like a 'British Kennedy', who would show Britain the way to the promised land, and the early days of his party's rule brought important political changes in terms of devolution at home and intervention abroad. In 1997 Hong Kong was handed back to China. Then plans were made for a devolution of power to Scotland, an assembly to aid regional autonomy for Wales, and a peace treaty with Northern Ireland, which diminished political violence in the home nations. The theme of devolution continued with a return of power to the London area and the establishing of the Greater London Authority with its own mayor and assembly. Labour supporters saw devolution of power as a democratic response to people's needs but critics said Blair was presiding over the break-up of the UK.

Since 1945 the Tory Party had presented a strong challenge to Labour, but now it was divided and incapable. In its place the press repositioned itself as the 'unofficial' opposition, subjecting the government to intense, critical scrutiny. Consequently, there was a need to maintain order to ensure party unity, which was often reported as Blair's obsession with centralisation and control. However, the government was now subject to more external controls than internal ones: big corporations and tycoons, the press, the European Union and the law now limit more than ever what government can do.

As the Cold War disappeared, so did political ideology in the Labour Party, which was no longer committed to programmes of nationalisation and high levels of taxation for the richest earners. With pragmatic economic

15

management the economy showed steady improvement, and the persistent post-war worries of inflation, unemployment and nuclear war disappeared. Economic stability continued, and by 2004 inflation was low at 2–3 per cent, and there was almost full employment for the first time since records were kept. Some 70 per cent of people owned their own homes, but between 1997 and 2002 house prices doubled.

New issues of education, health and social security came to dominate the domestic political agenda. In 1975 only 7 per cent of the population went to university, but in 2005 the figure was 33 per cent and rising. But education came at a price, as for the first time university fees were introduced, and students had to pay them with loans from the government. Health in particular was a major concern, as the government attempted to modernise and improve the National Health Service. Although hunger and malnutrition had once been the problem, in 2004 it was obesity, as 67.6 per cent of men and 56.4 per cent of women were classed as overweight. A related issue was the risk posed by eating 'fast' food such as burgers and frozen meals, and 'junk' food such as sweets and chocolates which exacerbated the problem, especially among school children. Alcohol consumption was also increasing, especially 'binge' drinking where large amounts of alcohol are consumed in a short time, often leading to anti-social behaviour and juvenile crime. The incidence of sexually transmitted diseases and cancer also rose, while the traditional pleasures of sex, smoking and sunshine were revealed to carry greater health risks than had earlier been suspected.

Despite economic stability and material prosperity, public confidence in politicians and the institutions of state continued to decline. In the election of 2001 only 39 per cent of people under 25 voted, and the total number of voters was the lowest since the election of 1918. Although institutions and corporations were now much more open, a more cynical press, communications technology and new legislation on the freedom of information had led to a fall in public trust and a growing cynicism, as people became more aware of the deficiencies in public bodies. Paradoxically, greater access to information appears to have made people disenchanted with government and politics.

The reputations of the monarchy, the Anglican church, the police, doctors, teachers and financial bodies all suffered, following investigations, exposures and scandals. The royal family was one of the first institutions to be affected in this way. The best of British family values were apparently embodied by the House of Windsor, and were accentuated by the glamour, style and romance of the royal wedding of Charles and Diana in 1981. But in confessional interviews to the media, Diana allegedly damaged the public image of the family, as did the many press intrusions and 'confessions' by former employees. However, Queen Elizabeth remains highly respected, and the movement for a British republic is currently weak. When Diana, Princess of Wales died in August 1997, millions were on the streets to throw flowers at the funeral car. Similarly, in 2002 when the Queen Mother died, a million people watched the funeral procession in London, and there was a two-mile queue to see her lying in state. Two months later, Queen Elizabeth's jubilee celebrations began with the lighting of beacons around the country, as in ancient times, and culminated in a pop concert in Buckingham Palace gardens. There has been no discussion of a different head of state, and in 2003 research by ITV and YouGov showed that 80 per cent of Britons wanted the monarchy to stay.

The Anglican church has also become less influential than 50 years ago. People feel it has been unable to give clear guidance on many modern-day issues from abortion to genetic research, and is incapable of readily accepting women and gay clergy, especially to senior positions. Public disenchantment may be reflected in the fact that in 1997 some 70 per cent of Britons professed religious faith, but not necessarily the traditional Christian one, and over 90 per cent said they did not go to church regularly, a statistic which remained barely changed in 2005.

To offset the growth in public knowledge and cynicism, the government and major organisations have all had quickly to learn the skills of advertising, public relations, and 'spinning' or manipulating stories in the media to protect their image. This has been a lesson which the Labour government has understood well, particularly in connection with foreign policy and war overseas. Initially, the government was able to rely on the size of its parliamentary majority for support, and the absence of any obvious foreign enemy gave a greater certainty about Britain's role in the world. Blair's sense of moral outrage led to several overseas interventions, beginning in Kosovo with the saving of Albanian lives. This encouraged his advocating the use of force across the world for humanitarian reasons. Subsequent events in America – commonly known as 9/11 – convinced Blair to support President Bush in the 'war on terror', which in 2003 involved the invasion of Iraq, despite a demonstration against it by over 2 million people in Britain. The strength of US technology ensured the country was swiftly overrun, but almost every day since the war ended there have been deaths and injuries of Iraqi civilians and British and US army personnel, as well as questions about Blair's judgement and honesty over the reason for the intervention – that Iraq held weapons of mass destruction.

The multicultural society

As in most successful countries immigration increases when the economy is strong, and in the new millennium the success of the British economy attracted the ambitious and the dispossessed from around the world. In earlier centuries movement took place from rural England, Ireland and Scotland to the industrial cities. Today, the movements are from Somalia, Afghanistan, Albania, Iraq and elsewhere. Those on the political right attempted to worry the public, claiming the country could not support more immigrants, while others argued that the economy and the public services would collapse *without* labour from overseas.

After the invasion of Iraq, fear of terrorism increased, and at the same time immigration and asylum seeking became even more controversial issues. Britain has a long history of immigration, and since the 1950s the numbers entering have grown substantially. In the Census of 2001, 4.6 million people described themselves as belonging to a minority ethnic group (defined by the Foreign and Commonwealth Office as 'black African, black Caribbean, black other, Chinese, Bangladeshi, Indian, Pakistani, other Asian'), who currently comprise 8 per cent of the UK population, and 9 per cent of the population of England. Of these, some 2.3 million described themselves as Asian or Asian British, and approximately 1.1 million described themselves as black or black British. Nearly half of the total minority ethnic population live in London, of whom almost 30 per cent were born outside the UK.

The Muslim population also constitutes a sizeable minority; there are around 2 million Muslims in the UK, mostly of Pakistani and Kashmiri descent, who make up just under 4 per cent of the population and live mostly in London, Bradford, Birmingham, Leicester and Oldham. There are mosques in most towns, and 'halal' shops and restaurants are easy to find. Many British Muslims have their family origins in Kashmir, and came to Britain in the 1960s with the aim of earning money before returning. But due to the unstable politics of their home region they were unable to do so and stayed on, forming communities in deprived areas where unemployment is high. Today, many have settled and formed young families; around 50 per cent of the community are aged under 25. But levels of integration and achievement are low; around one third of families have no qualifications, and around a fifth earned their living from taxi driving. Paradoxically, integration is a source of anxiety among some community elders. A poll in 2004 showed 26 per cent of Muslims felt their children had integrated too much into non-Muslim society, and nearly half of Muslim adults wanted their children to go to separate Muslim schools. As a result of ambivalent attitudes among community leaders and the younger generation, together with a suspicion of official organisations, relations between the authorities and local communities remain tense and deeply problematic in many urban areas.

Racism has continued to be a problem in several towns with large immigrant populations, and in recent years there has been an increase in the number of people reporting themselves as 'racist' or 'fairly racist' in surveys. In the past, British governments have responded to racial tensions in three main ways. First, limits on immigration include the Commonwealth Immigration Acts of 1962 and 1968, the Immigration Act 1971, and the Nationality Acts of 1981 and 1987. Second, there have also been several important Acts of Parliament introduced to prevent discrimination: the Race Relations Acts of 1965, 1968 and 1976, and afterwards the Race

Relations Board, the Community Relations Commission and the Commission for Racial Equality were established. Third, efforts have been made in the area of employment, most notably with the Equal Opportunities Act which aims to extend opportunities for ethnic and other minority groups.

The laws have helped facilitate integration, but their effects have been hampered by the findings of reports into allegations of racism even among the police, such as the Macpherson Report in 1999. Perhaps unsurprisingly there are periodic disturbances between whites, blacks, Asians and the police, for example in 2001 in Burnley, Oldham and Bradford, provincial towns with large ethnic populations of young, disaffected Asians.

The devastating events of 11 September 2001 in America when the country was attacked by suicide bombers, and the subsequent wars in Afghanistan and Iraq, as well as the second wave of mass asylum-driven immigration into Britain, and the emergence of closer surveillance and the electronic interconnected society have changed much. Tension has increased in communities with large populations of British Muslims, and was maintained following the suicide bombings in London during July 2005. At present the future seems uncertain, and the government is working with local communities to promote a sense of identification and involvement with wider society among young Muslims in deprived urban areas.

Gender issues

In spite of the progress made by the women's movement since the 1960s, Britain's institutions remain largely male dominated. Within Parliament there are still relatively few female MPs, with 24 in 1945, 41 in 1987, and of the 641 representatives in the 2005 election, there were only 125 women, along with 4 Muslim and 5 black MPs. Within the Church of England, women were first ordained in 1994, but today are still excluded from becoming Bishops, despite pressure to change. But compared with only 20 years ago, many women have been able to make considerable advances in their chosen careers, although, mostly, those who do so are white, middle-class, university graduates. However, women earn approximately 20 per cent less than men in business, industry and government, even when doing similar types of work. In 2005 only 5 per cent of company directors, 7 per cent of university professors and 10 per cent of judges were women, leading to allegations of a 'glass ceiling' for women – the illusion of the possibility of progress.

Within the domestic sphere, divorce rates have continued to rise, and in 2004 some 45 per cent of marriages ended in divorce. The figure increased from 1 in 3 in 1994 to almost 1 in 2 in 2004, leaving many women in single-parent households. Divorce, separation, delayed parenthood, work and job insecurity mean women tend to marry later and have children much later. Yet growing equality and liberation do not seem to equal happiness. A survey in 2005 found that a 25-year-old woman is between three and ten times more likely to be depressed than was her counterpart in 1950. One conclusion is that an incompatibility exists between home and working lives; that for many women, 'having it all' means doing it all, and frequently doing it alone.

Compared with only ten years ago, there has been a significant increase in the acceptance of gay and lesbian sexuality. The age of consent was reduced from 18 to 16 in 2000, the same as for heterosexual relationships. With greater public tolerance, and employment law which makes discrimination illegal, more individuals publicly declared their sexuality, even in traditional areas of employment such as parliament, the armed forces, the police and the Church. In 2004, MPs voted to give same-sex couples the same property, taxation and pension rights as married couples, and gay civil partnerships, or 'marriages', were officially recognised from 2005.

'Cool Britannia' and the revival of youth

In the mid-1990s it seemed as if the country was emerging from a cultural ice age, as Britain became more self-confident, diverse and expressive. The rapid changes in society and politics of the late 1990s reinvigorated the creative industries of fashion, design, architecture and pop music. After years of popular discontent with the Conservative government, many felt the time was right to express feelings of national pride again, a feeling heightened in 1996 when England hosted the Euro '96 football championship, the national team playing with character and spirit before passionate crowds. The flag of St George (rather than the Union flag) had been adopted by numerous England fans and was ubiquitous not only in the stadiums, but in cars and houses around the country, in a show of national unity rarely seen since 1966.

The Euro '96 tournament was the prelude to a powerful sense of renewal across the country, which was emphasised by the size of Labour's victory in the election of the following year. Blair's interest in the music scene (he had once played in a band called Ugly Rumours) helped create a sense of expectation across the arts, and in 1997 musicians and designers were invited to a reception in Downing Street echoing a similar gesture by former Labour Prime Minister Harold Wilson in 1964, who invited the Beatles and others to a reception there. Like Wilson, Blair was keen to present a new image of Britain as a youthful, progressive, dynamic place for pop, fashion, film and design.

The cultural ferment drew much press attention. In an article in the *Independent on Sunday*, 15 March 1998, entitled 'The Cool Economy', the journalist Peter Koenig referred to 'Cool Britannia', a pun on the patriotic song 'Rule Britannia'. The name quickly became used to label almost any cultural activity that renounced any American influences and stood proud and alone in splendid isolation.

This brief but significant period for the arts has since come to be understood as an expression of many things: a celebration of youthful communality; a reassertion of national identity through the arts and sport; a joyful reaction to 18 years of Tory rule and the class divide; a time when people seemed to express a desire to be part of a larger community which in the 1980s had almost been lost. On the other hand, the new trends were sometimes criticised as elitist, on the grounds that in a multicultural country they were mainly embraced by white, middle-class males, while the more ethnically diverse arts such as the sounds of British club culture went relatively ignored by the press. Moreover, the terms 'Britpop' and other 'BritArts' were inaccurate, as almost all the styles and trends were made in *England*, indicating a clear trend towards the centralisation of creative activity.

Culture and commerce

Britpop provided the background to the Millennium celebrations which centred around the construction of an enormous dome at Greenwich in London, while a programme of other public-sector projects including arts buildings, sports stadiums and transport schemes was created to greet the new century. In the area of arts administration, the Department for National Heritage was replaced by the Department for Culture, Media and Sport, which took responsibility for policy and expenditure on museums and galleries, the Arts Councils of England, Scotland, Wales and Northern Ireland, plus regulation of the film industry, broadcasting and the press.

But despite many centrally directed initiatives for the development of creative activity, public funding of the arts has declined, and an individualistic entrepreneurial ethic has become dominant. Most projects are now largely self-funded, although some are assisted with funds from the National Lottery, which began in 1994. Camelot – the company contracted to run it – pays 28 pence in every pound towards a variety of sports and arts projects around Britain. The main complaint is that a decline in funding has necessarily led to a commercialisation of the arts, and to a 'dumbing down'; that trying to attract large audiences leads to a reduction in quality and variety. However, others argue against a 'patrician' model of funding which only funds those projects that a small number of official 'specialists' think are good for 'the people'. Instead, they believe that limited funding enables works to be more responsive to public wants and needs, in turn leading to greater access and wider public involvement, as well as the freedom to be critical of officialdom.

The increasingly commercial nature of the arts, the rise of cultural studies in universities, a greater awareness of how the media and cultural industries operate, as well as political devolution to the regions of the UK,

21

have all contributed to growing debates about modern culture, its nature and its relationship with national identity. Social change, together with greater democratisation of the arts, has also led to a shift in the meaning of the word itself. Around 1960 'culture' was generally used in an elitist sense, and referred to 'the best' that had been thought, said, written, painted, played and patronised by the state: it was something closely associated with education and improvement. More recently its use has become widespread when referring to a diverse range of tastes and entertainments – both popular and specialised – and to all the media and signifying practices of different communities, as well as those of the country as a whole. But instead of citing canonical works and showing deference towards them, discussion of culture now involves questions of how such works emerged in the past, whose interests they served, how the public reacted, why popular entertainments and practices were frequently marginalised, derided and ignored, as well as the important realisation that traditions are not fixed and immutable, but have always been subject to evolution and change.

Moreover, increased educational opportunities and fewer social distinctions have created more diverse, fragmented and generally better educated audiences with a variety of tastes and preferences. Consequently, debates about 'high' and 'low' forms are now rarely heard, and there is greater emphasis on the role of the arts as entertainment and information, rather than as a source of improvement, as well as a recognition that both good and bad examples exist of different cultural forms.

As in the early 1960s, there is still some concern expressed among the public and critics about the political and moral emptiness of some modern works. This is perhaps unsurprising, given that the great common causes of religion, war and political ideology, which inspired writers and artists in the twentieth century, have diminished or disappeared altogether.

Today, society is more secular and ethnically diverse. The threat of a nuclear holocaust largely disappeared with the collapse of communism in the early 1990s, which in turn prompted the disappearance of political ideology. The polarisation between left and right, which had characterised British society since the 1970s, has now vanished; by 2005 the Labour Party was often accused by its own supporters of resembling the Tory Party and vice versa. Meanwhile, the 'tribal' identities of the main parties and their supporters have become much weaker. Today, home owners and business people no longer automatically vote Tory, while those who care about a more equal and tolerant society no longer can be relied upon to vote Labour, and in many cases may not even bother to vote at all.

Some of the most significant political advances of recent decades have been produced in the sphere of personal freedoms. In the 1960s and 1970s, demands for women's rights, abortion, divorce, gay rights and toleration of liberal lifestyles inspired many cultural works, which in turn helped to force change. As a result, legal reforms were gradually won that are now largely taken for granted. At the same time, traditional forms of authority, which for centuries had exerted control over personal liberty, such as the Church, government, family or simply 'custom', have been found lacking, ignored or forced to change.

Despite the advances made by the political left in the field of personal behaviour, business values of solvency, managerialism and public relations have become dominant in both the private and public sectors of the economy, as well as in sport and in the creative industries of film, theatre and television production, pop music and publishing. This indicates that although the arguments for individual liberty have been won by the political left, the economic arguments which divided British politics in the post-war era have been won by the political right. The result is a kind of 'controlled capitalism' with many checks and balances on business activity. These arguments have been replaced by new tensions and realities, which have come to the forefront particularly since events in America on 11 September 2001 (or '9/11' as it is widely known) when the country was attacked by suicide bombers, and following subsequent wars in Afghanistan and Iraq. This has especially affected communities with large numbers of British Muslims, such as the heavily urbanised cities around Britain, where racial tension has increased.

Politics, society and cultural life have thus changed greatly since the late 1970s, since 1985, and again since the mid-1990s. In 2006 British society is certainly less hierarchical, more liberal, tolerant, with higher living standards and improved levels of health and education than at any other time. Today, the British are said to be richer and more tolerant than ever before. They are pro-capitalist, pro-social solidarity, secular, individualistic and libertarian about personal behaviour. In economic terms, the country has never had it so good. But research also reveals them to be depressed, apathetic, celebrity obsessed, and in an age of uncertainty about the future, badly in debt. Moreover, surveys persistently show that social inequality is still extensive, and that the attempts to eradicate it have mainly favoured the middle classes. And despite the reforms in women's rights of the 1960s and 1970s, studies consistently show they have not been effective enough, as in 2005 women doing the same job as men still earned an average of 18 per cent less, while inadequate child benefit still forces many women into poverty and dependence on men and the state.

Many of Raymond Williams's predictions of 1961 have come true, as has his wish for a broader education in schools and universities, and today many courses include studies of society, the press, film, television and drama. In the twenty-first century, the subjects of cultural studies, media and communications are among the most commonly taught subjects in universities, and wide public and scholarly interest has led to their being the most rapidly growing fields of employment in Britain.

Discussion topics and activities

1   Briefly summarise the most important political and social changes in Britain since 1945. Which period do you find the most interesting from a political and economic point of view?

2   What social changes have taken place in your country in recent years? Think about different sections of the community such as young people, women and immigrants, their economic level and position in society.

3   Think of a distinctive period in your country's recent history. What cultural elements and symbols, such as songs, books, films and popular music, do you associate with it?

4   What changes can you see in the arts of your country compared with ten or fifteen years ago? What has caused those changes? Have they been positive?

5   Should the government subsidise the arts, or should they exist independently like any other commercial enterprise?

6   'The value of the arts is not merely in their worth as imaginative constructs, but in their relationship to political events and history.' Discuss.

Suggested further reading

Books

Booker, C. (1969) *The Neophiliacs*, London: Collins.

Booker, C. (1980) *The Seventies: The Decade that Changed the Future*, New York: Stein & Day.

Burston, P. and Richardson, C. (1995) *A Queer Romance: Lesbians, Gay Men and Popular Culture*, London: Routledge.

Caterall, P. and Obelkevitch, J. (eds) (1994) *Understanding Post-War British Society*, London: Routledge.

Chambers, I. (1986) *Popular Culture, the Metropolitan Experience*, London: Routledge.

Evans, E. (2004) *Thatcher and Thatcherism*, London: Routledge.

Gascoigne, B. (1993) *Encyclopaedia of Britain*, Basingstoke: Macmillan.

Green, J. (2002) *All Dressed Up: The Sixties and the Counterculture*, London: Pimlico.

Hall, S. (1988) *The Hard Road to Renewal – Thatcherism and the Crisis of the Left*, London: Verso.

Hoggart, R. (1957) *The Uses of Literacy*, London: Chatto & Windus.

Hunt, L. (1998) *British Low Culture: From Safari Suits to Sexploitation*, London: Routledge.

James, O. (2002) *Britain on the Couch*, London: Routledge.

Lewis, P. (1978) *The Fifties*, London: William Heinemann.

Marwick, A. (1998) *The Sixties*, Oxford: Oxford University Press.

Melly, G. (1970) *Revolt into Style*, Harmondsworth: Penguin Books.

Mirza, H.S. (ed.) (1997) *Black British Feminism: A Reader*, London: Routledge.

Morely, D. and Robins, K. (eds) (2001) *British Cultural Studies*, Oxford: Oxford University Press.

Oakland, J. (1998) *British Civilisation*, London: Routledge.

Phillips, M. and Phillips, T. (1998) *Windrush: The Irrisistible Rise of Multi-Racial Britain*, London: HarperCollins.

Rowbotham, S. (1997) *A Century of Women: The History of Women in Britain and the US*, London: Viking.

Sampson, A. (2004) *Who Runs This Place? The Anatomy of Britain in the Twenty-First Century*, London: John Murray.

Sked, A. and Cook, A. (1993) *Post-War Britain: A Political History*, London: Penguin.

Storey, J. (1993) *An Introductory Guide to Cultural Theory and Popular Culture*, Harvester-Wheatsheaf: Hemel Hempstead.

Strinati, D. and Wagg, J. (eds) (1992) *Come On Down? Popular Culture in Post War Britain*, London: Routledge.

Thorne, T. (1993) *Fads, Fashions and Cults*, London: Bloomsbury.

Wambu, O. (ed.) (1998) *Empire Windrush – 50 Years of Writing about Black Britain*, London: Gollancz.

Whitehead, P. (1985) *The Writing on the Wall – Britain in the Seventies*, London: Michael Joseph.

York, P. and Jennings, C. (1995) *Peter York's Eighties*, London: BBC Books.

Young, H. (1989) *One of Us – A Biography of Margaret Thatcher*, London: Macmillan.

The reference book *Britain 2006: An Official Handbook* (2006) London: The Stationery Office, appears every year with an update of statistics and a review of the previous year in politics, economics, society, cultural life and the arts.

Journals

The daily and weekly quality newspapers provide good sources of material to follow cultural trends, while journals such as *Prospect*, *The Economist* and the *Guardian Weekly* also contain articles on current affairs and cultural life.

Language in culture

Introduction

The past 400 years have seen an exponential growth in the number of English speakers worldwide. Over 1.4 billion people live in countries where English has official status. Around 400 million speak it as their first language, and around 500 million use it as their second language. Because of its usefulness as a second language, around 1 billion others study it in schools and colleges. Added together, around 2 billion people, or around one third of the world's population have some knowledge of English. It is the official or semi-official language in over 60 countries, and it has a significant role in 20 more.

Paradoxically, as English has become more widely spoken it has fractured into local dialects. The same process happened with Latin, which broke into French, Italian, Spanish, Portuguese and Romanian. People make it their own, and the language changes into a different form. Thus there are many varieties of English around the world, which are often known as creoles, for example in the Caribbean region and in Singapore. This is also the case within Britain where many dialects co-exist, and differences can be heard even after travelling just a few miles. Regional accents can also be heard on radio and television, but standard English grammar and vocabulary is retained for most types of public broadcasting, such as the reading of the news.

Despite the existence of a standard form which is taught in school, many native speakers have difficulty with the grammar and punctuation of English. Letters to national newspapers and to the BBC on such matters, together with comments and complaints about pronunciation in broad-casting, are common, and in 2003 public interest reached fever pitch as the book *Eats, Shoots and Leaves*, which takes a light-hearted look at punctuation, became an unexpected bestseller of the year.

Although English is spoken throughout Britain, the islands are also home to several other separate, indigenous languages, such as Welsh, Irish, Scottish-Gaelic and Scots, which have long histories and considerable liter-atures. Numerous other languages are also spoken by Britain's ethnic communities. The most common are from the Asian subcontinent, such as Urdu and Hindi, which each have over 100,000 speakers and are widely spoken in the larger cities. But perhaps the most surprising fact is that, according to a study in 2001, 66 per cent of the British population have absolutely no knowledge of any language other than English. This is despite the fact that some 74 per cent said they thought learning another language was useful.

A brief history of English

Like many of the world's languages, English is a hybrid, a linguistic 'stew' which has absorbed varied elements of speech brought by ancient con-quering tribes and nationalities. One of the most influential elements is Latin, introduced almost 2,000 years ago by the Romans, and for several hundred years it was the official language of the Church, government, education and the law. Although its influence gradually declined, in the nineteenth and twentieth centuries Latin was still taught in grammar schools (the 'grammar' of their name referred to Latin grammar), and knowledge of Latin was considered essential for entry into the medical and legal professions. To express their exclusive credentials, many universities, schools and colleges adopted mottoes which expressed their aims and ideals not in the language of the masses, but in Latin. Although it is rarely taught today, it is still used in some religious ceremonies, and on formal occasions at the Universities of Oxford and Cambridge.

Although Latin was used among Britain's ruling class for many years, it was never the only language spoken in Britain, and dialects were common. Around 450 AD Englisc was commonly used in parts of the east and south of England. This was based on the dialects of Angle, Saxon and Jute invaders who crossed the North Sea from lands which now form part of Holland, Germany and Denmark to an area now called Anglia. Englisc gradually spread around England and became Old English, which today seems rather like an exotic foreign language. But around 1150 it began to change, and over the next three centuries it expanded and evolved as population movements increased, and dialects from around the country mixed with each other and with Norman French (introduced into Britain with the conquest of 1066 from northern France) to form Middle English.

Thousands of new words were absorbed by government, Church, the law, the military, education, the arts and at all levels of society. In the fifteenth century society became more centrally organised. With the introduction of printing presses and the large-scale production of legal texts, newspapers and books, there was a further period of expansion and standardisation, and by 1500 the written language was beginning to resemble the English of today.

Over the next three centuries English was exported to the continents of North America, Africa, Asia and Australasia, on voyages of trade, discovery and imperial expansion. Around the world English became the language of the ruling class, but in isolation on four continents, different varieties began to emerge, such as American English and Australian English. Elsewhere in the world, for example in the Caribbean islands of the West Indies, English mixed with African dialects to form exotic hybrids known as 'pidgins' and 'creoles'.

In spite of its variation, both national and international, English has never had an academy or legislative body to control it. During the seventeenth and eighteenth centuries proposals for an academy regularly came from numerous poets and authors such as Pope, Swift, Dryden and Defoe. However, they were gradually abandoned when substantial, authoritative dictionaries began to appear, such as Dr Samuel Johnson's. Unlike earlier works Johnson's dictionary included many everyday words and used literary quotations to illustrate current usage and word meaning. This technique is still used in the compilation of dictionaries today, for example the *Oxford English Dictionary* (*OED*) records how language is actually used, and the meanings words hold for people.

The full version of today's *OED* consists of around 750,000 words, covering the period from Anglo-Saxon times to the present day. Once a word has entered the dictionary, it stays there as part of the history of the language. Until the mid-1970s mainly English and American English words were recorded, but today many different forms are recognised, such as Australian, Indian, South African, and even internet English, and slang words. For example, the *OED* in 2004 recorded a number of Hindi words entering general use, including many new ones related to food, such as 'balti' and 'masala', as well as others such as 'chuddies' (underpants), which it is claimed have entered usage from the TV comedy programmes *The Kumars at No. 42* and *Goodness Gracious Me*. However, this process of adoption and assimilation is not new and illustrates how Asians are influencing English, just as the Vikings, Normans and Irish did in the past. It is known as a descriptive approach to recording pronunciation and word meaning, and contrasts with a prescriptive approach, which gives ultimate, fixed meanings to words, describing how they should be used, rather than how they really are used when people communicate.

Speech and social background

Although English is widely spoken around the world, more variety is found among the regions of Britain. Among the most distinctive are the dialects of Glasgow, Liverpool, the West Midlands, Northern Ireland, Yorkshire, Newcastle and east London. They contain many non-standard words and their intonation and distinctive pronunciation of vowels makes them easy to recognise. In Liverpool the dialect is known as Scouse – a mixture of Lancashire, Irish and Welsh – while the vernacular speech of east London is Cockney, a dialect known for its rhyming slang. A different form of speech is used by some Afro-Caribbean immigrants and their descendants. This mixes dialect speech from the West Indies (Caribbean creole) with an English accent of the locality, and is known as black British English or black English vernacular.

Both accent and dialect thus give the listener clues about a speaker's geographical and social background. Non-standard features are commonly present in the speech of people who have had less formal education, and who have spent most or all their lives in the same locality. They are also more common in male speech. Since the eighteenth century this character-istic has often been exploited by novelists and dramatists who used dialect to create characters and make social comment. In his novels of London low-life, the Victorian storyteller Charles Dickens made frequent attempts to recreate Cockney, as did American novelists Herman Melville and Jack London during their time in Britain. The classic works of Thomas Hardy (Dorset), William Wordsworth (Cumberland) and later D.H. Lawrence (Nottingham) are all well known for their use of plain, everyday speech of the regions in which they lived and worked, and link language to the manners, morals and class of their characters.

While dialects in literature were becoming more common during the nineteenth century, there was also a growing interest in establishing common standards of spoken and written English, in a trend which had begun a century earlier. This was related to public demand for formal education and schooling. Moreover, the expansion of the British Empire required clear standards of language which would be intelligible to all foreigners. The Education Act of 1870 helped to meet this need. It made education compulsory for all children up to 11 years of age. Class sizes grew, demand for a more exclusive private education increased, and the number of public schools expanded. Children of the ruling class and of wealthy merchants from around Britain were brought together in the new schools where they were taught a standard form of written English, based on a variety used in government documents around the mid-fifteenth century.

But educators also wanted a pronunciation standard to eliminate what they saw as a cacophony of regional accents. Grammarians recommended the speech of London and the Court as the most correct and desirable. This carried many regional features found in speech of the south-eastern counties of England, as far north as Cambridge and as far west as Oxford. It was selected because it was spoken by the ruling class – by the aristocracy and Court – and therefore carried authority. It was sometimes called 'Queen's English' and later became known as 'received pronunciation' (often abbreviated to RP), which everyone was expected to 'receive', i.e. 'understand'.

The British Empire and its army, Church, government and administration, and later the BBC, all absorbed the products of the British public schools, many of whom went on to occupy positions of power and influence. RP thus became the voice of the ruling class, the voice of British authority, and for many it was and still is synonymous with prestige, power and education. Consequently, RP can be described not as a regional accent, but as a social one.

Dialects, society and the arts

A high degree of social significance came to be attached to English speech. The prestige and authority of RP implied the inferiority of regional accents and vocabulary. Dialect speakers became socially stigmatised as rustic, provincial, poor and uneducated. Linguistic differences came to be seen as linguistic errors, and the socially ambitious had to modify their speech towards that of their betters. This phenomenon was noted as early as 1912 when George Bernard Shaw observed that 'It is impossible for an Englishman to open his mouth without making another Englishman hate or despise him.' Shaw later wrote the play *Pygmalion* (1913), in which the language teacher Professor Higgins (based on the British phonetician Henry Sweet), convinces poor flower-seller Eliza Doolittle that with pronunciation lessons he can make her appear sophisticated and aristocratic. The play was later adapted into the 1964 Hollywood musical *My Fair Lady*.

The arrival of public broadcasting in 1922 helped to extend the social prestige of RP. Although it was spoken by only 2–3 per cent of the population, it was preferred by the BBC because it was widely understood and respected. An advisory committee was appointed to resolve any doubts about pronunciation. Their judgements on correctness helped to make the BBC an unofficial authority on language, and helped create 'BBC English'. Moreover, RP's clear vowel sounds and exaggerated intonation aided voice projection in large theatres, and it was later adopted in drama schools as a standard for teaching purposes. When the 'talkies' replaced silent films in Britain during the 1920s some actors had to retire because their accents were unsuitable.

Due to the dominance of RP, for many years non-standard regional speech was rarely heard on television, radio or at the cinema, except in the roles of 'character' actors: players and performers who were spontaneous and open, but usually had minor parts as poor, comic or deviant characters, such as backward rural farmworkers, or petty criminals. Similarly, in popular entertainment the success of 'figures of fun' such as Tommy Trinder (a Cockney) and George Formby (from Lancashire) largely depended on the comic effects produced by their strong regional accents. During the Second World War their unconventional speech was even used to fool the enemy. For a brief period the BBC radio news was read by the comedy actor Wilfred Pickles, whose strong Yorkshire accent could not be easily understood by German Intelligence.

However, a number of post-war education reforms, in particular the Butler Education Act of 1944, greatly improved educational opportunities for a generation of working-class and lower-middle-class children. There was an expansion of the university sector and improved access for students from all social backgrounds and regions. With growing social mobility, divisions between the classes became less rigid and movement between them easier. In this way, the old associations between accent and background began to be lost, and prejudice diminished.

There was greater openness and authenticity in post-war arts, and from the mid-1950s authentic representations of regional speech could be heard in theatre, television and film. Writers such as Harold Pinter and Joe Orton accurately used regional dialects to make their plays more realistic, as did television drama series such as *Armchair Theatre*, soap operas such as *Coronation Street* from Manchester and crime series such as *Z Cars* from Liverpool. All of these helped to present a more honest and complete view of British life, characters and accents to audiences around the country. In film, adaptations of 'realist' novels and plays such as *Saturday Night and Sunday Morning* and *The Loneliness of the Long Distance Runner* accurately portrayed working-class life, and to play the leading roles, well-known actors such as Albert Finney and Tom Courtney had to rediscover the northern accents they had lost at drama school.

The emergence of popular culture also promoted a wider acceptance of regional speech in the public sphere, where it was suddenly possible for less formally educated individuals to obtain social advancement in new professions such as popular music, photography, art, design and fashion. The Beatles from Liverpool, the Rolling Stones and the Who from London showed the way, and attracted intense public and media interest. New popular music radio stations, such as BBC Radio 1, and television shows such as *Ready Steady Go!* provided new stages for the amplification of accented speech in interviews and comment. Later in the decade, Sean Connery (Scottish), Richard Burton (Welsh) and Michael Caine (from London) became some of the most popular actors of the time, playing glamorous, sophisticated roles with non-RP accents. The talent, status and self-confidence of popular culture's new heroes helped regional speech become fashionable and frequently imitated, especially among the young.

32

Today, with changing social attitudes and greater social convergence and movement between the social classes, the RP accent has become less influential and is no longer regarded by everyone as the 'best' pronunciation. Indeed, the 'marked' or 'advanced' RP which linguists associate with the royal family and with high ranking members of the armed forces, civil service, Church and so on, tends to mark the speaker as being old fashioned, detached and remote from mainstream society, and is even rejected by some young people who see it as an unfashionable symbol of traditional values and authority. One consequence is that some speakers, including the Queen herself, are said to have modified their accents. After watching the Queen's Christmas broadcasts between the 1950s and the 1980s, one study found that her pronunciation of vowels tended to shift towards more modern and less old-fashioned forms. Similar shifts were also noted in the speech of the former Conservative Prime Minister Margaret Thatcher, who, it was said, modified her pronunciation in order to broaden her appeal to a larger number of voters. Similarly, although the accent was used some years ago by BBC newsreaders and commentators on prestigious cultural and artistic events, such as coronations, Wimbledon tennis, equestrian events and arts programmes, it is now considered antiquated, and is rarely heard except as the object of satire in comedy shows.

Today a more moderate RP accent is still widely used as a model for teaching English to foreign students, but it is still only spoken by around 3 per cent of the population (a figure which corresponds approximately to the percentage who attend public school). This sometimes causes confusion for overseas visitors, who may have studied English for many years, yet still have difficulty understanding many British native speakers.

Despite a wider acceptance of regional accents and dialects, there is evidence that some varieties may still carry negative connotations in the public sphere or, to put it another way, some accents may carry more positive connotations than others particularly in contexts where a high degree of credibility is required, such as advertising, public relations and news reporting. Thus, research suggests that within England a milder, 'moderate' RP accent is widely considered the most desirable, especially by those who have marked regional accents themselves. People claim to prefer the sound of it, and associate it with intelligence, ambition, occupational status and even good looks! Next to RP, the English are said to prefer the accent of an educated Scot over the accent of an educated Welshman or Irishman. Within Scotland, the educated Scottish accent is preferred over RP, while within England the accents of Yorkshire and Newcastle are highly rated, as are accents from rural areas such as Somerset and Devon. Among the least liked are those associated with large inner cities, especially those of Birmingham, Liverpool and London. The present situation is therefore a complex one, in which the most desirable accent is highly dependent on social context.

Preferences over accents are reflected in how businesses and other organisations speak to their public in advertisements. For example, Glasgow has some of the most distinctive voices in Britain, and in the 1990s many companies located their call-centres there because they thought that the softer version of the accent is one of the most friendly and trustworthy in the country. On the other hand, advertisers on national radio and television stations rarely choose local accents to promote their products, and generally prefer a mild RP accent. In contrast, if the goods have strong traditional or regional associations, such as beer or bread, they are sometimes promoted with accents that identify the product with the locality, for example Warburton's bread (Bolton, Lancashire), or Castlemaine beer (Australia).

English is thus adopting, borrowing and changing all the time. It has progressed from a small tribal dialect 1,500 years ago, to a language for the world. Yet it remains enormously varied both inside and outside Britain, a complex and varied mosaic of language in which differences in pronunciation, words and grammar reflect differences in region, social background and generation.

Languages of Britain

It is often imagined that Britain is a linguistically homogeneous country, but in 2001 at least twelve different languages could claim more than 100,000 speakers. Many of these, such as Urdu and Hindi, were spoken in families of immigrants from the Indian subcontinent who have settled in Britain since the late 1950s. But there are also several others which have been present in Britain for over 2,000 years: most of these are varieties of Gaelic, the language of the Gaels, Celtic invaders from Europe.

Gaelic is a separate language from English and has a long history in the British Isles. Its origins are obscure, but most accounts begin around the fourth century BC, following the earlier arrival of Gaelic-speaking Celts known as Gaels from central Europe. They settled in Ireland, Scotland, the Isle of Man, and later in southern England and parts of Wales. However, some 800 years later, around the fifth century AD, Britain suffered an invasion from the east and south by Anglo-Saxon tribes from northern Europe. They forced British Celts to go west and north, to the safety of the hills and mountains of Cornwall, Devon, Wales and Scotland, and to the Brittany region of France. The geographical separation of groups of Gaelic speakers led to linguistic and cultural differences, as Welsh, Irish and Scottish-Gaelic all developed independently. Others languages existed too: Cornish was spoken in the counties of Cornwall and Devon, and Manx in the Isle of Man. But the last speakers of Cornish as a living language died in the early nineteenth century, and the Manx language disappeared during the late 1940s. However, today there are periodic local initiatives to practise and celebrate them in areas where they were once spoken.

Welsh

Welsh is a Celtic language. For almost 1,000 years until the Act of Union with England in 1536, Welsh was the only language spoken in Wales. But until the mid-twentieth century it was marginalised as English became the language of government, education and trade. Welsh was only spoken at home and in church and the number of speakers slowly declined, hastened in the nineteenth century by the influx of workers from England to the coal-fields and steelworks of the south. Some Welsh people, however, were unwilling to adopt English ways, and in 1865 a party of 165 men and women emigrated to Patagonia in Argentina, where Patagonian Welsh is still spoken by their descendants.

In the twentieth century use of Welsh continued to decline until the 1960s, when an increase in political nationalism led to a rediscovery of Welsh identity through language. Perhaps surprisingly, the British government agreed to help the Nationalists, and in 1964 the government established BBC Radio Wales, the first regional service in Britain. Support for Welsh was secured in legislation with the Welsh Language Act of 1967, which ordered that all official documents be written in both languages. Consequently, the country is now comparatively well served by a Welsh-language mass media. Local newspapers in Welsh appeared in the 1970s and numerous radio stations now broadcast in Welsh. In 1982 the television channel S4C (Sianel Pedwar Cymru – Channel 4 Wales) began broadcasting. A significant part of its programme-making is in Welsh, and one of its most popular programmes is a soap opera *Pobl y Cwm* (People of the Valley).

Official support for the Welsh language was firmly established with the Welsh Language Act of 1993, which stipulated that Welsh and English should be considered as equal languages in public affairs and the administration of justice. Welsh is now studied in all Welsh schools, and several offer a Welsh-medium education.

Efforts to revive the language have been successful; in 2001, of a population of around 2.9 million, about 0.6 million were Welsh speakers, most aged under 35, and the language is widely used for official purposes, for example in most place names, road signs, job advertisements and public-information documents. Its literature is among the oldest in Europe, and is celebrated each year during a national festival of music, literature and drama known as the Royal National Eisteddfod, an event which originated in the twelfth century. It is held alternately each year in North and South Wales, during the first week of August, and is open to the public. An international festival of music and folk dancing is also held in Llangollen each year and is known as the International Music Eisteddfod. It attracts people from all over the world to recite poetry, sing and dance in a colourful expression of Welsh identity.

Irish

Around the UK and Ireland, language and politics have always been closely related, but tension between the two has been consistently high in Ireland. Irish is a Celtic language and was widely spoken in a united, independent Ireland until it became part of the United Kingdom with the Act of Union of 1803. Then its use in urban areas began a rapid decline. Following the death and emigration of millions of Irish speakers from rural areas during the tragic famine of 1845–48, there were even fewer speakers. But towards the end of the nineteenth century a Republican movement for independence from Britain emerged, whose supporters adopted Irish (*Erse*) as a distinctive symbol of their culture and identity.

In 1921 the south of Ireland gained partial independence from Britain, and its new government began to organise a revival of Irish. It is now taught in schools as a second language, and there is a small Irish media. Of some 3.5 million inhabitants, over 1 million speak both languages. However, Irish remains the first official language of the Irish Republic.

In Northern Ireland, language use remains strongly politicised. Since the Act of Union of 1803, the use of Irish has been linked with the nationalist cause. Because Irish has no official status, reliable data on the number of speakers has been difficult to obtain. But the 2001 Census found that 167,490 people (almost 10 per cent of the population of 1.7 million) in Northern Ireland had some knowledge of Irish. The British government recognises its importance, and provides financial support for activities to promote the language. In the capital Belfast there are bilingual schools, while the BBC and independent stations broadcast television and radio programmes in Irish. In 1981 an Irish daily newspaper '*La*' (meaning 'Day') was founded, and in 2004 the British government set up a fund to support Irish language film and television production in Northern Ireland.

However, as interest in Irish has grown in the north, it has declined in the more prosperous south. Irish literature has a long tradition going back to the sixth century, but today only around 5,000 monoglot Irish speakers remain, and most are elderly inhabitants of remote areas in the west of Ireland, known as *Gaeltacht*.

Scottish-Gaelic and Scots

Language in Scotland has a similar turbulent history, beginning around the fifth century AD when tribes of Gaels from Ireland and the north of England arrived in the Highlands and Western Isles of Scotland. Five hundred years later, their geographic isolation resulted in a different variety of language from that spoken in their former lands. But their remote rural location meant that over the years many speakers left in search of more prosperous lives in the cities, while others were forced to leave as landowners cleared their lands in preparation for more profitable sheep farming. This gradual depopulation of the countryside has left Scottish-Gaelic in steady decline from 250,000 speakers in 1891 to fewer than 60,000 in 2001 (1.2 per cent of the Scottish population) of whom some 5,000 are monoglot Gaelic speakers.

Until very recently Scottish Gaelic was neglected, and seen as a language spoken only by the rural poor, but today it is taught in schools and broadcast on television and radio, and receives financial support from the British government. It is also widely celebrated, and in 2004 there were 37 festivals or *Feisean* celebrating Gaelic culture, the largest being the curiously named *Royal National Mod*, held each October. Gaelic culture and language is celebrated at the annual Hebridean Celtic Festival in the grounds of Lewis Castle, Stornoway in mid-July, while Glasgow's *Celtic Connections* promotes Gaelic music. However, the literary corpus remains small, and is most noted for its eighteenth-century poetry, a tradition which Sorley Maclean and other writers continued into the mid-twentieth century.

In contrast to the Highlands where Gaelic is spoken, the Lowlands is home to Scots or 'Lallans' ('lowlands'), which is closely related to a dialect of Old English. Scots was widely spoken in the north of England and in many non-Gaelic parts of Scotland until the sixteenth century. However, after the abolition of the Scottish Parliament in 1707 and the transfer of power to London, English became the dominant language of the educated and merchant classes. As with Irish and Scottish-Gaelic, Scots was closely associated with people of poor rural areas, and was largely ignored. However, during the eighteenth and nineteenth centuries prestigious literary figures of Scotland such as Robert Louis Stevenson, Walter Scott and Robert Burns all wrote frequently in Scots. In their view, it was the authentic voice of the oppressed poor. Robert Burns remains one of Scotland's best-known literary and historical figures. His birthday is celebrated each year on Burns' Night (25 January), which typically features readings of his poetry and a haggis supper. His *Auld Lang Syne*, a song written in Scots about nostalgic reunion, is sung not only in Scotland but also by British people around the world at midnight on 31 December, and has become one of the most traditional and familiar of British anthems, even though it is written in words which, to most English speakers, resemble a foreign language.

In the twentieth century the best-known exponent of Scots poetry was Hugh MacDiarmid, a passionate Scot who founded the Scottish Nationalist Party. Today, the poet Tom Leonard and playwright Robert McLellan continue to write in various forms of Scots and to promote the language. However, its position remains precarious. Some critics argue it is a dialect of English, while others claim it is an artificial form which is only exploited for literary purposes. Because it is not recognised as an official language it is not recorded in national censuses. Therefore, data about the number of speakers is unreliable and few funds are available for its support.

However, in February 2004 the new Scottish Parliament elected its first national poet or Scots Makar – Professor Edwin Morgan – whose task it is to represent and promote Scots poetry.

Non-indigenous languages

Although Britain is a predominantly Anglo-Saxon country, ethnic diversity is a major characteristic of many towns and cities. Britain's global expansion over the past 500 years has resulted in a steady flow of immigration, and in the twentieth century the trend became more pronounced. Since the 1930s Jews, Russians and Italians have settled in Britain following persecution, war and poverty in Europe. Later, during the 1940s and 1950s the government invited Commonwealth citizens to fill job vacancies in the major towns and cities, and several periods of immigration followed. The new immigrants arrived mainly from West Africa, the Caribbean, India, Pakistan and Hong Kong, settling in areas where work was plentiful and housing cheap, for example in the central parts of London, Leicester, Slough, Birmingham and Bradford, as well as in the major ports of Bristol, Cardiff and Liverpool.

With people of Asian descent being the most numerous minorities of British cities, the most widely spoken foreign languages are those of the Asian subcontinent, such as Urdu from Pakistan, and Hindi, Bengali, Punjabi and Gujarati from India. They are well protected by an educational policy which provides tuition in the native language, and an established mass media of newspapers, radio and television programmes.

At the same time, however, many Asians have a complex relationship with English, which often varies according to age: for example, the inner London borough of Tower Hamlets is 25 per cent Bangladeshi, but less than two-thirds of the community speak English. The most proficient speakers of English are children, the majority of whom grow up speaking both English and the community language. In contrast, the community elders often have a poor command of English, for example only one in ten Bangladeshi women between the ages of 50 and 74 speaks English.

The cultural distance and difference between many younger immigrants and British society often provides the inspiration for new forms of creative expression. Novels, films, plays and music by British Asians and Afro-Caribbeans frequently propose a complex new British identity, one composed of varied cultural, political and historical influences. This is amply demonstrated in the works of numerous artists and writers who appear in the following chapters, whose presence helps to make cultural life in Britain among the most diverse and dynamic in the world.

Discussion topics and activities

1   There has never been an academy to regulate the English language. What do you think are the advantages and disadvantages of such an authority?

2   Should regional speech forms be allowed in the classroom, or should children be encouraged to use the 'prestige' dialect of the south-east, as they are at present?

3   Which is the 'correct' or 'prestige' accent in your country? What attitudes do people have towards speakers of regional accents and minority languages? Are such languages found in advertising, the mass media and certain types of role in films and plays? What connotations do they carry?

4   Listen carefully to the varieties of speech you hear spoken in buses, bars and other public places. Does language use vary according to the region, social background and educational level of the speaker? If so, how? What are some of the characteristics associated with speakers of this kind of accent?

5   There is a saying among linguists that 'a language is a dialect with an army and navy'. What do you think this means, and to what extent is it true?

6   If your first language is not English, how has that language been affected by English in recent years? Is diversity and change good for a language? What are the possible advantages and disadvantages?

7   Around 2001/02 a new type of English was observed in phone 'text' messages. The following extract appeared in the *Guardian* newspaper early in 2003, composed by John Mullan of University College London. Look at it and translate it into standard English. Would it be useful to reform the spelling system like this?

> Dnt u sumX rekn eng lang v lngwindd? 2 mny wds & ltrs? ?nt we b usng lss time & papr? ? we b 4wd tnking + txt? 13 yr grl frim w scot 2ndry schl sd ok. Sh rote GCSE eng as (abt hr smmr hols in NY) in txt spk. (NO!) Sh sd sh 4t txt spk was 'easr thn standard eng'. Sh 4t hr tcher wd b :) Hr tcher 4t it was nt so gr8! Sh was :(& talked 2 newsppprs (but askd 2 b anon). 'I cdnt bleve wot I was cing! :o' -!-!-! OW2TE. Sh hd NI@A wot grl was on abut. Sh 4t her pupl was ritng in 'hieroglyphics'.

8   Use the internet to find the words to the famous song *Auld Lang Syne* by Robert Burns. Translate it into modern English, and try to find the music to accompany it. What can you discover about its historical and social significance?

9   Cricket has given birth to a number of idioms such as 'it's not cricket', a 'sticky wicket', 'knocked for six', 'caught out', 'play with a straight bat' and 'play the game', which are all commonly used in everyday English. Look up their meanings, and make appropriate sentences. If your first language is not English, does it contain any similar metaphors concerned with sport?

Suggested further reading

Books

Baugh, A. and Cable, T. (1993) *A History of the English Language*, 4th edn, London: Routledge.

Blake, N.F. (1996) *A History of the English Language*, Basingstoke: Macmillan.

Bryson, B. (1990) *Mother Tongue*, Harmondsworth: Penguin.

Coates, J. (1986) *Men, Women and Language*, London: Longman.

Crystal, D. (1987) *Cambridge Encyclopaedia of the English Language*, Cambridge: Cambridge University Press.

Crystal, D. (1997) *English as a Global Language*, Cambridge: Cambridge University Press.

Honey, J. (1997) *The Story of Standard English and its Enemies*, London: Faber & Faber.

Hughes, A. and Trudgill, P. (1996) *English Accents and Dialects*, London: Arnold.

Kay, B. (1993) *Scots: The Mither Tongue*, Darvel: Alloway Publishing.

Leith, D. (1983) *A Social History of English*, London: Routledge.

Montgomery, M. (1995) *An Introduction to Language and Society*, London: Routledge.

Sutcliffe, D. (1982) *British Black English*, London: Blackwell.

Wells, J.C. (1982) *Accents of English*, Cambridge: Cambridge University Press.

3

Newspapers, magazines and journalism

NEWSPAPERS IN BRITAIN

Introduction

There is a wide choice of press in Britain, with approximately 130 daily and 1,800 weekly newspapers. Many dailies also publish a Saturday or Sunday edition with special colour supplements on homes, cars, fashion, finance gardening, travel, and so on. The national newspapers have an average total circulation of 13 million on weekdays, and about 14.5 million on Sundays, and with each copy often read by more than one person. There are also some 900 free newspapers which are financed by advertising and appear weekly. In 2002/03 some 63 per cent of the population aged over 15 read a national newspaper every day (66 per cent of men and 59 per cent of women) and 85 per cent a regional or local paper.

Current newspapers and back issues can often be consulted free in public libraries, but are only rarely available in pubs and cafés. Instead, many people have them delivered to the house, and breakfast over a newspaper has become a ritual in millions of kitchens. This intimacy has helped to create a special bond between the British and their newspapers. The newspaper owners target their press not so much to a particular age group, region or ethnic majority, but to a particular social class and political affiliation, and for this reason they have said as much about the people who read them as the world they report. The political leanings of different newspapers as well as the conspicuous difference between larger broadsheets and smaller tabloids, have ensured that for many readers their newspaper has become a badge of social identity.

The *Guardian*, the *Independent*, the *Daily Telegraph*, *The Times* and the *Financial Times* have been considered as the most prestigious papers, as they were traditionally read by wealthier and more educated social classes. However, these only account for around 15 per cent of all newspapers sold in Britain, as the mid-market papers of the *Daily Mail* and *Daily Express*, and the popular daily press of the *Sun*, *Daily Mirror* and the *Daily Star* all sell far more (see Table 3.1).

By tradition, the British national press is free of political control. No newspaper is owned by the government, and the press is able openly to criticise any political party and its policies. However, the press has never been impartial. There is no legal requirement for it to be so, unlike with the television and BBC radio news which is more strictly regulated. Consequently, outspoken political views are often found in newspaper editorial articles and columns. These are most clearly stated at election time, and derive from the interests of their owners. Despite their freedom, the newspapers are usually careful to avoid criticising the business of the advertisers, as the press also depends heavily on sales and advertising for its income.

One of the most consistent characteristics of the British press is its language, which features much inventive wordplay in its headlines and style of writing. The language used is often witty and imaginative, with alliteration, puns, amusing misspellings, references to literature and history. This serves to capture the reader's eye, raise a smile and stimulate the imagination, but for foreign readers it can sometimes render simple stories unintelligible.

Most articles and reports are written by men, but in the past 30 years female journalists and editors have become more numerous. However, with the exception of opinion columns, the kind of articles written by women are predominently on lighter issues, such as family, marriage, the intimate lives of celebrities and royalty. In contrast, coverage of serious political issues remains a male-dominated field of journalism. Moreover, there has been little evidence that female editors make the content or editorial style of the paper more appealing or accessible to female readers.

Until the 1980s most of the national newspapers were based in London's Fleet Street in the heart of the city, but now many are based in modern premises in the outskirts. The London base means they are often accused of having a strong bias towards London politics, economics and culture. The *London Evening Standard* has the highest sales among local and regional papers with currently around 400,000 sales per edition. However, the importance of the regional press is indicated by the fact that there are approximately 1,300 local or regional newspapers serving other parts of Britain, which are read by 90 per cent of the population. The *Daily Record* has the highest circulation of the Scottish newspapers, and the *Western Mail* has the highest circulation in Wales. The Welsh press also includes bilingual newspapers, and papers solely in Welsh which receive an annual grant from central government. Across in Northern Ireland, papers

Table 3.1 Newspaper circulation in Britain

Title	Year first published	Controlled by	Circulation
Popular dailies			
Daily Mirror	1903	Trinity Mirror plc	1,748,026
Daily Star	1978	Express Newspapers Ltd	846,169
Sun	1964	News International Newspapers Ltd	3,239,041
Mid-market dailies			
Daily Mail	1896	Associated Newspapers Ltd	2,403,073
Daily Express	1900	Express Newspapers Ltd	892,533
Quality dailies			
Financial Times	1888	Financial Times Ltd	425,259
Daily Telegraph	1855	Telegraph Group Ltd	917,001
Guardian	1821	Guardian Newspapers Ltd	377,292
Independent	1986	Independent Newspapers (UK) Ltd	262,293
The Times	1785	News International Newspapers Ltd	682,109
National Sunday newspapers			
Popular Sundays			
News of the World	1843	News International Newspapers Ltd	3,631,057
Sunday Mirror	1963	Trinity Mirror plc	1,591,708
People	1881	Trinity Mirror plc	931,019
Mid-market Sundays			
Mail on Sunday	1982	Associated Newspapers Ltd	2,531,928
Sunday Express	1918	United News & Media plc	996,049
Quality Sundays			
Sunday Telegraph	1961	Telegraph Group Ltd	694,304
Independent on Sunday	1990	Independent Newspapers (UK) Ltd	212,172
The Observer	1791	Guardian Newspapers Ltd	459,952
Sunday Times	1822	News International Newspapers Ltd	1,363,512

Source: Audit Bureau of Circulations, November 2004.

43

from the British mainland as well as the Irish Republic are widely available. In addition, most national and local newspapers now have websites; these have expanded greatly in recent years, and in 2003 there were over 600.

Since 1945 the British press, like mass communications in general, has changed greatly. The number of newspapers has declined, sales have fallen, and the nature of journalism has changed, becoming generally more populist, and it is said, dumbed down. There are also fewer owners, and their individual power has grown. Nevertheless, public and academic interest in the media is strong, and courses in mass communications, media studies, journalism and public relations are among the most popular courses read by undergraduates and postgraduates in British universities.

Pioneers

Until the eighteenth century news was commonly spread by a 'town crier' who would walk through towns and villages making public announcements. Most people could not read, but his familiar cry of 'Oyez! Oyez! Oyez!' (from old French, meaning 'listen!') drew attention to major news of wars, crimes, tax increases and so on. Production costs, transport difficulties and general illiteracy prevented large-scale publication, distribution and sale of newspapers, but gradually they began to appear for a small, educated, wealthy readership.

The first English newspaper – the *Daily Courant* – was published in 1702, although newspapers of today were established much later. *The Times* (1785), the *Observer* (1791) and the *Sunday Times* (1822) are among the oldest which are still in print. Initially their circulations were very small as literacy levels were low. However, after the introduction of the Education Act of 1870, standards improved and there was a new, expanding lower-middle class of literate clerical workers. They had little interest in the papers written for an educated, wealthy elite, but there was demand for simple, interesting stories in print. In response, a popular national press began to grow, with papers such as the *News of the World* (1843) and the *People* (1881).

At first, newspapers were printed only in the larger, broadsheet style, due to a government tax on the number of pages. But in the late nineteenth century, prices fell and cheap popular newspapers for the less wealthy were mass produced in a smaller, more manageable 'tabloid' size. The larger broadsheets, however, kept their traditional format, creating a distinction between the two. Since then, the quality press has gained a reputation for greater focus on economic, political and cultural coverage, in longer articles written with longer sentences, and with more formal vocabulary. In contrast, the popular press has become synonymous with sensational, lighter stories, presented in shorter articles with more colloquial vocabulary, and with more emphasis on pictures and news of well-known people from show business and sports. Both kinds of paper also carry cartoons. Political satire has a long history in Britain, from the images drawn by Hogarth and Gillray in the eighteenth and nineteenth century, to those of Steve Bell, Heath and many others of the present day.

'Read all about it!' – the influence of the press

The new popular press sold well, and an expanding industry attracted a new class of business people or 'press barons' who saw the possibilities for profits and self-advancement, as well as the chance to influence the political and economic affairs of the time. Many of the family names associated with the industry in the beginning are still involved today. The Irishman Alfred Harmsworth (who later became Lord Northcliffe) was the first British press entrepreneur. He wanted to produce a newspaper like those being published in the USA, and in 1896 founded the *Daily Mail*, before later buying the *Observer* and *The Times*.

But in the early decades of the twentieth century the public had few opportunities to gain and exchange information about what was happening in the world. There was still no radio or television, and most newspapers supported the politics of the right and opposed demands for reform from organised labour and women. Moreover, standards of education were generally poor, and the majority of students left school with little more than a basic ability to read and write. Consequently, those with control of information were able easily to influence people and politics.

As the owner of several popular newspapers Harmsworth enjoyed great power, and saw his readers as his voters. During the First World War he entered government and took charge of propaganda. The family's influence became more established when his brother Harold (who later became Lord Rothermere) took control of several newspapers following Alfred's death in 1922. To frighten the British public, before the 1924 General Election he published the 'Zinoviev Letter', a document allegedly from the Russian government which urged British communists in the Labour Party to start a revolution. Although the document was subsequently exposed as a forgery, it succeeded in its aim and contributed to the defeat of Labour. Some years later, during the 1930s, Harmsworth supported Oswald Mosley's National Union of Fascists. He later met Adolf Hitler, and used his newspaper columns to excuse Hitler's persecution of the Jews.

A reputation was established among the most popular British press for supporting conservative, right-wing interests, and being hostile to progressive attempts at redistribution of wealth, social reform and equal rights for women. However, one of the few papers which traditionally supported the Labour Party is the *Daily Mirror*. When it was founded by Harmsworth in 1903 it was initially aimed at a new readership of literate women, but sales fell until the paper became a picture paper which was sympathetic to the Labour Party, and soon it became one of the most popular papers in Britain. It remained so until the mid-1980s, when a change of politics under its new owner, Robert Maxwell, led to falling sales, high levels of debt, theft from *Mirror* employees, and finally the mysterious and dramatic death of its owner, who drowned at night off his yacht in the Mediterranean.

Britain is one of the few countries which allows foreign ownership of major media enterprises, and since 1945 there has been substantial involvement by non-British owners. Robert Maxwell was born Jan Ludwig Hoch, a Czech. More recently, until 2004 the Canadian businessman Conrad Black held various media interests in the USA, as well as the *Daily Telegraph*, the mouthpiece of the Tory Party. Rupert Murdoch (originally an Australian and now a naturalised American) currently holds substantial media interests, including the *Sun*, *The Times*, the *News of the World*, the *Sunday Times*, as well as Sky TV, and other American media companies.

The well-defined political views on current topics held by newspaper owners can usually be found in press editorials, as well as in the selection and coverage of news stories. The political 'line' of the paper can be seen most clearly at election time, when readers are urged to support one or other one of the major parties. However, since the mid-1990s press allegiances have become less clearly defined. Most are critical of the current Labour government, and to some extent this is due to journalists who see it as their duty to criticise the government of the day, and also because their owners want to express their own right-wing political views. Another reason is that, since the mid-1990s, the Tory Party has become so weak and incapable that the press appears to have taken on the role of unofficial opposition. Yet at the last three elections of 1997, 2001 and 2005 most of the press supported Labour – despite the critical stance of the owners of the newspapers. This is because the press barons are shrewd and pragmatic individuals who, in troubled times of falling sales, fully understand the need to 'back the winner' and be popular in order to sell papers and remain solvent.

Another common criticism is that the Conservative-supporting press sometimes sensationalise and exaggerate certain types of behaviour, giving the impression that it is something new, dangerous and more common than it really is, in order to sell newspapers and strengthen a conservative view of the world. Dramatic headlines, stories and pictures are published, together with lurid descriptions and labels, and debates about the topic are based on stereotypes and prejudice against the alleged behaviour rather than facts. In consequence, members of the public become worried and demand tough action from the police and politicians. However, close examination often shows reports to be exaggerated or untrue, and photos to be staged or posed, in episodes known as 'moral panics'.

During the past 50 years there have been panics over various youth subcultures such as Teds, mods, rockers and 'New Age' travellers, as well as drug takers, inner-city black youths and asylum seekers. These very different groups could not defend themselves against vicious press attacks, and people who had no direct experience of them became angry and worried. They demanded tough political action, and created a situation which the political right could exploit by promising tough measures and 'zero tolerance' against what was essentially a minor or trivial threat, compared, for example, with the consequences of unemployment, the erosion of welfare benefits or the unavailability of affordable housing.

It is often discussed to what extent the newspapers influence voters. Results of recent British election study surveys suggest two things: that people vote according to the advice given in their newspapers, and that editors and proprietors reflect the views of their readers. If both things are happening at the same time, it means that editors and newspaper owners are exercising real political power through their ability to influence people's political preferences. However, another view – often held by those who work in the media – is that people buy a newspaper because they like its tone, the pictures and the sports coverage, rather than its attitude to the political parties.

The press under pressure

Clearly, newspapers have become important 'players' in British politics. They are sometimes referred to as the 'Fourth Estate', after the three principal institutions of Church, Crown and Parliament. But since 1971 the sales of British daily and Sunday newspapers have been falling gradually. Commentators suggest this is for a number of reasons. First, an increase in the number of daily papers has created more competition. Television has also had a substantial impact, and with the gradual deregulation of broadcasting since the 1990s, a multitude of different news, sport and entertainment channels has appeared. These receive news on a 24-hour feed, which is more up-to-date, convenient, and sometimes more reliable than newspapers from the day before. Other sources of information and entertainment such as the internet have grown rapidly, providing news which is both up-to-date and fun to use. Most important, however, is the disappearance of political ideology and dogma from British politics, reflecting the broader changes in world politics after the fall of communism.

In the past newspapers have forged their identities around the traditional political certainties of left and right, but they now need to find new ways of attracting readers, whose own politics have fragmented and diversified, and who now look less and less to their newspapers to find ideas and information about the major issues of the day. The main way in which newspapers have addressed this problem is to carry more light, popular news to the point where they begin to resemble magazines, with 'celebrity' stories and scandals about people in sport, television, music and popular culture in general, together with attempts to seduce readers with discounts and free gifts, cheap air tickets and restaurant meals, CDs and price cuts.

Thus, commentators argue that the British press, and other cultural products, have become more like a form of entertainment, rather than a source of news and education.

Increased competition and financial pressure has also heightened the need to look for stories and to be the first to report them. In recent years this has produced important revelations of corruption, hypocrisy and abuses of power among Tory officials, especially in the 1990s when many members of the Conservative government including Jeffrey Archer, Jonathan Aitken, David Mellor, Neil Hamilton and others were forced to resign following newspaper investigations into their financial and personal affairs.

Increased pressure has also brought a greater vulnerability to hoaxes. Some of the most notorious include a *Sunday Times* story in 1983, claiming that the paper had obtained a 62-volume collection of Adolf Hitler's diaries, but in reality they were fakes produced by a German antique dealer. In 1996 the *Sun* claimed to have a video tape of Princess Diana and her lover James Hewitt enjoying life, but in fact it was made with amateur actors in a suburban living room. More seriously, in 2004 the *Daily Mirror* published photos which it claimed were of Iraqi prisoners of war being abused by British troops. Again, the photos were a hoax, and the editor Piers Morgan was forced to resign. The same year, the *Daily Telegraph* was sued and forced to pay £1.2 million after claiming that the then Labour MP George Galloway had been financed by Iraqi President Saddam Hussein.

An important aspect of press freedom is that there is no law of privacy to protect public figures. Although the press is not allowed to publish false information that is likely to damage an individual's reputation, they frequently publish photos of well-known 'personalities' in contexts which are private. This trend became pronounced in the 1980s, particularly with the fervent interest surrounding the wedding of Prince Charles and Diana, Princess of Wales. When the marriage began to fail, interest in royal affairs became more acute, and in the pages of some of the popular press it was caricatured as a soap opera. This presented an enormous contrast to the serious, deferential reporting which had previously characterised press coverage of the royal family, but nevertheless helped to sell many newspapers.

Since the 1960s British society has become much more open, less deferential and hierarchical, and today the public demand to know 'the facts' about the behaviour of those in positions of authority and influence. However, it is not only the politicians and the royal family being pursued and photographed by the 'paparazzi' and 'undercover' reporters, but also a new celebrity culture of stars of television, pop and sport who are regularly photographed and reported on in a range of newspapers and magazines as if this were a matter of public interest. This has led to many high-profile cases in which private individuals have sued the press to gain redress for false allegations made about them. For example, in one case the

Daily Mirror published photographs of the model Naomi Campbell leaving a clinic for Alcoholics Anonymous. Campbell subsequently sued the paper and won a substantial amount of money. However, litigation is usually long, very expensive and involves further publicity, so most individuals feel it is not worthwhile.

The *Sun*

The best-selling newspaper in the history of Britain is the *Sun*. It has become famous for its funny, sharp headlines, its wordplay, for capturing the mood of its readers, influencing their views, and often forcing the government to listen. Its supporters say it is the common voice of the country, but its critics argue that it has nasty politics and an aggressive populism, which in the past has often been mischievous and malevolent.

The paper began in 1964, when the left-wing *Daily Herald* was relaunched as the *Sun*. In 1969 it was bought by Australian-American billionaire Rupert Murdoch, who currently owns the paper. Murdoch wanted to expand the appeal of the *Sun* to a wider audience, and began to attract readers by focusing on sex and sport. A picture of a topless model was published every day on Page 3, and the paper began to include coverage of all major sports events. Its new formula proved popular, and by 1978 its circulation had increased to 4 million copies per day.

Until 1979 the *Sun* had supported the trade unions and the Labour Party, but it switched its political allegiance to the Conservatives before the election of that year. Its leading article proclaimed:

> Vote Tory this time. It's the only way to stop the rot. This is 'D' Day. 'D' for decision. The choice you have to make today, is quite simply between freedom and shackle. With Margaret Thatcher there is a chance for us to look to the skies.
>
> (2 May 1979: 2)

The election was won by Margaret Thatcher and brought the start of 18 years of Tory rule. The *Sun* became Thatcherite propaganda. Stories were carefully chosen, oversimplified and presented as 'black and white' in a way that avoided complexity or careful analysis, while a popular diet of celebrity and sport amused its readers. Meanwhile, the newspaper damaged the Labour Party with humour and often inaccurate reporting.

During Britain's war with Argentina over the Falkland Islands (Malvinas), the paper enthusiastically ran competitions for the best anti-Argentinian jokes. It also sponsored a missile, encouraged a boycott of Argentinian corned beef, and published crass, insensitive headlines such as 'Gotcha' when 1,200 Argentines were killed as the warship *Belgrano* was sunk. But despite criticism for becoming aggressive, prejudiced and jingoistic, it became the most popular newspaper of its time.

After the defeat of Argentina the *Sun* began to attack those Thatcher called 'the enemy within'. Gay rights, women's rights and Labour Party attempts to promote a fairer, more equal and tolerant society were all criticised and ridiculed as the politics of the 'loony left'. But despite sometimes violent police action in industrial disputes with print workers, miners and others, the authorities were rarely criticised.

By the mid-1980s the economy began to improve and conspicuous consumption became fashionable. In 1989 the new four-channel satellite television service Sky Television began broadcasting, launched by Rupert Murdock's company News International, and the *Sun* contained frequent 'plugs' for its news and sports programmes, as well as adverts for the dish needed to receive them. Meanwhile, Tory minister Norman Tebbit praised the paper's topless 'Page 3' girl, telling readers she was really the working man's Venus de Milo, to much public amusement.

During the time of its highest circulation (1981–94) the editor was Kelvin MacKenzie, who introduced a mixture of gossip, celebrity, television, sport and reality TV. But its popularity has not always been constant: for example in 1989 the *Sun* reported the news that 74 Liverpool fans had died at a football match at Hillsborough in Sheffield. The paper implied the fans were to blame, in reports which offended the people of Liverpool, who had not liked its Thatcherite politics and anti-trade unionism. In protest on Merseyside, copies were publicly burnt and newsagents refused to sell it.

In the 1990s sales of the *Sun* fell, as the Tory government became more and more unpopular. Eventually, in 1997, the paper realised that it could not tell people to vote for the party likely to lose the election, and so advised its readers to vote for Labour. It was a pragmatic gesture, which showed the paper's need for sales and popularity.

Since then, in response to changes in social attitudes and a less politically polarised society, the *Sun* has gradually become much less aggressive than in the 1980s. There has been a gradual shift towards attacking government policies rather than personalities. However, it still claims to defend values that are said to be 'British' but are often those of the newspaper or its owner. For example, a campaign against asylum seekers in 2003 was carried out under sensational, populist headlines such as 'Our Heritage is Crumbling', 'Migrant Horde in Hospital Rampage' and 'Richest Town in Britain Swamped by Illegals'. In a similar vein, a flavour of the *Sun*'s attitude towards

Europe can be seen in its 'Guide to the EU Constitution' published on 22/04/04 (p. 13) which states 'Our army will have to follow EU orders', 'We will be ordered what to say at the UN: the new EU foreign minister will speak for Britain at the Security Council', 'We will lose control of our borders and have no say in who enters the country', all of which seem unlikely.

Today, as with many other popular newspapers, 'showbiz' stories, drama, sex, money and sports stories still take up most of the paper, largely reflecting the content, style and tone of Sky TV. But in spite of its crude, brash populism its circulation (like that of many newspapers) continues to decline. Nevertheless, politicians of all the main parties still see it as a potentially important ally in a general election. Meanwhile, critics observe that although the newspaper has produced some witty tabloid journalism, good light entertainment and wide sports coverage, it has also produced stories which are unreliable, exaggerated and untrue.

The press and public confidence

Critics argue that for too long the press has exercised power without responsibility, and has had too much freedom to publish stories about those in public life as well as those outside it. This is because there is no state control or censorship of the press, and reporters are subject to English law in the same way as other citizens.

Complaints about press invasion into people's private lives are investigated by the Press Complaints Commission, which was set up in 1990. It operates a code of practice agreed by editors, which covers inaccuracy, invasion of privacy, harassment and misrepresentation by the press. In 2002 the Commission received 2,630 complaints (a decrease of 13 per cent on the previous year). Over half related to national newspapers. Most were resolved by the editors beforehand, and only 17 were upheld. Despite this, a MORI survey found that in 2003 more people were dissatisfied than satisfied with the press, and public demands for tougher rules to control press behaviour are common. Consequently, it is argued that British journalists face no real sanctions from the current policy of press self-regulation, or from the Press Complaints Commission, and also that editors and proprietors encourage their inaccuracies, exaggerations and invasions of privacy in a bid to win readers and arrest falling sales. Nevertheless, there are some important restrictions on press freedom, for example newspapers may not give opinions about or influence legal proceedings while they are taking place; if they do they can be prosecuted for 'contempt of court'. They are also prohibited from revealing official secrets.

In spite of their frequent, detailed, forensic analyses of other institutions and individuals, journalists' and newspapers' own ways of working are seldom exposed to the public. Newspapers rarely carry any critical comments about other journalists, or the way the press works. They are naturally reluctant to encourage criticism of their own industry, and the 'press barons' are shady figures who are rarely seen. Moreover, all governments fear them and want their support. If they openly criticise the press or demand new laws to limit its freedom, they risk a hostile reaction which could damage the party's reputation and its popularity with voters. Thus, in the twenty-first century there were serious concerns about the concentration of newspapers, magazines and TV stations into the hands of fewer and fewer global corporations or 'big brothers', and questions about how impartial the news services would remain in future.

The lack of openness may be another reason why the press is gradually losing the confidence of its readers. The public finds journalists among the least trusted members of society, along with politicians and estate agents. This view was supported in one poll for the *Observer* newspaper, conducted by the market research company ICM in 2003. It found that broadsheet newspapers such as *The Times*, *Telegraph* and *Guardian* are widely trusted by 59 per cent of Britons in general, and by 83 per cent of those who read them. But papers such as the *Mirror*, *Sun* and *News of the World* are in a different category; only 17 per cent trust them while 78 per cent do not. Among readers of those papers, 68 per cent do not, and just 30 per cent say they trust them 'a lot or a fair amount'. It seems that most people do not buy the popular press expecting responsible, truthful journalism, but instead seek entertainment from the tone of the paper, the sport and the pictures.

Ethnic and alternative publications

Many newspapers published in Britain are prepared by and for different ethnic communities, such as the Chinese newspaper *Sing Tao*, the Arabic paper *Al-Arab*, and the *Jewish Chronicle*, a long-established paper founded in 1841. Other dailies include the *Asian Times*, an English language weekly for people of Asian descent, and *Q-News*, a progressive journal for young Muslims with religious, political and lifestyle features. Afro-Caribbean publications include *The Voice*, the *Caribbean Times* and *New Nation*, while several other publications appear in Bengali, Gujarati, Hindi, Punjabi and Urdu.

Some ethnic newspapers have been produced in response to what was seen as unfair representation in the British press. For example, during the early 1980s much attention was given in the papers to an association between race and crime, and racist reports in the mainstream popular press alleged that black people caused trouble and took white people's homes and jobs. In response, black communities wanted a newspaper which would represent their interests more fairly, and in 1982 *The Voice* was launched, a weekly paper that aims to project positive images about and for the black community to a younger readership aged mainly between 15 and 34. It has also gained a strong reputation as a populist newspaper which campaigns to correct miscarriages of justice involving black people. It currently has a circulation of around 45,000, and a readership of almost 200,000.

Another magazine produced in response to poor coverage in the main-stream press is the *Big Issue*, a popular weekly magazine that originally focused on the issue of homelessness, but now addresses wider social issues. It is unique in that homeless men and women are trained as vendors of the magazine, and can be seen selling it on the streets of most large towns and cities.

During the 1980s most of the mainstream press and other publications supported the Tory government, and it was difficult for other, dissenting voices to be heard. There was still no internet, but communication across the counter-culture was facilitated by the production of home-produced journals and 'fanzines' which were printed or written by hand and photo-copied in sheds and bedrooms around Britain. Fanzines aimed to cover topics which the commercial, mainstream press often ignored. They first appeared in the 1970s in response to the mainstream's sensational, exaggerated reporting of the punk phenomenon. Fans of the scene felt it was being misrepresented, and that commercial motives prevented accurate reporting by the press. Instead, new publications were created by fans for fans and in the language of fans. *Sniffin' Glue* was among the first. It was rarely sold in newsagents, but could be bought directly from the people who wrote it, whose mission was aided by the development of photocopying which offered a cheap means of publishing.

Later in the 1980s and 1990s football fanzines appeared in response to what fans saw as the game's domination by money and celebrity. They carried lively, humorous articles written by and for *supporters*, who were passionate about the game, not *consumers* of it. Some of the most notable have evolved to become more mainstream publications such as the informa-tive, irreverent *When Saturday Comes*, while many other publications and forums have become widely available on the internet. Today, a wide range of fanzines cover music, sport and sometimes cinema, and are found mainly on the internet. Most are witty, apolitical and written with an infec-tious enthusiasm, as an antidote to the increasingly commercial nature of commentary, journalism and public relations surrounding many aspects of popular culture.

The boom in political satire in the late 1950s and early 1960s led to the creation of *Private Eye*, a humourous and irreverent magazine dedicated to the satire of people and events in politics, business and the media. However, it also features serious, investigative reports into the same areas, exposing events which the mainstream press are often reluctant to report. The magazine is readily identified by its covers, which traditionally show a picture of someone in the news with a comic speech 'bubble' attached. Meanwhile, the bleaker, more desperate aspects of British life are humorously detailed in *Viz*, founded in 1979, the year Margaret Thatcher was first elected, as an anarchic, darkly humorous, chillingly bleak and occasionally surreal commentary on urban life in the north-east, through the adventures of politically incorrect, dysfunctional characters who include 'Roger Mellie the Man on the Telly', '8 Ace' and the 'Fat Slags'.

MAGAZINES

There is an enormous market in Britain for light reading on leisure and entertainment, and a glance at the shelves of any newsagent reveals a huge variety of magazines directed at people's interests, wants, needs and fantasies. Numerous titles cater for education, culture and the arts, such as the *Times Higher Educational Supplement*, the *Times Literary Supplement* and *Granta*, while journals of opinion include *The Economist* (a mostly independent analysis of current affairs), the *New Statesman* (a socialist review of current affairs, politics and the arts) and the *Spectator* (a more conservative review of daily life). But the vast majority of magazines are 'consumer' titles, which consist of about 7,000 separate publications with information on cars, computers, hobbies and so on, as well as business and professional titles with information relevant to people's work.

The business of magazine publishing is very much subject to fashion and change and new titles are constantly appearing, particularly in the field of magazines for women where there are about 80 different journals which traditionally enjoy a large readership. Many, such as *Cosmopolitan* and *Marie Claire*, are produced to offer advice on contemporary issues such as money, sex and contraception, as well as more general subjects such as fashion, travel, the law and so on. Another category includes magazines featuring photographs and gossip about the 'new aristocracy' of television, pop and sports stars, shown for example going to a party, getting married, or cooking Sunday lunch. They include well-known titles such as *Hello!* and *OK!*; however, their popularity is small compared with the top-selling *Take a Break*, a puzzle magazine with 'true life stories', which enjoys weekly UK sales of around 1.4 million.

The freedom and independence enjoyed by British teenagers is high-lighted in the subject matter of publications available for younger teenage girls, such as *Sugar* and *Just Seventeen*, which feature pop music, fashion, romance, pin-ups, romantic photostrips and frank discussion of teenage girls' problems. For younger boys and girls there are titles such as the *Beano* and the *Dandy*, traditional comics founded in the mid-1930s which still feature many of their original cartoon characters such as Dennis the Menace, Little Plum and Biffo the Bear.

For many years women's magazines and titles for young readers have been traditional categories of the magazine market, but among the newest trends is the appearance of men's 'lifestyle' or general interest magazines, such as *FHM*, *Loaded* and *Maxim*. Popularly known as 'lad mags', the number of titles has expanded greatly since the 1990s, and they carry a mixture of general interest features, humour and numerous pictures of bikini-clad girls for a male readership aged mainly under 35.

Most magazines are sold in newsagents and supermarkets, as well as in bookshops, or through regular subscriptions direct to readers' homes. Many also have internet sites where readers can get information or preview the latest edition. The sales figures of magazines are important to advertisers, and are published every six months by the Audit Bureau of Circulations. Advertisers also want to know what kind of readers buy a particular magazine, and the National Readership Survey analyses readers' social class, age, sex, as well as the magazine's similarity to other titles. This information is then used by advertising agencies to target appropriate titles with information about their products.

Despite the variety of titles aimed at carefully selected demographics of the market, according to age, gender and social background, the top-selling magazines are general publications carrying details of forthcoming television and radio programmes on terrestrial and satellite stations, such as *Radio Times* and *TV Times*. They regularly sell more than a million copies each, and reflect the importance, popularity and centrality of television in everyday life.

When people do decide to go out, they can get information on the dates, times and locations of all kinds of events, from sport, cinema and theatre, to gay and lesbian events in London and elsewhere in *Time Out*, a weekly magazine available in most of the larger cities.

Women's magazines

After TV magazines, women's magazines are the most popular category in terms of sales. They have a long history, and changes in society and the position of women have been reflected in different types of publication. As with newspapers, the early magazines were directed towards the wealthy and educated, as this was the only class that could afford them and read well. Content reflected the lifestyle of ladies of leisure, for example the *Ladies' Mercury*, launched in 1693, claimed to provide answers to all 'the most nice and curious questions concerning love, marriage, behaviour, dress and humour of the female sex, whether virgins, wives or widows'. Since then, many magazines have come and gone, leaving the *Tatler* (1709) and *The Lady* (1885) as two of Britain's oldest.

During the mid-nineteenth century demand grew for printed matter of all kinds, and there was an expansion in the number of women's titles. Despite calls in parliament for more equality for women, most press ignored feminist politics, revolutionary thought and demands for universal suffrage, believing it could put readers off. Queen Victoria agreed, and gave permission for her title to be used for the magazine *Queen* in 1861, a publication aimed at upper-class young women, which lasted until it merged with *Harper's Bazaar* in 1970 and became *Harpers & Queen*.

In the early twentieth century new types of popular press appeared when more women began to work outside the home. For many years domestic service in large households had been a great employer of young, single women, but during the Great War of 1914–18 the majority had gone out to do factory work. This was better paid and often easier, and consequently many women did not want to return to housework. Literacy rates had also improved, and magazines began to appear for younger readers, such as *Pegs's Paper* (1919), a light, chatty publication which allowed girls to relax and float away on a romantic white horse, in stories featuring, for example, a doctor who meets a young factory girl while on holiday at the seaside.

In contrast, the more established, traditional magazines of *The Lady*, *Queen* and *Vogue* continued to feature stories and articles by the best-known literary authors of the day, such as Aldous Huxley, Evelyn Waugh, Wyndham Lewis and Somerset Maugham. These were mixed in with news about the movements of aristocrats and illustrations of international fashion, written for women who had no need to go out to work or be involved in politics.

During the years of the Second World War magazines aimed to boost the morale of women, who were suffering on the 'home front'. They encouraged women to be determined, with features on how to survive a bombing, the splitting up of families, the evacuation of children and life after bereavement. In 1941 *Ideal Home* magazine even ran a feature on rebuilding a bombed home. But the austerity of the war and post-war years gradually gave way to a feeling of optimism, most notably reflected in new magazines such as *Vanity Fair*. Launched in 1949 and describing itself as 'for the younger, smarter woman', it contained cheaper youthful fashion ideas which could even be copied. This was a new development, as fashion had previously followed the 'canon' of 'haute couture' as dictated by the major fashion houses. In 1955 *She* was launched, with less emphasis on fashion and more on entertainment, with a variety of topics of interest to the 1950s' woman, namely, films, photography, camping, caravanning and DIY.

The 1950s witnessed a number of social and cultural developments affecting the style and content of future women's magazines. Better public health and information campaigns conducted through the National Health Service were beginning to make women more health conscious. Obesity rather than malnutrition was identified as a problem, prompting features on slimming, weight-watching and health in general. Women were also becoming more politicised, gaining more freedom and equality, and the first female peers were taking their seats in the House of Lords. Moreover, the economy was booming, and rationing was a distant memory. Far more women were now going to university and earning a living, and commercial television, which had begun in 1955, was popular with viewers and advertisers, helping to create a new generation of aspirational female consumers.

Magazines for women were changing in consonance with the social changes, often inspired by the *Sunday Times Magazine*, which was launched to accompany the paper in 1964. Innovative and stylish, it carried strong photo-journalism and features on varied aspects of contemporary life, as well as aspirational adverts for high quality consumer products, jewellery, drinks and cars. *Nova* (1965) had a similar style, with pictures of contemporary stars by leading photographers such as Terry Donovan and Helmut Newton. It also became more daring; one famous cover advertised 'how to undress in front of your husband', and a feature inside explained how 'inside every woman is a stripper longing to get out'. In contrast, magazines such as *Queen* still retained more traditional elements, such as pictures of guests at horse events and debutantes' balls; the difference between the two was said to be that '*Queen* readers drive out of town at weekends, while *Nova* readers drive in', in an attempt to illustrate a growing cultural divide between the traditional and modern young woman.

By the mid-1960s not only women in their 20s and 30s were looking for a new style of magazine, but adolescents too. Teenagers had more freedom and money to spend, and a new popular culture was beginning to appeal to their tastes and preferences, reflected in weeklies such as *Honey* (1960–86), *Jackie* (1963–93) and *Fab* (1964–80). *Jackie* was named after the wife of the American president John F. Kennedy, who was seen as a fashionable role model by many young girls. Aimed at 10–15 year olds, it was typical of many magazines of the era. On the cover of the first edition was the pop star Cliff Richard and free inside was a 'twin heart' ring. Content included colour pictures of the Beatles, picture love stories, and a page of readers' problems answered by an 'agony aunt'. The formula was highly successful attracting over 1 million young readers by 1970. It changed little in 30 years, and its influence on the attitudes and behaviour of young girls has been the subject of much analysis by cultural historians and other academics keen to analyse the attitudes and values reflected and encouraged in its pages.

Women's liberation was a predominant theme of the 1970s and many magazines for women aged 18 and over were launched to promote its agenda. The first one to do so in a mainstream, commercial way was *Cosmopolitan*, first imported from the USA in 1972. The magazine was not new, having begun almost a century earlier in 1886. But during the late 1960s under the progressive young editor Helen Gurley Brown it promoted independence self-improvement and self-confidence in a bright, colourful, glossy magazine which showed how young women could get the best for themselves, their careers and their sex lives. The magazine enjoyed enormous commercial success, and set the standard for others to follow.

In contrast, new non-commercial 'underground' magazines such as *Shrew* and *Spare Rib* (1972–93) gave coverage and support to a different kind of women's liberation. Unlike most other magazines for women, *Spare Rib* was not glossy, not commercial, but radically feminist. There were no adverts or features on fragrances, fashion or cosmetics, only small adverts for folk festivals, political rallies, lesbian events and shoes made by collectives. Its contributors argued that the mainstream advertisers in *Cosmopolitan* and other magazines made women feel insecure about themselves in order to make profits.

Cosmopolitan's radical style was influential and other magazines appeared with a similar agenda, but they were generally less successful. One exception has been the *Feminist Review*, which began in 1979 as a socialist-feminist monthly, and later attempted to bridge the divide between what it called academic and active feminism. The appearance of such magazines reflected a broader trend towards more specialised publications with different agendas aimed at different types of women. This continued with the launching of magazines for women in Britain's various ethnic communities. *Sheba* (1979–80) appeared briefly for Arab women domiciled in the UK. *Black Beauty and Hair* (1987–) continues to report on exactly what its name suggests. But there have been few successful specialist magazines for ethnic groups, and circulations remain small, which in turn makes it difficult to attract advertising. This is because some women feel they want to integrate into the British mainstream by reading mainstream magazines. Moreover, the women of some immigrant groups have only limited possibilities for learning the English language, and are thus unable to access publications in English.

Guilty pleasures? Magazines in Britain today

Magazines are highly profitable, and several large international media concerns dominate the market, such as EMAP, Condé Nast, OPC, National Magazines, Gruhner and Jahr, Bauer, and DC Thompson, while several other independent companies publish on a smaller scale.

Some of the most popular magazines are consumer 'lifestyle' titles, in particular those dealing with houses and gardens. Since the 1980s and the boom in house prices, property development became a popular means of generating income. For many people, home improvements, DIY and interior design changed from being a hobby and a means of building a more comfortable domestic environment, to a way of expressing individuality and identity. The house became not just a place to live but a fashionable commodity. For many Britons, the vast array of furnishings, fittings, accessories and components have fuelled this new aspect of consumerism, and to meet and accentuate demand the range of magazines covering houses and gardens has expanded greatly. In the 1980s the fashionable 'look' was a traditional, countrified one, heavily influenced by conservative values, and the 'ideal type' of Charles and Diana. It was heavily promoted in new magazines which appeared throughout the decade. Titles such as *Traditional Homes* (1984), *Country Living* (1985), *Country Homes and Interiors* (1986) and *County* (1988) all featured the aspirational country lifestyle and consumer aspects of dreamlike affluent rural existence. This was despite the fact that the vast majority of the population live in towns and cities, and of those living in the countryside, many do so on low incomes. But the dream still sold well, and the magazines thrived.

Aspiration seemed to be an invention of the 1980s, and while many new consumer magazines took off in that decade, the biggest new publishing phenomenon was the arrival of magazines dedicated not to the consumption of goods, but to celebrities and their lifestyles. Until then, the more snobbish British magazines such as *Tatler* and *Harpers* had traditionally carried news of the social lives of British royals, but in 1988 *Hello!* arrived from Spain, filled with gossipy photo-journalism of the 'new aristocracy' of television and film stars, footballers and models. It was published by a Spanish family company which saw the potential of a version of *¡Hola!* for British consumers. The result was one of the most successful magazines of the past half-century, with many similar publications appearing soon afterwards in what has become the most profitable sector of the British market.

Although half the female population never reads a magazine, women remain significant consumers of leisure material. Some of the popular titles of the 1960s and 1970s were produced in response to feminism, but today many titles for women reflect independence, potential to consume and potential to aspire. Women now buy houses, cars, investments and travel packages, and these changes are reflected in the choice of magazines available. The popularity of these publications has been assisted by programmes on the BBC, which often produce a magazine to complement their television series. There has also been a general trend towards greater coverage of these topics in newspapers, and many now provide glossy colour supplements with a range of features and content unconnected with the news of the day.

Another category of reading bought mainly by women is puzzle magazines. Their popularity is followed by the celebrity and gossip magazines, such as *Hello!* and *OK!*. This is a new development in British publishing; in 1994 *Hello!* was the only celebrity magazine, but 10 years later there were six others. Recent new arrivals, such as *Heat* and *Closer*, have specialised in less flattering photographs of their subjects, for example revealing fake tans, body hair and signs of cosmetic surgery. They have created a new, realistic, less admiring and less deferential relationship between readers and the rich and famous, in a trend which seems set to continue.

The progressive women's weeklies such as *Cosmopolitan* and *Marie Claire* still retain a mixture of features and tips on fashion, beauty, travel and consumer features, as well as emphasis on relationships and sexual matters. But recent years have seen a change in the style of the 'problem pages' of many modern publications. Until the late 1990s readers would write and ask a resident 'agony aunt' to solve their problems. But now, other readers often contribute their own, differing solutions, which are published alongside the original problem. This allows the reader to select which course of action would be most appropriate.

Faced with a rapidly changing world, sales of more traditional women's weeklies such as *Women's Own* with their recipes, romantic stories and knitting patterns have fallen, while the sexual explicitness of *Cosmopolitan* and others have increased sales. This trend has spread down to younger teenage magazines where sex has become a predominant topic, along with romantic descriptions and illustrations. This has attracted criticism from parents and teachers, and titles such as *More, Sugar, Mizz, Just Seventeen* are often accused of being obsessed with sexual matters. The magazine editors, however, argue that many teenagers are already sexually active, and so it is important to give them the information they need. In this way, they argue, teenagers can be encouraged to respect themselves and their health, and have confidence to say 'no' if they want to.

For many years 'adult' or 'men's' magazines were synonymous with pornography. The less sexually explicit 'soft-core' type were sold in news-agents, and could usually be found on the 'top shelf' (hence their nickname), while more explicit 'hard-core' magazines were sold in specially licensed shops. Other magazines bought mainly by men dealt with specific interests, such as sport, cars, music or computers. They were mostly aspirational, consumer magazines with relatively low sales. But in the mid-1990s a new trend in magazine publishing appeared, with the launching of a new type of magazine for men aged 18–35, such as *Loaded, Maxim, FHM* and *GQ*.

The magazine *Loaded* started the trend in 1994 with a mixture of glossy colour features on all the topics traditionally popular with men, such as beer, clothes, cars, and pictures of provocative, bikini-clad girls. Articles were witty, ironic and apolitical, written with spirit and attitude. Previously, men's magazines had talked down to their readers, but *Loaded* spoke to men using the same informal language as the readers themselves. The magazine even had a men's problem page, a piece of satire complete with an 'agony uncle'. A typical piece ran as follows: a man writes to the magazine complaining that his girlfriend annoys him by wearing short skirts. The agony uncle replies: 'Tell her she looks fat.' Today, such maga-zines, popularly known as 'lad mags', sell approximately 2.2 million copies per month, and several titles are exported overseas.

The success of 'lad mags' at a time when feminism was becoming estab-lished in the mainstream has perplexed cultural commentators. Some said the new magazines had a sense of escapism and fun, freedom and inde-pendence, which celebrated being young and male in the mid-1990s, when the country was beginning to regain cultural confidence after years of recession and Tory government. Others said that men felt insecure after years of political correctness, and the magazines were an aggressive, misogynistic and negative response to their changing roles and identities. In other words, some men felt anxious about threats to their identity as feminism entered the mainstream, and found solace in 'lad mags'. Whatever the reasons, they have become one of the most surprising and successful publishing events of recent years, and one of the most popular kinds of magazine in Britain today.

Discussion topics and activities

1 (a) The political preferences of newspapers and their content and style of writing attract different kinds of readers. This was humorously illustrated in an anonymous quote:

> Don't tell me about the press, I know exactly who reads the papers. The *Mirror* is read by people who think they run the country. The *Guardian* is read by people who think they ought to run the country. *The Times* is read by people who actually do run the country, the *Daily Mail* is read by the wives of those who run the country. The *Financial Times* is read by those who own the country, the *Morning Star* is read by those who think the country ought to be run by another country, and the *Daily Telegraph* is read by those who think it already is! And the *Sun* is read by those who don't care who runs the country as long as there's a topless pin-up on page 3!

In Britain of the early 1980s who do you think these groups were?

(b) Who reads the principal newspapers and magazines in your country? Think about their occupations, age and gender, etc. Why are they popular with these groups?

2 In groups, obtain copies of as many daily and weekly newspapers and magazines as you can. Do they have different sorts of stories in terms of content, style, tone of language? Why do you think this is? Think about the target audience(s) for each one. Who do you think they are?

3 (a) Choose one story in the news. Contrast the coverage of it in three different national newspapers. How is it presented differently?

(b) Do the same with three different ethnic newspapers. What can you notice about the treatment of the story?

4 Newspaper reporters sometimes set up situations and use hidden microphones in order to trap people into making confessions, or committing illegal acts. Do you think reporters should act in this way?

Is it in the public interest? Should greater controls be placed on news reporting?

5 Compare quality and popular newspaper websites. What do you notice about the 'news values' (in other words, factors affecting newspapers' acceptance or rejection of stories, and the importance they are given) in each paper/website, and who do you think the typical readers would be? Think about their age, social and educational background, and level of income.

6 Compare four celebrities and the reasons for their fame, and how positively they are represented in each newspaper/magazine/website.

7 Design the perfect tabloid front page. Think about and create news stories about famous people, and include surprise, sensation, gossip, scandals and so on.

8 (a) Look through a selection of women's magazines. What themes can you find in the contents?

  (b) Do the same with a selection of men's magazines? Are there any differences from themes in women's magazines? Why do you think this is?

9 Can you think of any news stories about groups of people in your country where the press has discussed events in an unfair, inaccurate or disproportionate way? Think about coverage of young people, gypsies and the various nationalities and ethnic groups in your country. Why might this happen?

10 Can you think of any stories which were reported about you or your friends or family, or issues which you are familiar with, where the published story was quite different to what you expected? Why do you think this was?

Suggested further reading

Books

Benjamin, I. (1995) *The Black Press in Britain*, Stoke on Trent: Trentham Books.

Boyce, G., Curran, J. and Wingate, P. (eds) (1978) *Newspaper History: From the 17th Century to the Present*, London: Constable.

Braithwaite, B. (1995) *Women's Magazines*, London: Peter Owen.

Cohen, S. (2002) *Folk Devils and Moral Panics*, 3rd edn, London: Routledge.

Curran, J. and Seaton, J. (1997) *Power Without Responsibility*, 5th edn, London: Routledge.

Ferguson, M. (1979) 'Social Change and the Content of Women's Magazines 1949–78' (Department of Sociology Thesis, London School of Economics).

Ferguson, M. (1983) *Forever Feminine: Women's Magazines and the Cult of Femininity*, London: Heinemann.

Fowler, R. (1991) *Language in the News: Discourse and Ideology in the British Press*, London and New York: Routledge.

Franklin, B. (1997) *Newszak and News Media*, London: Edward Arnold.

Greenslade, R. (2004) *Press Gang: How Newspapers Make Profits from Propaganda*, London: Pan.

Griffiths, D. (ed.) (1992) *The Encyclopaedia of the British Press 1422–1992*, London: Macmillan.

Horrie, C. (2003) *Tabloid Nation*, London: Carlton Books.

Jones, N. (1996) *Soundbites and Spin Doctors*, London: Indigo.

Koss, S. (1990) *The Rise and Fall of the Political Press in Britain*, London: Fontana.

Lee, A. (1976) *The Origins of the Popular Press 1855–1914*, London: Croom Helm.

Linton, D. and Boston, R. (1987) (eds) *The Newspaper Press in Britain: An Annotated Bibliography*, London: Mansell.

Lloyd, J. (2004) *What the Media are Doing to Our Politics*, London: Constable & Robinson.

McRobbie, A. (1991) '*Jackie* Magazine: Romantic Individualism and the Teenage Girl' in *Feminism and Youth Culture: From* Jackie *to* Just Seventeen, Houndmills: Macmillan.

Marr, A. (2004) *My Trade: A Short History of British Journalism*, London: Macmillan.

Negrine, R. (1994) *Politics and the Mass Media in Britain*, 2nd edn, London: Routledge.

Poole, E. (2002) *Reporting Islam: Media Representations of British Muslims*, London: I.B. Tauris.

Seymour-Ure, C. (1996) *The Press and Broadcasting in Britain since 1945*, 2nd edn, Oxford: Blackwell.

Taylor, S.J. (1996) *The Great Outsiders: Northcliffe, Rothermere and the* Daily Mail, London: Weidenfeld & Nicolson.

Tunstall, J. (1995) *Newspaper Power: The New National Press in Britain*, Oxford: Oxford University Press.

4

Literature

Introduction

Some of the most illustrious authors in English, such as William Shake-speare, Charles Dickens, Jane Austen and Virginia Woolf, have helped to establish a long and distinguished literary tradition. Their works are exten-sively studied in schools, colleges and universities in Britain and overseas, and are frequently adapted into well-known films, television series and plays for theatre and radio. Similarly, a lively children's literature has also provoked public curiosity and academic respect, from the time of Lewis Carroll's *Alice's Adventures in Wonderland* (1865), to the phenomenal success of J.K. Rowling's Harry Potter stories, which have contributed to renewed interest around the world of young and old readers alike in mystery, myth and magic.

The publishing and retailing of classic and modern works have become major industries, and in 2004 some 125,000 new and revised titles were published. Around 6,000 of these are new works of fiction. There are numerous awards for new books and authors, such as the Whitbread Prize, the Orange Prize for Fiction (awarded to female authors) and the Carnegie Medal, which is awarded each year to the best children's book written in English and published in the UK. But the most prestigious for English fiction by a British or Commonwealth author is the Booker Prize, which has been offered annually since 1969. It is judged by a panel of publishers, novelists and critics, and ensures wide publicity for the winning author.

Recently published books and information on literary and cultural trends can easily be found in Britain's libraries. The local authorities in

Great Britain and education and library boards in Northern Ireland have a duty to provide lending and reference library services free of charge. In 2001/02 there were almost 5,000 public libraries in the UK, and in Great Britain more than 34 million people (60 per cent of the population) were registered members. Around 10 million people make a visit to their local library at least once every two weeks. Those who are not registered can also use the facilities, which often consist of works in foreign languages, local history documents, children's books, CDs, DVDs, audio and video cassettes as well as access to the internet.

There are also many literary societies and book clubs dedicated to the discussion of a variety of authors' works. But for those more interested in creativity than reading or criticism, several centres offer specialised courses. One of the most famous is at the University of East Anglia in Norwich, founded by Malcolm Bradbury, and where contemporary authors such as Ian McEwan and Kazuo Ishiguro have studied.

Most writers in Britain use English in order to reach a national and international audience. However, in Wales there is a strong tradition of writing in the Welsh language. This has been maintained for centuries in the annual cultural festival of the Royal Eisteddfod, and since the 1960s Welsh has been supported by the British government. In Scotland, Scots-Gaelic and Scots also have long histories, and some authors continue to write in those languages to help preserve the literary tradition.

Early influences

Until the late 1800s Christian belief exerted a powerful influence over literary ideas, but towards the end of the century its influence gradually declined. A growing knowledge of the natural and social world led to a reaction against the traditional certainties which it offered, and enthusiasm for the exploration of new subjects and experimentation with new forms grew. The works of Rudyard Kipling took inspiration from the achievements of the British Empire and the creation of a wealthy new civilisation. His work earned him a reputation as 'Poet of Empire', and in 1907 he became the first English author to win the Nobel Prize for Literature.

Kipling's optimism was shared by George Bernard Shaw and H.G. Wells, who wrote enthusiastically about the benefits of progress and increased knowledge of the social and scientific world. But some authors were pessimistic about the future unless the state intervened to prevent exploitation and suffering. George Orwell's novels frequently expressed the need for socialism, although later in his career his views became closer to those of E.M. Forster, whose novels stressed the importance of individual rights and freedoms over the collective demands of the state.

In contrast, other authors were more sceptical about the ability of religion, politics or science to create a better world, for example Oscar Wilde was inspired and sustained by natural beauty, hedonism and decadent living. Thomas Hardy preferred the simplicity and authenticity of rural life and nature, believing they were important sources of human happiness. D.H. Lawrence and Aldous Huxley saw modern civilisation as having a dehumanising effect on man. For them, personal fulfilment lay within, and could only be achieved by exploring the senses and obeying the instincts.

English literature has always been diverse and marked by a plurality of influences, and in the twentieth century ways of telling stories grew more experimental. Some authors such as James Joyce and Virginia Woolf found traditional, descriptive methods too conventional. They wanted a more liberating style of expression and developed a technique known as 'stream of consciousness'. It consists of a mixture of verse and prose but without traditional grammar or logical sequence, which creates the sensation of a dream or interior monologue. It seemed a more natural way to represent human thoughts and impressions, and was given full expression in Joyce's *Ulysses* (1921), which is one of the most original and highly praised works of English literature. In contrast, for many years some of the most established and respected authors such as William Golding, Graham Greene and Evelyn Waugh continued to take inspiration from their religious beliefs.

Since 1945 British society has been transformed from a conservative imperial power to a progressive, dynamic multicultural nation, and the influence of youth, the emergence of feminism, migration and growing cultural diversity have all produced new waves of literary energy. The influx of immigrants from the Caribbean, India, Pakistan and East Africa created a variety of religious and ethnic groups within the wider British society, and the experience of growing up bi-cultural has produced new perspectives which have invigorated English literature and became its most distinctive feature since the 1980s.

New arrivals: working-class youth, immigrants and teenagers

In the late 1940s following the horrific losses of six years of war, the public looked not for brave new ideas and styles, but for comfort and reassurance in literature. However, by 1955 the old values and certainties which religion and nation had traditionally provided were being questioned, and a new generation of critical young novelists, playwrights and artists was emerging.

Playwright John Osborne and novelists Colin Wilson, John Wain, Stan Barstow, Alan Sillitoe, Keith Waterhouse, Kingsley Amis and others were mostly aged under 30, and like many of the British public at the time, they shared an impatience with tradition, authority and the ruling class. Their works reflected their anger and frustrations in novels such as John Wain's *Hurry on Down* (1953), Kingsley Amis's *Lucky Jim* (1954), Colin Wilson's *The Outsider* (1956), John Braine's *Room at the Top* (1957) and Alan Sillitoe's *Saturday Night and Sunday Morning* (1958). Many are set in working-class areas of depressed cities in the industrial north, and contain sexually explicit scenes. Dialogue is often in regional dialect, giving a strong sense of the characters' identity and social background. The protagonists of these novels were 'outsiders'; they did not identify with modern society. Like the authors themselves, they were impatient, dissatisfied and critical of conventional morality and behaviour. They felt resentful and powerless, and sometimes were violent.

In Britain of the mid-1950s it was considered provocative and subversive to write on themes of frustrated ambition, sexuality and class conflict. The revelations of uncomfortable truths about an unequal society through realistic portrayals of everyday life were seen as dangerous and threatening to the British establishment, which feared it could lead to political change and even communism. Moreover, the creation of uneducated, undisciplined heroes was a departure from literary convention, and angered many critics. But it meant that dissent, honesty and openness were introduced into literature, theatre, television and film by a group of writers who became known as the 'angry young men'.

The new currents of social realism in novels of the 1950s also extended to poetry. In 1956 Robert Conquest edited *New Lines*. The contributors became known as 'the Movement', and were identified by their popular image of pipe-smoking, beer drinking, a love of jazz, and a dislike of what they saw as the pretensions and elitism of modern writing. Thom Gunn contributed *Fighting Terms* about motorcycle gangs, a literary act seen as daring and provocative in Britain at the time. In contrast, Philip Larkin ignored stylistic experimentation and wrote clear, economical observations about daily life in Britain. He went on to produce three major collections: *The Less Deceived* (1955), *The Whitsun Weddings* (1964) and *High Windows* (1974), which established his reputation as a major poet. In the satirical *Whitsun Weddings*, Larkin describes a train journey from Hull to London and comments on a sad England of false merriment, cheap fashions and joyless weddings, in a style which could belong to the new millennium. His subject matter was a revelation, and created new territory for English poetry. Larkin was also a fan of jazz music and in *All What Jazz?* (1970) presented a collection of reviews criticising the freedom and experimentation of modern styles.

Jazz music has always had a following in Britain, though this was still quite small in the mid-1950s when a steady flow of Afro-Caribbean immigrants began to arrive from the West Indies. Britain offered an exciting new world of freedom and adventure, which is captured in Samuel Selvon's comic masterpiece *The Lonely Londoners* (1956), a series of narratives about West Indian immigrants in London. Another early portrait of immigrants' experiences is drawn by Colin MacInnes in the nostalgic *City of Spades* (1957). MacInnes grew up in Australia, but in *Absolute Beginners* (1959) and *Mr Love and Justice* (1960) he depicts a newly emergent English youth culture of coffee bars, jazz clubs, teenage fashions and conflict with authority in London of the period. MacInnes's three novels form the *London Trilogy* and together with his fascinating collection of essays, *England, Half-English* (1961), were the first works to recognise the emergence of pop culture and how it provided a young generation with a sense of identity and belonging.

Literature of the 1960s and 1970s

During the 1960s the resentment and frustration of the 1950s began to develop into a counter-cultural movement. At the same time, some of the most highly praised authors of recent times began to receive critical recognition as major writers. Their themes were diverse but freedom and equality tended to predominate, for example in the work of John Fowles. He made his debut with an exciting psychological thriller *The Collector* (1963), about a butterfly collector who kidnaps an attractive young art student, and although the male character is stronger, Fowles shows that it is the young girl who is the more powerful of the two. Later, *The Magus* (1966, revised 1977) involves a young teacher of English in what seems the ideal post on a remote Greek island, whose sense of perception becomes distorted following an unusual sexual encounter. In this and several other of Fowles's works, heroines feature prominently, combining femininity with mental strength to conquer their circumstances, as in *The French Lieutenant's Woman* (1969). This is told in a highly original way, with the author showing a self-awareness of how he uses language and imagination to shape the reader's reality. The book was made into a successful film, and Fowles is one of the few British authors who has written serious, experimental fiction while remaining on the bestseller list.

Like those of Fowles, Iris Murdoch's novels are often concerned with human freedom, and question how goodness can triumph over evil. She also lectured in philosophy, and her novels frequently combine philosophical questions with detailed observations of middle-class life and academic intrigue. The first of her many works was the comedy *Under the Net* (1954), while one of her finest – *The Bell* (1958) – looks at a declining religious community. The humour and surprises in stories such as *A Fairly Honourable Defeat* (1970) and *An Accidental Man* (1971) were also popular with critics and the public. All her novels are noted for their intense descriptions of her characters, who are often possessed by erotic fantasies. These are mixed with unexpected and bizarre incidents which sometimes involve cats, dogs, mice and spiders to create comic effect. During a prolific career she won numerous awards, including the prestigious Booker Prize for *The Sea, the Sea* (1978).

Issues of personal morality in challenging and liberated times were frequently expressed in stories of the 1960s and 1970s, and are central themes to many works of Anthony Burgess. His experiences as an English teacher in Malaya and Brunei provided inspiration for his early writing, such as the *Malayan Trilogy* (1972), later reissued as *The Long Day Wanes* (1982). However, it was *A Clockwork Orange* (1962) which brought him fame. It is set in a future England, where an aggressive gang of young delinquents rob, rape, torture and murder. The gang speak *nadsat*, a private teenage slang, an 'inhuman' language invented by the author (but based on Russian) to emphasise the gang's collective identity and their distance from conventional society. Eventually, their leader Alex is captured and treated, but he begins to produce mechanical, robotic responses to the things that make him human: sex, violence and the arts. The story's main concern is morality and how to deal with transgressions of it, in a tale which satirises both totalitarian and liberal humanist approaches. In 1971 the story was made into a highly successful film by Stanley Kubrick.

Burgess also wrote articles, memoirs, music and several comic stories, such as his four 'Enderby' novels (1963–84) which describe the humorous adventures of a middle-aged university lecturer and poet. The liberal, progressive, permissive atmosphere of the university campus, with its own petty problems, rivalries and jealousies, inspired many writers of the 1970s to write satirical tales in stories known as 'campus' novels, and helped to establish the careers of several modern authors, among them Malcolm Bradbury and David Lodge. In contrast to Iris Murdoch's frequent setting within the ancient walls of Oxford University, their stories take place in the new, red-brick universities of the 1970s.

One of David Lodge's most successful campus novels is *Changing Places* (1975), a comical story about an academic exchange between the universities of 'Euphoria State' in America and 'Rummidge' based on Lodge's own teaching base at Birmingham University in the English Midlands. It marked the first of a trilogy on campus life, and was followed by *Small Worlds* (1984), a humorous tale of intrigue at an academic conference, and *Nice Work* (1988), another comical tale of a collision between town and gown. Lodge's stories are also imaginative and playful, offering a strong social satire, for example his earlier *How Far Can You Go?* (1980) examines the Catholic faith's impact on sex and marriage for British Catholics growing up in a secular, permissive society.

Lodge is a former professor of English literature who is also well known for his extensive work on literary criticism. Malcolm Bradbury was also a distinguished academic, and is remembered for founding Britain's first course in creative writing at the University of East Anglia, where between 1970 and 1995 he was professor of American Studies. His best-known works include *Stepping Westward* (1965), a humorous comparison between American and British university life, and *The History Man* (1975).

The permissive youth culture of the early 1970s could be found not only on the university campus, but in the tough, mean streets of Britain's industrial conurbations. These are the setting for Richard Allen's *Boot-Boy* (1970), *Suedehead* (1971), *Glam* (1973) and others, sensationalised, mass-produced stories based on the imagined lifestyles of teenage gangs. Set in bleak, urban Britain of the 1970s, they depicted closed, mean, brutal worlds of youth with no future, and include many detailed descriptions of vandalism, violence and sex. Critics complained that they encouraged imitative, 'copycat' behaviour. Nevertheless, the simply written fantasies remain raw, energetic, adrenaline-fuelled adventures, which were popular with many teenagers of the period, and have been rediscovered in recent years as popular artefacts of 1970s youth culture.

The work of the Mersey Poets from Liverpool was also popular with a younger, non-literary audience. The success of the Beatles and other Liverpool groups helped to generate interest in the local popular culture, and during the mid-1960s poets such as Roger McGough, Adrian Henri and Brian Patten pioneered a new style of light, satirical verse. Unlike many poets they were funny, irreverent and streetwise. They wore fashionable clothes, mixed with pop stars and wrote pop poetry: poetry with a performance, pop music without the music. A flavour of their work is captured in the anthology *The Mersey Sound* (1967).

Feminism and fiction

By the mid-1960s the impact of feminism was being widely felt in politics, law, social and family life. Traditional attitudes towards women's sexuality, marriage, work and many other aspects of their lives began to change, and there was a new recognition of women's role in society. Germaine Greer's *The Female Eunuch* (1970) gave popular literary expression to feminist theory. Its provocative and outspoken text offered a clear, untheoretical manifesto which was accessible to everyone. Its impact was enormous, and soon afterwards a significant new body of women's literature emerged. This contained powerful descriptions of women's experience, and feminist writing quickly became an influential new genre.

Literature had been a male-dominated field, but new feminist publishing houses opened to energetically encourage women's writing. Virago, the Women's Press and Pandora contracted new feminist authors and began promoting others, such as Stevie Smith, Storm Jameson, Rebecca West, Rose Macaulay, Barbara Pym and Jean Rhys, whose work had passed largely unnoticed earlier in the twentieth century. There were also important changes in the universities. Departments of Women's Studies were established and departments of literature began to study themes and imagery in women's writing.

The position of women in society, social injustice and the search for equality with men were some of the dominant themes in the early novels of many new authors. Earlier in the 1960s many female writers still did not openly identify with the new intellectual and political currents of feminism, although some were sympathetic to its messages in their work. One such author is Muriel Spark, who was born into a Scottish family of

Jewish descent and who later converted to Catholicism. Her short, stylish funny stories emphasise the roles of the female characters, her best-known work being *The Prime of Miss Jean Brodie* (1961), a story set in her native Edinburgh of the 1930s. It features a charismatic teacher who is proud, cultured and romantic, who inspires and transforms a group of young girls who begin to follow her example.

In contrast, social injustice and the need for equality with men came to dominate the novels of many later authors. Fay Weldon's robustly feminist novels deal with female resentment, anger and revenge in a way that is detached and often ironic. *Down Among the Women* (1971) draws attention to the repetitive nature of most women's lives, spent cooking, cleaning and looking after children. Told in a colloquial present tense, the narrative produces a realistic, documentary effect, as if the action is actually taking place.

More conventional themes of inequality and oppression are found in the highly praised novels of Margaret Drabble. These often have female protagonists whose education, careers and family relationships are described in detail, and often reflect the experiences of the author. In *The Millstone* (1965) the heroine has to fight against various distractions to gain her independence. Then she has an unplanned baby daughter which both helps and limits her development. The trilogy *The Radiant Way* (1987), *A Natural Curiosity* (1989) and *The Gates of Ivory* (1991), in which three women look back on their younger selves, also provides a clear account of a difficult, confrontational and politically polarised country. *The Ice Age* (1977) is considered by many critics to be her finest work. It deals not only with women's liberation, but also social deprivation and the faltering welfare state in mid-1970s Britain. The period's contradictions are embodied in the person of Mike Morgan, a comedian with a 'rat-clown face' who comments here on the way the country seemed to be destroying itself in the 1970s:

> The English are guilty, they are self-denigrating, they are masochists, they love to be kicked, he said, because of their deeply ingrained inalienable disgusting certainty of superiority. They are island xenophobes, and they love to be kicked because they know it does not hurt. They are rich bitches who like to be degraded.
>
> (Drabble 1977: 214)

While many early feminist writers focused on themes of social strife and inequality, others were more concerned with women's domestic lives and their relationships with men. The fiction of Edna O'Brien portrays women as having a frustrating choice between either loneliness or slavery to men and the family. This is apparent in her early trilogy *The Country Girls* (1960–3), in which sexual desires conflict with the heroine's Catholic upbringing. This uncertainty again finds expression in *Casualties of Peace*

(1966), a story told with wit and pace. The eroticism of her stories brought to the novel a frank exposure of women's sexual needs and amplified the spectrum of women's writing.

Several highly regarded authors such as Penelope Lively and Anita Brookner write about women's issues in a simple, direct way. Before she became a respected author of feminist novels, Penelope Lively wrote children's fiction, for example *A House Inside Out* (1987). Her adult novels began with *The Road to Lichfield* (1977) and in 1987 she won the Booker Prize for *Moon Tiger*. Anita Brookner's style of writing is elegant and sometimes funny. She began her career as an art historian, but later wrote stories which often feature a lonely, intellectual woman who lives unhappily, such as *A Friend from England* (1987) and *Fraud* (1992). Instead of rebelling against society, her characters accept their situation and cannot be described as feminists. But in *Hotel du Lac* (1984) the heroine makes the brave decision not to get married on her wedding day. *Hotel du Lac* won the Booker Prize in 1984 and was later made into a successful television series of the same name.

Doris Lessing

Doris Lessing (b. 1919) is among the most highly respected of contemporary British writers, the author of prolific and varied works. As well as many novels she has also written short stories, poetry and travel writing. At the beginning of her career, her left-wing politics and sense of realism identified her with the social realists of the 1950s. But she later adopted a more imaginative style, characterised by fantasy, interior monologues and multiple realities.

Lessing grew up in South Africa and moved to England in 1937. The country of her childhood is the setting for her early stories and novels which include the five-volume *Children of Violence* (1952–69). The story begins in Rhodesia, where the first volume, *Martha Quest*, tells the story of women's 'absence' from history. The setting later moves to England and forward to the year 2000. The novels aim to present the arguments of feminists who witnessed the bigotry and apartheid of South African politics of the 1960s. But the author also expresses her cynicism about communism, doubting it could provide a more just or equal society.

The Golden Notebook (1962) is a work of politics and psychology. The heroine, Anna Freeman Wulf, suffers a crisis in her personal life and eventually has a nervous breakdown. But after recovering she takes an American lover and becomes involved in socialist politics. Her feelings as a liberated woman, private individual and author are explored in different sections of the novel, which is seen by many critics as one of the most significant contributions to the literature of women's emancipation in the twentieth century.

73

Lessing's interest in experimental storytelling extends into her work as a writer of science fiction. *Canopus in Argos: Archives* (1979–83) is an allegorical story which tells how fantastic beasts on distant planets affect life on earth. It is both subtle and feminist, but its argument is not that women are superior to men. Instead, hers is the more contemporary view that traditional feminine qualities are suppressed or ignored by society, and that many current problems could be solved if these qualities were given greater expression. In the mid-1980s Lessing returned to realistic narrative, publishing several more novels, poetry, travel writing and the first volume of her autobiography *Under My Skin* (1994).

New directions in women's writing

Although some authors such as Maureen Duffy, Penelope Fitzgerald, Penelope Mortimer and Rose Tremain continued to write about women in a similar, conventional manner, several others began to explore new, experimental styles of language and storytelling. They believed that, in a society dominated by men, women had to free themselves from traditional, established practices in thought, language and literary style. In this way, they could find a more natural, authentic voice.

The writing of Jean Rhys and Eva Figes is characterised by the frequent use of split narrative, in which the story is sometimes told in the first person and sometimes in the third. This creates the sense of a divided self and of fantasy. Rhys wrote her early novels during the 1920s, but was 'rediscovered' during the 1960s. Her novel *The Wide Sargasso Sea* (1966) was published when she was aged 72. It is set in the 1830s and is a highly imaginative, tragic story about Rochester's mad wife, a character from Charlotte Brontë's *Jane Eyre* (1847). The technique of 'reworking' a traditional story has become a distinctive characteristic of many novels of recent years. It involves the changing of numerous details to create an imaginative and accessible tale with contemporary relevance. Some examples include Fay Weldon's *The Cloning of Joanna May* (1989), a reworking of Mary Shelley's classic tale *Frankenstein* (1818), and Emma Tennant's *Tess* (1993), in which she took as her subjects the female characters of classic novelist Thomas Hardy (1840–1928).

The novels and short stories of A.S. Byatt demonstrate her interests in both imaginative experimental literature and historical fact, especially her later works, which became more fictional and fantastic: for example *Possession* (1990) is part fairy tale, part journal, part academic essay, part verse, which together tell the story of an imaginary poet of the nineteenth century. It was awarded the Booker Prize in 1990. In contrast, a more vigorous attack on accepted notions of reality is found in the works of Angela Carter, an energetic mixture of fairy tales, eroticism and transsexuality, in which characters regularly change role and sex. This is a characteristic of magic realism, a technique associated with South American writers such as Gabriel García Márquez, whose stories mix extravagant fantasy and fable with everyday events.

Jeanette Winterson is another contemporary author who has also combined historical fact with fantasy in several imaginative novels. *Boating for Beginners* (1985) is based on the biblical story of Noah's Ark, but is given a modern emphasis by presenting Noah as a businessman who builds boats. *Sexing the Cherry* (1989) is a mixture of history and fiction, set between the English Civil War of the seventeenth century and present time, while *The Passion* (1987) is set in Venice, as well as in Russia during Napoleon's march on Moscow. Winterson's imaginative fiction is often described as magic realism, in which her sentimental, intense style is frequently used to explore lesbian sexuality. *Oranges Are Not the Only Fruit* (1985) is widely interpreted as the conflict between her traditional, evangelical Pentecostal upbringing and her own lesbian sexuality, in a novel which won a Whitbread Prize and was made into an acclaimed BBC TV series. Subsequent books include *The Powerbook* (2000) which is part autobiographical, and *Written on the Body* (1992) a love story, about an anonymous narrator whose female lover is dying from leukaemia. In the following intimate dialogue, the narrator addresses her lover:

> 'Explore me,' you said and I collected my ropes, flasks and maps, expecting to be back home soon. I dropped into the mass of you and I cannot find the way out. Sometimes I think I'm free, coughed up like Jonah from the whale, but then I turn a corner and recognise myself again. Myself in your skin, myself lodged in your bones, myself floating in the cavities that decorate every surgeon's wall. That is how I know you. You are what I know.
>
> (Winterson 1992: 120)

Since the late 1970s, women's writing has continued to be distinctive, influential and increasingly diverse. Different experimental styles have been widely developed in the work of Angela Carter, Zoë Fairbairns, Marina Warner, Sara Maitland and others. This indicates that modern women's writing is frequently both feminist and feminine: women expect material equality in law, employment and in relations with men, but authors also want to develop a distinct, more liberated and natural way of expressing the world through a more extensive narrative range and a wider variety of techniques.

Fiction and popular genres since 1980

During the 1980s the most right-wing government in living memory resulted in a torrent of creativity, and over the next 20 years English literature witnessed several profound changes. Early in the decade, publishing became one of Britain's few growth industries. In 1980 there were 48,158 new titles published in the UK. By 2000 this had risen to 100,000, in 2004 to 119,000, with some 6,000 new fictional works being published each year. The number of chain-store bookshops in the high street increased, and chains of book retailers became established such as Waterstones and Borders.

Many new prizes were introduced to encourage new authors and to draw attention to important new works, while established ones like the Booker, attracted wide attention across the mass media. The only time this had happened previously was in 1972, when John Berger won with his novel *G* and donated the prize money to the Black Panthers in America. The marketing and publicity of new books became fine arts, while literary festivals such as the one at Hay-on-Wye became major events. There was much comment in the media about new works, as well as gossip about the size of writers' advances. For the first time, works of literature and popular fiction began to compete with each other in the bestseller lists and the novel became a popular, fashionable object.

The breaking of social barriers during previous decades led to a vigorous expansion of literary themes in the 1980s. Techniques of storytelling continued to diversify, as some writers looked to the past and took inspiration from earlier traditions, while others combined different narrative styles such as fact, fiction, or the past and the present in the same story, in a style known as 'magic realism'. Lesbian writing became increasingly established, but fiction dealing with homosexual themes has been slow to gain recognition and acceptance. Some of the best-known exponents include Alan Hollinghurst and Adam Mars-Jones. Hollinghurst's *The Swimming Pool Library* (1988) was widely praised by critics, but novels about gay identities and relationships are said to be unappealing to critics and literary judges, and consequently have been slower to gain recognition amongst a conservative British literary establishment and readership.

Other dominant styles of the 1980s were imaginative and escapist, but often in a dark, sinister way. Throughout the 'age of greed' fantastic, grotesque scenarios involving themes of corruption of innocence and 'paradise lost' were common. One of the most representative novelists of this trend is Martin Amis. The son of Kingsley Amis, he is a satirical, witty author, and sharp social commentary is a characteristic of all his novels. His two early works *The Rachel Papers* (1973) and *Dead Babies* (1975) deal with decay, deprivation and sexuality in a declining Britain, while later titles, such as *Success* (1979) and *Money* (1984), ironically reflect the spirit of the times. For Amis, the prosperity enjoyed by some during the 1980s appeared to extinguish all moral obligation to others, as people became more selfish, envious and greedy. He writes of a class system based on money and privilege, in which the spirit is starved and disaster is imminent. His *London Fields* (1989) is a murder story set in west London's pubs and streets. *Einstein's Monsters* (1986) is a collection of short stories about nuclear war, while *Time's Arrow* (1991) narrates the story of the Second

World War and describes its effects on the present. Its imaginative technique tells the story in reverse, beginning in the present time and regressing.

Like Amis, Ian McEwan's early work seemed to demonstrate a wish to shock. His earlier work used precise, elegant prose to write about dark, sinister themes such as incest and infanticide. But his later work is broader, often beginning with realistic descriptions of a calm, everyday life which is suddenly disrupted, such as *Enduring Love* (1997) and *Atonement* (2001). His novel *Saturday* (2005) continues this pattern, and tells the story of a day in the life of a successful brain surgeon, Henry Perowne. His wife is a top media lawyer, his teenage daughter a published poet, and his son a blues guitarist, which together make his life almost complete until the Saturday of the title. This is 15 February 2003, the day of the great march in central London against the forthcoming war in Iraq. Perowne is a perfectionist and all seems well in his life. In the following extract the main character is alone with his thoughts, driving around the streets of central London in his comfortable Mercedes S500, while reflecting on the threat of Islamic terrorism:

> Shamelessly, he always enjoys the city from inside his car, where the air is filtered and hi-fi music confers pathos on the humblest details. . . . He is heading a couple of blocks south in order to loop eastwards across the Tottenham Court Road. Cleveland Street used to be known for garment sweatshops and prostitutes, now it has Greek, Turkish and Italian restaurants – the local sort that never get mentioned in the guides. . . . There's a man who repairs old computers, a cobbler's, and further down a wig emporium, much visited by transvestites. This is a fair embodiment of an inner city by-way – diverse, self confident, obscure. And it's at this point that he remembers the source of his vague sense of shame and embarrassment: his readiness to be persuaded that the world has changed beyond recall, that harmless streets like this and the tolerant life they embody can be destroyed by the new enemy – well organised, tentacular, full of hatred and focused zeal.
>
> (McEwan 2006: 76)

Events in *Saturday* take a sudden turn for the worse when Perowne has a small traffic accident with a car driven by three men who have just emerged from a lap dancing club, and the protagonist's secure world of contentment and plenty seems vulnerable and threatened.

The gradual globalisation of life in Britain in the late twentieth century has brought many opportunities, but it has also brought greater insecurity and the threats of terrorism and environmental catastrophe. In the 1980s and '90s, feelings of insecurity were largely about the Cold War, unemployment and social unrest, which were compounded by the greed and selfishness which the government seemed to encourage through policies of privatisation, reductions in public spending and a gradual dismantling of the welfare state. These economic and social trends made many authors pessimistic about the future, despite the optimism of the Tory government about the new world of freedom and opportunity which it had attempted to create.

Dark themes, including the effects of abortion and murder during adolescence on the writer as a grown man, are found in Graham Swift's *Waterland* (1983), which has been critically praised as one of the decade's finest novels. Set in the Fenlands of Cambridgeshire, Swift's theme is that people often live in the shadow of a suspect past, a corrupted history. Concerns with history and place are also central to Peter Ackroyd's *Hawksmoor* (1985), a novel about the London architect Nicholas Hawksmoor (1661–1736) who worked with Sir Christopher Wren, the renowned architect of St Paul's Cathedral. Chapters are alternately set in London of the eighteenth and twentieth centuries, each in the language and style of the period. London was also the setting for his first work *The Great Fire of London* (1982), an imaginary story which deals with the making of a film of Charles Dickens's *Little Dorrit*, while his second novel *The Last Testament of Oscar Wilde* (1983) tells the story of the last four months of the dramatist's troubled life, as recorded in his own diary. London-born Ackroyd is considered to be one of the most original writers of the 1980s and is also well known as a poet, biographer and reviewer.

Most authors of the 1980s were concerned with life in Britain. However, Julian Barnes's light, confident, humorous style demonstrated his interest in France and its culture in *Metroland* (1980), *Flaubert's Parrot* (1984) and *Cross Channel* (1996). Closer to home, *England, England* (1998) is a humorous tale set in the near future, when the nation's major tourist attractions of Big Ben, Stonehenge, Buckingham Palace and Hadrian's Wall are reconstructed on the Isle of Wight to ease the itinerary of the Americans and Japanese tourists who come to see them. The island is a remarkable success, being cleaner, more convenient, friendlier and more efficient, and far more popular than the real thing, suggesting that a packaged, tourist version of England is what visitors are really seeking. As well as his fictional novels, Barnes has also written several crime novels under the pseudonym of Dan Kavanagh.

As levels of crime increased sharply in the 1980s and 1990s, so did interest in crime and detective stories. The tradition originated in the 1890s with Sir Arthur Conan Doyle and his fictitious sleuth Sherlock Holmes. But during the twentieth century the genre has been largely maintained by women authors, such as Agatha Christie with her detective heroes Miss Marple and Poirot. Stories are set in a remote country house and involve an affluent, middle-class group in a type of intellectual puzzle popularly known as a 'whodunit'. The traditional detective story projected a morality which everyone could agree with and created a psychological tension through suggestion and subtlety. In the 1990s some of the most widely appreciated authors included P.D. James (with her sleuths Adam Dalgleish and Delia Gray), Ruth Rendell (Inspector Wexford), Colin Dexter (Inspector Morse), Richard Hill (Dalziel and Pascoe), Caroline Graham (Inspector Barnaby) and Ian Rankin (Inspector Rebus).

Ruth Rendell has been writing detective fiction since 1965. Some of her stories are conventional 'police procedurals' in which there is a puzzle to be solved, while others emphasise the shocking and disturbing aspects of violent crime. Her recent detective novel *Thirteen Steps Down* (2005) is one of the latter. Its protagonist is a disturbed and lonely young man – Cellini – a semi-educated mechanic who repairs exercise machines, drinks heavily and stalks celebrities. He becomes obsessed by the true story of the mass murderer John Christie, who killed six women at his home in Rillington Place, in London's North Kensington in the early 1950s. Some years later, a film was made of the murders and starred Richard Attenborough in the lead role. In this extract, the author describes how the film triggered Cellini's psychotic behaviour.

> It was seeing the film that started him off. He was still living at home then and he watched it on his mother's old black and white television. Never much for reading, he had found the book of the film on a stall outside a junk shop. It came as a surprise when he looked at the photographs and saw that John Reginald Halliday Christie looked not like Attenborough, but far more like himself, and it was from that time that he began referring to him in his mind as Reggie rather than Christie. After all, what had he done that was so terrible? Rid the world of a bunch of useless women, hookers, street hookers most of them.
>
> (Rendell 2005: pp. 21–22)

While crime fiction and detective novels have increased in popularity, the numbers of spy 'thrillers' – closely related to the detective novel – have declined. They were especially popular during the years of the Cold War, when Graham Greene, John Le Carré, Len Deighton and Ian Fleming were among the most respected authors. In the 1970s they provided some critical commentary on the condition of British institutions, such as their secrecy, inefficiency and resistance to change. But as the Cold War disappeared, interest in the spy novel diminished, leaving their works as monuments to an era. Declining interest in spy stories has contrasted with a growth in the popularity of science fiction novels. The freedom of 'sci-fi' to create time, place and plot exposes some of the limitations of the more conventional novels and has provided authors, such as J.G. Ballard, Brian Aldiss, Ray Bradbury, Michael Moorcock and others, with limitless possibilities for creative writing. But the landscapes of the next century and beyond were often represented as sad, bad, uneasy places, with an absence of community or values, as dark speculation about life in space began to mirror that of life in England.

In Scotland too, the 1990s were characterised by a bleak social realism in several prominent works, most notably in the novels of James Kelman, which deal with hard realities on the streets of Glasgow. But unlike many other Scottish authors, Kelman rejects standard English prose and writes mainly in the local dialect, which he peppers with numerous expletives to create more authentic dialogue. His style has made him controversial with critics, and often difficult to evaluate. But his novel *How Late it Was, How Late* (1994) won the Booker Prize in the same year. Like Glasgow, the city of Edinburgh also has high levels of social problems, drug addiction and AIDS, themes frankly revealed in Irving Welsh's *Trainspotting* (1993) and *The Acid House* (1994). These are dark tales of violence, deprivation and drug addiction, but are lifted by the author's lively, witty style.

Complex expressions of identity are common characteristics of several novels by Scottish novelists, for example Alisdair Gray's distinctive *Lanark* (1981), which makes humorous comparisons between the Scottish and the English. It describes the author as a young Glaswegian, but the story is told in a dual style, indicating the presence of a split personality or identity. Similarly, Iain Banks's *The Bridge* (1986) mixes hallucination, fantasy and reality in a tale set around the Forth Road Bridge near Edinburgh. His novels and science fiction stories (the latter written by his 'alter ego' of Iain M. Banks) have made him one of the most critically and publicly admired authors of the 1980s and 1990s, from the sexuality and violence of *The Wasp Factory* (1984) to the dual narrative and mysticism of *Inversions* (1998).

The continuing tensions in Northern Ireland between the violent demands for independence and the maintenance of union with Britain provided the basis for several novels of the 1980s and 1990s by Bernard McLaverty, Alan Judd and others. There is also a strong tradition of verse, maintained by poets such as Tom Paulin, Paul Durcan, Paul Muldoon and Derek Mahon, whose works have examined the problems and pressures of life in the Northern Counties in the late twentieth century.

Historical novels grew in popularity in the 1990s, as it seemed that the public had tired of experimental forms of writing, and now wanted the certainty offered by more conventional, linear styles of storytelling. There was also a suggestion that people mattered because of the great things they did, for example Anthony Beevor's *Stalingrad* (1999), about the siege of the city, and Simon Schama's three-volume *History of Britain* (2000–02) and various works on royalty by David Starkey, who, like Schama, brilliantly brought his subjects to life in major television series.

Biography is another genre to have grown in popularity. Many public figures have written about themselves or employed a 'ghost writer' to assist them. This may be due to the growing appetite for personal details, trivia and information about different lifestyles, especially with the increasing interest in 'celebrity culture'. Paradoxically, books about famous people often sell more than books by them, perhaps because the former are more critical and revealing. But together with crime, the genre which still has the largest women's readership is escapist, romantic writing. Traditional romances and historical dramas with their carefully observed speech, manners and dress style are consistently appreciated by British readers, and authors such as Jilly Cooper and the late Catherine Cookson are endlessly popular. As well as romance, other popular genres include astrology, health and alternative medicine, areas in which the contribution of women authors is consistently greater than that of men. There is also a growing number of gay and lesbian fiction writers who were inspired by the new perspectives offered by 'queer' literature in America. However, the genre has been slow to develop in Britain, where it generally carries less political importance or critical interest.

The millennium also showed increasing public interest in literary themes and creative writing. In the BBC show *The Big Read* (2005), viewers were invited to vote for their favourite book of all time. Some 750,000 votes were received, and the winner was the classic J.R.R. Tolkien novel *The Lord of the Rings*. In another literary 'show' 17,000 viewers responded to a short story-writing competition, *End of Story* (2004), in which the challenge was to write the ending for one of eight, half-written stories by several bestselling authors.

There was a new fashion for book clubs, informally set up around the country, in which members choose particular books and meet regularly to discuss them. Meanwhile, literary festivals such as the annual event at Hay-on-Wye, the small country town which has more bookshops per head of population than anywhere else in Britain, have continued to grow in popularity.

New identities

In the mid-twentieth century Britain became a multicultural society, as migrants from countries in Asia and the Caribbean region came to live and work in the major industrial cities. Around the same time, the British withdrew from many of their overseas territories which became independent after years of colonial rule. The presence of new realities brought by migration from a religious, patriarchal society into a secular, individualist British one, and the process of adaptation to a new independence following the British withdrawal, introduced new creative impulses into English literature, which have remained a distinguishing feature in the early twenty-first century.

Salman Rushdie, Hanif Kureishi, Kazuo Ishiguro, Caryl Phillips and Timothy Mo are some of the authors whose stories deal with experiences of displacement, and loss and rediscovery following cultural upheaval. Theirs is often an 'outsider's' view of the world – the expression of someone in it, but not always of it – and has been compared to some women's writing of the 1970s and 1980s, when the feminist movement and equality

81

in law brought similar life-changing experiences for many British women. Both influences have become powerful creative forces in English literature of the past 30 years, as authors asked questions about how people adapt to changed political and cultural circumstances, and the new realities they bring.

Some of the liveliest and most colourful accounts of growing up in a multiracial society are found in the works of Hanif Kureishi. These frequently draw on his own childhood experiences in the suburbs of south London. His highly praised *Buddha of Suburbia* (1990) is part-autobiographical, and tells the humorous story a young boy born into a Pakistani family and growing up in Britain, wondering how he can successfully integrate his dual heritage into his London life. Early in the book he introduces himself and immediately makes the reader aware of his bi-cultural identity, indicating the importance it has for him:

> My name is Karim Amir, and I am an Englishman born and bred, almost. I am often considered to be a funny kind of Englishman, a new breed as it were, having emerged from two old histories. But I don't care – Englishman I am (though not proud of it), from the South London suburbs and going somewhere. Perhaps it is the odd mixture of continents and blood, of here and there, of belonging and not, that makes me restless and easily bored. Or perhaps it was being brought up in the suburbs that did it. Anyway, why search the inner room when it's enough to say that I was looking for trouble, any kind of movement, action and sexual interest I could find, because things were so gloomy, so slow and heavy, in our family . . .
>
> (Kureishi: 1990: 3)

His later novel *The Black Album* (1995) is a thriller set in London in 1989 and tells a story of drugs, religion and sexual passion. As well as writing novels, Kureishi has also written screenplays and television dramas, which include the critically praised film *My Beautiful Laundrette* (1985), and his witty, insightful and accessible work has made him a leading cultural commentator of his generation.

Other examples of writing from a similar viewpoint include Caryl Phillips's *The Final Passage* (1985), a tale about the Caribbean community in London during the 1950s and the kind of life which Leila, a young woman, finds when she arrives. Suburban London is also the setting for David Dabydeen's *The Intended* (1991), which depicts a young man from Guyana trying to make sense of his different heritage as he grows up, and Amit Chauderi's *Afternoon Raag* (1993), set in Oxford, about the sense of dislocation experienced by a young Indian who has come to study in the ancient seat of learning.

Kazuo Ishiguro arrived in Britain from Japan at an early age, and later studied creative writing under Malcolm Bradbury at the University of East

Anglia. His Japanese parentage and attachments to the country feature in many of his works, for example *An Artist of the Floating World* (1986) which explores Japanese attitudes towards the Second World War through the eyes of an ageing artist. But Ishiguro's most successful novel is set in Britain. *The Remains of the Day* (1989) is set in an English country house of the mid-twentieth century, and uses precise and detailed observation of an elderly butler to present a portrait of British life and society. His fine observations of class distinctions and social behaviour won the Booker Prize of the same year and the book was later made into a successful film.

Like Ishiguro, Timothy Mo brings to his work a unique vision which is derived from his experience of growing up in Hong Kong and England. In *Monkey King* (1980) and *Insular Possession* (1986) the author observes the ancient and modern traditions of his native Hong Kong, while *Sour Sweet* (1982) describes the closed, distant character of the Chinese community in the London district of Soho. The Far East is also the setting for *Redundancy of Courage* (1991), which describes how the island of East Timor was abandoned by the Portuguese colonial power, leaving it in chaos and anarchy.

Salman Rushdie

One of the most critically praised writers of the past 50 years is Salman Rushdie (b. 1947). He was born into a Muslim family in Bombay, India, and emigrated to Britain in 1965. His homeland provides the setting for *Midnight's Children* (1981), the title of which refers to a new generation of Indians born at midnight on 15 August 1947, when India became an independent republic. The story is a mixture of fantasy and magic, and narrates the key events in the story of modern India through the life of Saleem Sinai, who works in a pickle factory. The story is widely acclaimed as original, clever and observant, and twice won the Booker Prize: once in 1981, and again in 1993 as the best novel during the first 25 years of Booker awards. However, its real significance lies in the way it shone a critical light on the new, divided post-imperial identities that independence from Britain created, and the sense of dislocation and rediscovery which it produced: an original perspective which made the book highly influential.

Later works include *Shame* (1983), a story set in Pakistan, and *The Jaguar Smile* (1987), a travel book about life in Nicaragua under the Sandinistas. But it was *The Satanic Verses* (1988) for which the author became renowned. The verses of the title are verses from the Koran, the Muslim holy book. Set in Arabia, India and Britain, the verses are central to a complex, imaginative story about the act of storytelling. Central to the text is a discussion of the ways in which migrants can and should change in order to adapt to their new environment. For those with strong religious convictions, this raises important questions, as Rushdie describes in the following passage:

A man who sets out to make himself up is taking on the Creator's role, according to one way of seeing things; he's unnatural, a blasphemer, an abomination of abominations. From another angle, you could see pathos in him, heroism in his struggle, in his willingness to take risks: not all mutants survive. Or, consider him sociopolitically: most migrants learn, and can become disguises. Our own false descriptions to counter the falsehoods invented about us, concealing for reasons of security our secret selves.

(Rushdie 1988: 49)

The book was widely praised, but some Muslims found in it a blasphemous abuse of their religion, and Ayatollah Khomeini of Iran demanded that the author be killed. An Italian translator of the book was subsequently attacked, the publisher in Norway was shot, and a Japanese translator murdered. In Britain, Muslims publicly burned the book, and many bookshops withdrew it from sale. But around the world thousands of authors pledged their support for Rushdie, who could make only very rare public appearances.

Since the late 1980s he has continued to produce a variety of books which have included children's stories, *Haroun and the Sea of Stories* (1990), collected essays in *Imaginary Homelands* (1991) and a volume of short stories *East, West* (1994). In September 1998, on the tenth anniversary of the publication of *Satanic Verses*, the death threat was finally withdrawn by the Iranian government.

His most interesting and successful work of recent years has been *The Ground Beneath Her Feet* (1999). Set in the world of rock 'n' roll in the 1970s, it follows two Indian pop stars from Bombay to London and on to New York. Rushdie subsequently worked with the rock band U2, touring with them and working with the singer Bono to write a song named after the novel.

Rushdie's examination of new cultural realities and how they change people's way of seeing and interpreting the world marked a new literary departure, and helped create post-colonial studies, one of the most important areas of literary study in Britain today.

The search for the self

Earlier in the century the novel had often been seen as a contribution to intellectual thought on a particular subject. The erudite views of respected authors were read and discussed enthusiastically, assisted by a shared morality between author and readers. But with the collapse of communism and the gradual disappearance of ideology, people began to question authority of all kinds: political, religious and scientific. Morality, attitudes, values and behaviour gradually became more personal, individual matters. Novels gradually came to be read less as a manifesto for social change or

84

a radical new piece of 'legislation', and more for entertainment. The result was a fragmentation of styles and subjects, as the public wanted stories it could relate to.

This lack of an authoritative 'compass' made many critics despair over the state of modern fiction. They complained about the absence of political voices or moral direction in modern writing, and were frustrated by a growing inability to distinguish serious literature from sensational novels or 'pulp' fiction and by the absence of any clear sense of British or English identity in the novel. But the lack of a compass was itself a source of inspiration for many authors, who continued to write of being culturally adrift, of being out of place in the world. This has been the theme of bestselling new work by Monica Ali, Zadie Smith and Hari Kunzru. For example in Monica Ali's *Brick Lane* (2002) a native Bangladeshi bride arrives in London's East End and finds her horizons changing rapidly in a moving, honest account of life as a Muslim woman in an unhappy marriage.

However, questions about how people respond to and are changed by the process of migration and growing up bi-cultural appears to be not just the preserve of ethnic communities, but of society more generally, in the sense that modern life can produce a genuine feeling of dislocation, when very little is given, permanent or stable.

The search for a clear sense of identity and belonging was the theme of Nick Hornby's *Fever Pitch* (1992), one of the most critically praised books of the early 1990s. Set in the 1970s, this is the autobiographical story of a young man brought up in suburbia, whose complex emotions are expressed in his passionate, almost religious obsession with Arsenal Football Club. He is in his mid-30s when he begins to analyse these emotions. The book became a bestseller, and one of the most talked-about novels of its time.

In this extract, Hornby recalls his experience of growing up in a dull Home Counties suburb, and his feelings of dislocation and being 'out of place'. Like many immigrants to new countries, he changed the way he spoke, in this case to show his identification with another community – that of the Arsenal supporters on the terraces of their north London stadium.

ISLINGTON[1] BOY

The white south of England middle-class Englishman and woman is the most rootless creature on earth ... Yorkshiremen, Lancastrians, Scots, the Irish, blacks, the rich, the poor, even Americans and Australians have something they can sit in pubs and bars and weep about, songs to sing, things they can grab for and squeeze hard when they feel like it, but we have nothing, or at least nothing we want. ... Hence the phenomenon of mock-belonging, whereby pasts and backgrounds are manufactured and massaged to provide some kind of acceptable cultural identity. .... In the mid-seventies young, intelligent, and otherwise self-aware white young men and women in London began to adopt a Jamaican patois. . . . How we all wished we came from the Chicago Projects, or the Kingston Ghettos, or the mean streets of north London or Glasgow! All those aitch-dropping, vowel-mangling punk rockers with a public school education! All those Hampshire girls with grandparents in Liverpool or Brum! All those Pogues[2] fans from Hertfordshire singing Irish rebel songs! . . .

Ever since I have been old enough to understand what it means to be suburban I have wanted to come from somewhere else, preferably north London. I have already dropped as many aitches as I can . . . and I use plural verb forms with singular subjects whenever possible. This was a process which started shortly after my first visits to Highbury,[3] continued throughout my suburban grammar school career, and escalated alarmingly when I arrived at university. My sister, on the other hand, who also has problems with her suburban roots, went the other way when she went to college, and suddenly started to speak like the Duchess of Devonshire.[4] . . .

Post-war . . . none of the available cultures seemed to belong to us, and we had to pinch one quick. And what is suburban post-war middle-class English culture anyway? Jeffrey Archer and *Evita*, Flanders and Swann[5] and the Goons, Adrian Mole and Merchant–Ivory . . . and John Cleese's silly walk?[6] It's no wonder we all wanted to be Muddy Waters or Charlie George.[7]

(Hornby 1993: 47–9)

His subsequent novels *High Fidelity* (1994) and *About a Boy* (1997) are also part-autobiographical, and provide realistic, amusing explorations of suburban youth culture in the 1970s and 1980s. They also highlight his search for a sense of belonging, and raise questions as to what extent white British men and women share the migrant condition, in the sense of feeling adrift and rootless in modern society.

Poetry

Ted Hughes is considered by many critics to be the finest poet of the post-war generation. His work is frequently concerned with the birds, beasts, insects and fish of his native countryside, which provide the inspiration for many of his poems. His early collection *The Hawk in the Rain* (1957) announced the arrival of a major British poet. After this he wrote volumes of poetry for children, verse plays for radio and several works of criticism. In 1984 he succeeded Sir John Betjeman to become Poet Laureate. This title is held by an 'official' poet to the royal household, a position created in 1616 so that poems would be written for important state occasions. His collection *Rain Charm for the Duchy* (1992) contains his Laureate verse, but some of his finest work appeared later in his career, such as *Birthday*

Letters (1995) in which he described his troubled marriage to the American poet Sylvia Plath, who committed suicide in 1963.

Today, Andrew Motion, Tony Harrison, Geoffrey Hill, Tom Paulin and James Fenton all write highly praised poetry about contemporary themes with rich, anecdotal narrative. However, in recent years poetry has been neglected and there currently exists a general feeling that traditional forms of verse have little to say about modern themes. Consequently, poets have found it increasingly difficult to have their work published and many publishing houses have been forced to close their poetry sections, or reluctantly have maintained them simply for reasons of prestige.

But despite the difficulties, poetry has continued to evolve with popular new styles such as 'performance poetry' – verse which is written to be performed aloud by elaborately dressed performers who read their dramatic poems about topical urban themes such as sex, drugs and fame, to an appreciative, youthful, non-literary audience. Poetry as performance was pioneered by the Mersey Poets in the 1960s, and was developed during the 1970s and 1980s by Manchester-born 'punk' poet John Cooper-Clarke. During the 1980s black musical styles were incorporated, and a leading exponent is the British Rastafarian poet Benjamin Zephaniah, whose 'rap' is performed in sharp, urgent volleys of politically charged verse. When punks and Rastafarians were protesting about high unemployment, homelessness and the National Front in the early 1980s, his poems could be heard at demonstrations, outside police stations and even on the dance floor. Collections include *Pen Rhythm* (1980), *The Dread Affair* (1985), *Inna Liverpool* (1988) and *Propa Propaganda* (1996). In 1998 he was a shortlisted candidate for the prestigious post of Poet Laureate, following the death of Ted Hughes, and in the new century remains one of the few poets widely recognised by young, black non-specialists, as well as by the literary 'establishment'.

A related type of performance poetry is 'dub', a verse-form with the distinctive rhythms of reggae but without the music. A prime exponent is Linton Kwesi Johnson, who has written several volumes of dub poetry. He was born in Jamaica, but came to Britain in 1963. His poems are set in urban areas, and are often dark and violent. *Inglan is a Bitch* (1980) is one of his best-known collections. He has also made records of his poetry, including *Bass Culture* (1980) and *Making History* (1984).

A more recent development is 'slam' which is a mixture of poetry and rap created by Afro-Americans and adopted by young British Afro-Caribbeans. Slam poetry is delivered vigorously, with attitude and energy, by slammers who stand alone or work in pairs or groups to deliver their message on topics as varied as racial pride, female self-respect, friendship, crime and body image. The main difference from rap is that it is competitive, with judges being drawn from the audience.

Attitudes towards the new verse have varied. While younger readers found it accessible and enjoyable, many older critics claimed it was shallow, populist and had little substance. However, the new forms have inspired many young people to creativity, and brought about a new appreciation for the written and spoken word.

Children's literature and the rise of Harry Potter

Before the early twentieth century children often read stories which were written originally for adults, but a literature for the very young began to develop with the growth of mass literacy and cheaper publishing. Some of the best-known books are classic stories of imaginative, escapist fiction, such as J.M. Barrie's *Peter Pan* and Kenneth Grahame's *Wind in the Willows*. Later in the 1920s Beatrix Potter's animal tales were especially popular with children, who did not seem to mind the author's frank treatment of danger and death their characters sometimes encountered.

Richmal Crompton's *Just William* books of the 1920s, and Enid Blyton's bestselling children's stories of the 1940s, which feature groups of friends such as *The Famous Five*, *The Secret Seven*, and the fictional gnome *Noddy*, were pure escapism, in which nothing bad ever happened to the characters. Despite some criticism that her stories were bland, as well as snobbish and sometimes racist, Blyton became the bestselling English language author of the twentieth century. In her career she authored nearly 700 books, and in 2005 – 35 years after her death – she still sold around 7 million per year, making a total of over 400 million worldwide.

In the post-war period there was a greater concern with removing social prejudice from children's books. Realistic stories expressed egalitarian values and community solidarity. But in the 1960s this began to give way to more imaginative and escapist fiction, for example Alan Garner's *Owl Service* (1967) with its magic and legend, which also became a successful television series. In recent years public concerns over what children should be taught, and the international popularity of J.K. Rowling's Harry Potter stories, have made children's books one of the most high-profile areas of literature.

Rowling's books have been phenomenally successful. After studying for a degree in French and working as an English teacher in Portugal, her first book *Harry Potter and the Philosopher's Stone* was published in 1997. Harry is a bespectacled schoolboy who has lost his parents and lives in a cupboard under the stairs of his aunt and uncle's house. Fear of loss and separation are common themes in the stories, which feature witches, potions, a mysterious owl, and lessons in magic at the Hogwarts School of Wizardry and Witchcraft.

Success came quickly, as did the books, and the fourth Harry Potter book *Harry Potter and the Goblet of Fire* became the fastest selling hardback in history when it was launched in 2000. Today, her six books are published in over 200 countries and almost 50 languages, in an achievement as fantastic as the adventures of her hero. The books have also been

Figure 4.1
J.K. Rowling, the author
of the Harry Potter series of
children's books

made into phenomenally successful films, which together have earned their author an estimated £65m, and an award of OBE.

Today, the range of stories available to children has been influenced by a desire to encourage positive social attitudes towards people of different backgrounds and circumstances, for example the social realism of Jacqueline Wilson's *The Bed and Breakfast Star* (1995), which tells the story of a child without a proper home, and *The Story of Tracy Beaker* (1991) about a girl who is in foster care. The ethnic diversity of Britain is also reflected in stories in which black children are central, for instance stories by Malorie Blackman, Jamela Gavin and Benjamin Zephaniah. The broad range of writing for an intelligent and thoughtful modern audience has increased demand for children's literature, which is written to make learning fun, promote social awareness, and reflect a diverse and multicultural society.

Discussion topics and activities

1   What do you consider to be the most distinctive aspects of English literature since the mid-1950s? Which kind of literature would you prefer to read?

2   How do the themes and style of the literature of your country differ from those of English literature? Think about women's writing, migrants' stories and writing with a strong regional flavour.

3   Imagine you are a book critic for a popular magazine. Write a critical review of a novel which you know well, explaining what you like or dislike about it.

4   Most people in Britain live in suburban areas of towns and cities. What do you think it is like to live there? What sort of image does it have? Refer back to the extracts in the text from Hanif Kureishi's *Buddha of Suburbia* and Nick Hornby's *Fever Pitch*.

   (a) How do the authors feel about living in suburbia? Why do you think they feel that way?

   (b) Why do many young people in Britain feel the need for a sense of belonging and roots in their lives? Is it similar where you live? Can similar themes be found in the literature of your country?

Suggested further reading

Books

Bradbury, M. (1992) *The Modern British Novel*, Harmondsworth: Penguin.

Breen, J. (1990) *In Her Own Write: Twentieth-Century Women's Fiction*, London: Macmillan.

Cairns, C. (1987) *The History of Scottish Literature*, vol. 4, *The Twentieth Century*, Aberdeen: Aberdeen University Press.

Carter, R. and McRae, J. (1997) *The Routledge History of Literature in English: Britain and Ireland*, London and New York: Routledge.

Connor, S. (1996) *The English Novel in History*, London and New York: Routledge.

Dabydeen, D. (ed.) (1985) *The Black Presence in English Literature*, Manchester: Manchester University Press.

Drabble, M. (1977) *The Ice Age*, Harmondsworth: Penguin.

Hornby, N. (1993) *Fever Pitch*, London: Gollancz.

King, B. (2004) *The Oxford English Literary History Series*, vol. 13, *1948–2000: The Internationalization of English Literature*, Oxford: Oxford University Press.

Kureishi, H. (1990) *The Buddha of Suburbia*, London: Faber & Faber.

McEwan, I. (2006) *Saturday*, London: Vintage.

Munt, S.M. (1994) *Murder by the Book: Feminism and the Crime Novel*, London: Routledge.

Rendell, R. (2005) *Thirteen Steps Down*, London: Arrow.

Rushdie, S. (1988) *The Satanic Verses*, London: Vintage.

Sanders, A. (1994) *The Short Oxford History of English Literature*, Oxford: Oxford University Press.

Stevenson, R. (1993) *A Reader's Guide to the Twentieth-Century Novel in Britain*, Hemel Hempstead: Harvester-Wheatsheaf.

Stevenson, R. (2004) *The Oxford English Literary History Series*, vol. 12, *1960–2000: The Last of England?*, Oxford: Oxford University Press.

Thieme, J. (ed.) (1996) *Post-Colonial Literatures in English*, London: Arnold.

Wallace, G. and Stevenson, R. (eds) (1993) *The Scottish Novel since the Seventies: New Visions, Old Dreams*, Edinburgh: Edinburgh University Press.

Waugh, P. (1995) *Harvest of the Sixties: English Literature and its Background 1960–90*, Oxford: Oxford University Press.

Winterson, J. (1992) *Written on the Body*, London: Vintage.

Journals

Granta, the *Literary Review*, the *London Magazine*, the *London Review of Books*, *Strand* and the *Times Literary Supplement* all carry up-to-date information, news and comment on current developments. The British Council has a regular newsletter *Literature Matters*, which includes recent information on academic conferences, publications and so on, as well as analysis of the latest trends in English literature.

Notes

1 A suburb of north London, close to the Arsenal stadium.
2 A London-Irish band.
3 Then the home of Arsenal Football Club.
4 An aristocrat renowned for her distinctive R.P. accent.
5 A genteel music hall comedy duo popular in the mid-1950s.
6 A comedy sketch from the satirical show *Monty Python's Flying Circus*.
7 A talented, flamboyant Arsenal footballer of the 1970s.

Theatre

Introduction

British drama is consistently admired for its variety and vitality. Traditional productions, novel reinterpretations, brave new works, lively musicals and pantomime are all elements of contemporary theatre, in which creativity and evolution are highly valued and the work of young playwrights is strongly encouraged.

Plays are performed in many different places. Settings vary from the intimacy of a small room above a village pub to the formality of London's Royal National Theatre, whose company of actors and staff is among the most prestigious in the country. There are approximately 300 theatres in Britain and more than 40 have resident companies of actors, playwrights and other staff. These are known as repertory or 'rep' theatres, and offer a variety of plays for short periods. They generally receive a subsidy from the Arts Council, which enables them to be more creative and free from commercial pressures.

Repertory theatres are found in all the major cities. Some of the largest are Glasgow Citizens', Sheffield Crucible, Bristol Old Vic and the Liverpool Playhouse. They have a reputation for original, varied and high-quality plays. The most successful often transfer to London, which is important for any director seeking a larger audience and national publicity. Some are even exported abroad, where there is always strong demand for traditional works. However, with the exception of American shows, foreign productions on the British stage are rare.

London has around 100 theatres, with around half in the West End, of which 15 are occupied by subsidised companies. The large commercial

Figure 5.1 Shaftesbury Avenue, at the heart of London's West End

theatres, such as the Theatre Royal in Drury Lane, are situated in the West End, the capital's focal point for night-life. These theatres generally offer a familiar programme of light entertainment, such as musicals and comedy shows, while plays with more individual themes are offered in smaller theatres, such as the Donmar Warehouse or the Tricycle, which are situated off-West End. But the most innovative and experimental work is usually found in the 'fringe' theatres. These are smaller, simple stages which specialise in small-scale works of quality. Their shows often feature unconventional, experimental plays, or works which deal with controversial themes; they are found in all parts of the city.

Drama schools offer specialised training for the stage. Among the best known are the Royal Academy for Dramatic Art (RADA), the Central School for Speech and Drama and the London Academy of Music and Dramatic Art. Numerous other colleges, art schools and universities also offer courses in drama, theatre design and related subjects, as well as training for technicians and directors. Afterwards, many actors go to work in 'rep' before working in film and television, where for the lucky few, the fame and financial rewards can be much greater.

But drama is also a popular spare-time activity, and many provincial towns have amateur dramatics societies which put on an annual play for the local community. Schools, colleges and universities have drama societies too, where students can exercise their dramatic talent and where many famous actors began their careers. Plays are also made available in other media such as television, film and book form. So although the *stage* may not have the same appeal it had early in the twentieth century, it can be said that drama is more popular in the twenty-first century than it has ever been.

Historical influences

Theatre in Britain originated in Roman times, but the tradition of British theatre probably originates in the tenth century, when priests used drama as a tool of religious and political education, teaching biblical stories which were developed into 'Miracle Plays' to coincide with town feasts and festivals. By the sixteenth century professional actors were travelling in small groups from town to town, performing in the squares and pubs, and in 1576 London had its first permanent theatre in Shoreditch. Although it was closed by the authorities due to the unruly crowds it was attracting, it later moved to Bankside on the edge of the River Thames, where it was rebuilt and renamed 'the Globe'. In recent years this has been carefully reconstructed, and it is now open to the public once again.

At one time theatres were built all over London, but since the seventeenth century the city's West End has been 'theatreland', where many of the country's most prestigious stages are packed into a maze of narrow streets. Many of today's grand old establishments were built around 1900, often on the sites of much older ones, such as the Theatre Royal and the Royal Opera House. Modern theatres include the National on London's South Bank, and the Barbican Centre to the east of the city.

Outside the capital, Stratford-on-Avon is home to the Royal Shakespeare Company (RSC), and is the town where the playwright was born and died. The RSC primarily interprets works by William Shakespeare (1564–1616) and presents works throughout the year. His plays are still the most performed of any British dramatist, and fresh interpretations are constantly appearing, which the RSC also shows in London, Newcastle and other cities in Britain and abroad.

Although British theatre is often considered to be synonymous with Shakespeare, most contemporary dramas are influenced by plays from the mid-nineteenth century. The political and social themes of Henrik Ibsen (1828–1906) had a great impact on British drama. Ibsen was a Norwegian playwright whose 'problem plays' examined controversial themes, such as the effects of the social environment on the individual, and the oppression of women in marriage. Plays such as *Hedda Gabler* (1890) shocked audiences and critics, but Ibsen was supported by the influential dramatist George Bernard Shaw (1856–1950), who similarly proposed that British drama should be influenced more by social ideas than by spectacle and comedy.

Shaw was an Irish playwright and a master of language. He often mixed different styles, for example colloquial and biblical, to great dramatic effect in works which were witty, provocative and political. At a time when it was unfashionable and even eccentric, he was a feminist, vegetarian and abstemious, and his inventive works such as *Man and Superman* (1903) and *Pygmalion* (1913) frequently attacked conventional morality and ideas. Shaw's influence has been enduring, and in 1925 he received the Nobel Prize for Literature.

Social realism

During the late 1940s and early 1950s the public did not want to be challenged and provoked by its theatre. In times of austerity and when the pain of war was still close to the surface, the most popular works were light, comfortable and reassuring. Consequently, theatre was dominated by bland populist plays such as weak thrillers, and comedies which gently poked fun at the old social order. During and after the war patriotic, film adaptations of historical dramas were also popular with audiences, such as *Henry V* (1944), *Hamlet* (1948) and *Richard III* (1955), which all featured Laurence Olivier in a starring role and helped cement his reputation as the leading actor of his time.

By the mid-1950s the economy was slowly beginning to improve after the devastation of the war years. But many young people felt a sense of dissatisfaction with the government, which was seen as old-fashioned and remote from society. There was a feeling of discontent with the safe, complacent, conservative state of things, and a desire for honesty and a fresh start. By 1955 this had found expression in a new wave of activity across the arts. Creative young authors began to write plays and novels whose characters spoke directly and honestly, and were loudly critical of the ruling class of government, Church and business-leaders. The authors became known as the 'angry young men', a description originally used in the publicity for John Osborne's *Look Back in Anger* (1956) at London's Royal Court Theatre, a stage known for its adventurous and experimental plays.

Osborne's play tells the story of Jimmy Porter, a university graduate who lives in a small Midlands town. Porter is angry with the modern world, which he sees as dull and false. His concerns are those of many young people at that time: a desire for social change and the need for new values and causes. Much of the action takes place in his cheap, untidy bed-sitting room and centres on his chaotic marriage.

The play was highly successful. It caught the mood of the times, and young audiences crowded to hear the new voices speaking from the heart. Forceful plays followed, expressing the discontent, frustration and anger of the post-war young in a style that had not been seen before. Among those were Shelagh Delaney's *A Taste of Honey* (1962) and Ann Jellicoe's *The Knack* (1962), which both dealt with unmarried couples living together, a subject considered taboo in the Britain of the early 1960s. Many scenes are set in a small, scruffy room, which is simply furnished with a double bed, ironing board, table, fireplace and sink. They became such common props that the plays and stories were nicknamed 'kitchen sink dramas' after an earlier term for a style of painting which for the first time realistically portrayed mundane, everyday life.

Such dramatic portrayals of ordinary people had never been seen before, and plays were often received by audiences with bemusement, shock and disdain. But the new movement put on the stage the concerns and problems of ordinary people and not just those of a better-educated, affluent minority, as had been the case until before the war. It introduced dissent into the arts and provided British audiences with a more complete theatre of social experience.

Harold Pinter

The late 1950s was a fertile period for British drama and several new writers emerged, who would go on to have long and successful careers. One is Harold Pinter, the longest established among prominent dramatists, and who is regarded by many critics as Britain's finest living playwright. The action in Pinter's plays often takes place in one room, where the characters attempt to express their feelings, irrational thoughts and ideas. His first major play was *The Birthday Party* (1958), in which the two protagonists are forced into a situation which they cannot control. It has humour, sex and menace, but *The Homecoming* (1965) is one of his best-known works. It is about a divided family in which the father does not get on well with his son Jayston, who works at an American university. Jayston returns home with his new wife Ruth, an educated 'career woman', who has strong views on women's equality and liberation. But as in many families of the early 1960s, she is seen only in terms of her sexuality and her domestic role, and the other men in the family regard her as a mother, a wife and a whore. In this scene she is alone with her brother-in-law Lenny, and uses her sexuality to defend herself against Lenny's attempt to control her.

Lenny: Excuse me, shall I take that ash-tray out of your way?
Ruth: It's not in my way.
Lenny: It's seems to be in the way of your glass. The glass is about to fall. Or the ash-tray. I'm rather worried about the carpet ... it's not me ... it's my father. He is obsessed with order. And clarity. He doesn't like mess. So, as I don't believe you're smoking at the moment, I'm sure you won't object if I move this ash-tray. And then, perhaps I'll relieve you of your glass.
Ruth: I haven't quite finished.
Lenny: You've consumed quite enough in my opinion.
Ruth: No I haven't.

Lenny: Quite sufficient in my own opinion.
Ruth: Not in mine.
Lenny: Just give me the glass.
Ruth: No.
Lenny: I'll take it then.
Ruth: If you take the glass, I'll take you.
Lenny: How about me taking the glass without you taking me?
Ruth: Why don't I just take you?
Lenny: You're joking!

(Pinter [1965] 1991: 50–52)

One of Pinter's most notable contributions to drama is in the writing of dialogue. Earlier playwrights wrote it in an extravagant and impressive manner, but Pinter's dialogue is naturalistic and includes many pauses, hesitations and changes of subject, as in real life. He allows the audience to use its imagination and decide what the play is about. This was considered radical in the 1950s, but since then it has become a characteristic of dialogue in many British mainstream plays and films.

His later works often deal with questions of self-identity and knowledge of others, for example *Old Times* (1971) and *No Man's Land* (1975). But since the late 1980s his works have become more explicitly political, in response to what he sees as the encroachment upon personal freedom and the desire for war by successive governments in Britain and America. *Mountain Language* (1988) is set in an unnamed dictatorial, totalitarian state where people are imprisoned for using their own language, which has been prohibited by the authorities. The play warns of the dangers of a centralised culture and authority where local differences and identities are not merely ignored, but actively repressed. *New World Order* (1991) is a short play based on the first Gulf War, in which the author expresses his profound doubts about the conflict.

Pinter is a prolific writer who has written extensively for film, radio and television, and won numerous awards including in 2005 the Nobel Prize for Literature. The uniqueness of his style led to the adoption of the term 'Pinteresque', commonly used to describe dark threatening situations in which people become victims of their own feelings, desires and guilts, even though their lives seem superficially normal.

Censorship

Until 1968 the content of dramatic works was still closely controlled by laws limiting what could be shown on stage. All public performances required a licence from the Lord Chamberlain, an official of the royal household. The practice originated in the sixteenth century to control political content in drama. During the nineteenth century there was more concern over moral censorship, and licences were used to prevent obscene and blasphemous plays. Theatres without a licence could only offer musical shows and so, to avoid problems with the law, lively dramas of crime, violence, sadism and seduction were combined with background music. Owing to their combination of melody and drama, these popular spectacles became known as 'melodramas'.

In 1843 the government introduced the Theatre Regulating Act which allowed small theatres to offer a variety of plays. The new freedoms encouraged the writing of many new works, but there were few dramatists of quality. However, later in the century some of the most popular and talented playwrights of recent times emerged, such as the Irish playwright Oscar Wilde. His imaginative, witty plays were based on sharp social observation, the best known being his comedy of manners *The Importance of Being Earnest* (1895). W.S. Gilbert and A. Sullivan combined lyrics and music in numerous comic operas, for example *H.M.S. Pinafore* (1878) and *The Mikado* (1885).

Censorship remained unchanged until 1968, when at a time of reform and more permissive attitudes, plays were subjected to the same tests as works of literature under the Obscene Publications Act of 1959, and prosecution depended on whether or not the book or play might be seen by someone who could be depraved or corrupted by it.

Shocks of the new: theatre in the 1960s and 1970s

Although many new works of the late 1950s were critical of authority, none had yet followed in the long British tradition of satire until 1960, when the highly original and entertaining new comedy show *Beyond the Fringe* appeared at the Edinburgh Festival. The team of Peter Cook, Jonathan Miller, Alan Bennett and Dudley Moore wrote and performed in a series of irreverent, satirical sketches on English manners, eccentricities, and the government of the time. This had not been done in recent years, as during and after the war there had been a tradition of patriotism, deference and a profound conservatism, which had seen a Tory government in power since 1951. However, the British were becoming more self-confident and began to doubt the calibre and judgement of their leaders, in particular after the Suez crisis of 1956, which emphasised just how much Britain had declined as a world power.

In 1961 *Beyond the Fringe* transferred to London where it continued until 1966. It was an immediate success and marked a new beginning for political satire on stage and later on television, with programmes such as *That Was the Week That Was* and later *Monty Python's Flying Circus*. The show marked what future Tory Prime Minister called 'the death of deference'. Many agreed, and thought it could not come soon enough.

In the cultural ferment of the 1960s, drama was becoming braver and more provocative, and Joe Orton was a leading exponent of the trend. Orton disliked authority and control by the state, and his works were created to alarm as well as to amuse respectable, bourgeois audiences. Although his works were comedies, they also had a dark side to them. *Loot* (1966) deals with murder and robbery; *What the Butler Saw* (1969), Orton's final farce, considers questions of authority, sexual identity and the role of psychoanalysis. Tragically, his life was cut short when he was murdered at the age of 34 by his lover Kenneth Halliwell.

The 1970s were years of conflict and struggle between several opposed forces: the unions, the government, the IRA, the SPG (Special Patrol Group), the National Front. The decade also saw a rising tide of racist violence and also 'white on white' violence among subcultures such as football supporters. Aided by a relaxation in the censorship laws in 1968, allowing authors to write more shocking, violent and explicit works, playwrights began more accurately to represent the times in which they lived. Playwrights such as David Edgar, Edward Bond, Trevor Griffiths and Peter Schaffer wrote radical, intentionally shocking works, and argued that deviant and violent behaviour was a natural consequence of a corrupt, decaying society. Fine descriptions of character and attention to dialogue were considered less important than visual 'shock tactics', with cold depictions of murder, torture, rape and cannibalism. One of the most disturbing was Peter Schaffer's *Equus* (1973). Its theme of spiritual and mental decline was developed by showing a young boy who expresses his affection for horses by blinding them.

Howard Brenton and David Hare were both closely associated with radical drama at the beginning of their careers and since the 1970s they have both become major dramatists. Brenton had an early success with *Magnificence* (1973), an angry play about urban terrorism. His later play *Romans in Britain* (1980) featured the simulated homosexual rape of a Druid priest by a Roman soldier. Many critics saw it as gratuitous sexual violence, a cynical attempt to gain publicity. But he defended it as an exploration of empire-building, a critique of colonialism and of the British military presence in Ireland. In contrast, David Hare's approach has been less controversial than Brenton's, and his works reflect his philosophy that political plays should not be used for direct protest, but should create opportunities for debate and discussion, a point of view reflected in *Slag* (1970), *Fanshen* (1975) and the television play *Licking Hitler* (1978), which emphasised the ways in which individuals change as a consequence of their social environments.

Faced with provocative new drama and often distasteful subject matter, many older members of the public stopped going to the theatre. But radical playwrights argued that they needed to write controversial material in order to shock their middle-class, middle-aged audiences out of their sense of complacency. On the other hand, a younger, more liberal audience found such plays daring and attractive, and it provided them with fresh ideas on how to develop their own material.

New perspectives: alternative drama

Many of the freedoms taken for granted in the twenty-first century, such as gay rights and equality for women, in the 1960s were still considered subversive, even dangerous drama topics, which the mainstream theatres would not touch. For example, homosexuality was illegal until 1967, as was abortion, and contraceptives for women were not freely available until 1974. Equal pay for women did not become a reality in law until 1975, and it was legal to discriminate against women in employment until the same year.

Plays about such issues were still part of the 'underground' and were often held in small, non-profit-making studios known as 'arts labs', where like-minded artists of all kinds could meet and work. Some theatre groups such as Hull Truck, Red Ladder and Café La Mama had no permanent base and toured continually, putting on shows in smaller studio theatres, schools and community buildings. One of the most vigorous and vocal of the new theatre trends was women's theatre. Around 1970 the Women's Theatre Group, the Sadista Sisters, the Chuffinelles, Cunning Stunts and others toured schools and performed in the street. Their works dealt openly with questions of gender, sexuality and identity, and aimed to raise awareness of the harsh realities of many women's everyday lives, for example by contrasting them with what they saw as young women's unrealistic, fairy-tale expectations.

The pioneering nature of women's theatre, its new voices and identities gave impetus to the gay theatre movement. The newspaper *Gay News* was used to recruit theatre staff and actors, and in 1976 a mixed-sex company Gay Sweatshop was formed. Women worked on plays which addressed issues such as lesbian parenting rights, while men worked on plays dealing with issues such as lowering the age of homosexual consent. By 1978 the movement had been sufficiently confident and successful to produce a play with an openly homosexual theme. This was *Bent* by Martin Sherman, which dealt with the Nazi persecution of homosexuals in Berlin of 1934.

The platform created by alternative drama led to a greater representation of ethnic minorities in the mainstream. Until the early 1970s, the only plays dealing with the experience of racism had been presented by visiting playwrights from the USA and South Africa, such as South African Athol Fugard's *Sizwe Bansi is Dead* (1972), about the apartheid system. But new black playwrights gradually made their mark, such as Michael Abbensetts, whose *Alterations* (1978) presented an authentic West Indian view of life in Britain. However, by the end of the decade, British drama was still predominantly organised and performed by white British males on the London stage, and black voices were still marginalised, as they were in many other areas of the arts.

101

'Radical' drama was sometimes difficult to understand for British audiences, and because many plays could not be easily enjoyed by a non-specialised public, there was a feeling that drama was becoming too experimental, and at the same time remote from society. Competition from popular music and television intensified the financial pressures. Consequently, theatre attendances continued to fall, and some theatres were faced with closure.

Musicals

In contrast to the specialised, 'niche' appeal of radical drama were the large-scale, commercially driven 'blockbuster' musicals. Those of the 1960s and 1970s had enormous appeal to the young, who were bringing about a revolution in British society. The nudity and androgynous sexuality on display in many performances reflected the 'permissive' society and the increased tolerance shown by the 1968 Theatres Act, which had removed the need for each play to have an individual licence. As the theatre became one of the few places where progressive, provocative and daring new shows could be seen, ecstatic audiences regularly filled the palatial West End playhouses.

In America, Galt MacDermot, Gerome Ragni and James Rado created *Hair*, a successful musical which used elements of rock music, circus and dance. Big, confident and impudent, it captured the mood of the times, announcing the imminent arrival of a new age – the 'age of Aquarius' – and its associated values of liberality and freedom. In 1968 *Hair* opened in London and was an immediate success. It was also the first time that nudity had been seen in a theatrical production. But some critics and members of the public claimed the shows were blasphemous and pornographic, which in turn generated even more publicity and interest. Others remarked that the nudity and swearing were carefully adjusted to shock nobody, and that the press were over-reacting in order to boost newspaper sales.

Several other shows with nudity, song and dance appeared, such as *Oh! Calcutta!* (1969, Kenneth Tynan) and *Godspell* (1971, Steven Schwarz), and since then the format of pop songs, dance and spectacular visual effects has been regularly exploited by Tim Rice and Andrew Lloyd-Webber in musicals which have been popular around the world. Their *Jesus Christ Superstar* (1971) combined rock with religion to make a modern version of the story of Jesus, and built on the success of *Joseph and the Amazing Technicolour Dreamcoat* (1968), another biblical drama attracting huge audiences of young people. The duo had another big success with *Evita* (1978), which tells in grand style the story of Argentinian 'first lady' Eva Peron.

The new musicals proved highly successful and many of those involved with them went on to successful careers. In 1981 Lloyd-Webber went solo to make *Cats*, which celebrated poems from T.S. Eliot's *Old Possum's*

Book of Practical Cats. Then came *Starlight Express* (1984), a train race on roller-skates, and *Phantom of the Opera* (1986), which tells the story of a disfigured composer who haunts an opera house and falls in love with a beautiful singer. The colourful, high-tech stage sets and accessible lyrics, lively music and energetic dancing guaranteed their popularity and made enormous profits, quickly transferring to New York's Broadway and other theatres around the world, where they have been successful for many years.

In the 1990s almost half the total number of productions showing in the West End were musicals, a record number. Their combination of stories and songs and the absence of political themes or difficult dialogue have proved popular with British audiences and overseas visitors. But despite their commercial success, many critics remain unenthusiastic. They refuse to take seriously a form of entertainment which mixes technology and pop songs, in which the actors could be changed without affecting the show, and similarly have difficulty in taking seriously a play which is completely uncritical and made simply for commercial consumption.

Theatre and Thatcherism

In the 1980s the Conservative government reduced spending on the arts more than any previous administration. Provoked by the oppositional nature of most productions, in 1982 the Secretary General of the Arts Council asked why artists should 'expect public money to advocate the overthrow, not of the particular party in power, but of the whole system of parliamentary democracy'. Local government was reorganised, the funding of drama was altered or removed, and political works became scarce and more moderate. Radical, alternative theatre groups such as 7:84 (a name which reflects the fact that in the early 1980s, 7 per cent of the population held 84 per cent of the wealth in Britain) continued to write plays and tour. But they lost financial support from the Arts Council and many similar groups disappeared. As the government began to expose the theatre fully to market forces, the years of critical, state-subsidised theatre for the people appeared to be over.

However, some writers continued to make commercially successful plays that were highly critical of Thatcherism, such as David Hare, one of the most respected writers of the period. His career began in the late 1960s, and as he matured, his plays reflected interests in politics and society, such as *A Map of the World* (1983) which looks at issues of exploitation in the Third World. Between 1985 and 1991 he focused on aspects of British society with four 'state of the nation' plays, which take a close look at British institutions: the Church, the legal system, Parliament and the 'fourth estate' of the press. The first of these was *Pravda: A Fleet Street Comedy* (1985), which was co-authored by Howard Brenton and deals with corruption of the mass media by their rich owners. The second was *Secret Rapture*

(1988), which contrasts a female Conservative Member of Parliament and her unambitious, 'good' sister, while in the third play *Racing Demon* (1990), Hare examines the Church of England in a time of crisis. The fourth play, *Murmuring Judges* (1991), looks at the legal system and its weaknesses. It goes into the law courts and a busy south London police station, where the professionals are involved in their daily routine. Although these plays are not satires, they emphasise the comical aspects of public life in Britain. But they also discuss deeper questions, such as how one can do good in the world and how difficult it can be to do so.

In *Pravda,* newspaper editor Lampert Laroux was cast by Hare to closely resemble the press baron Rupert Murdoch, a portrayal said to be potentially libellous, although no legal action was taken. In the following extract Laroux responds to allegations that his paper is full of lies:

> What on earth is this stuff all about the truth? Why, when everywhere you go, people tell lies; in pubs, to each other, to their wives, to the children, to the dying. Thank God they do. No one tells the truth! Why single out newspapers? Oh, a 'special standard' . . . everyone can tell lies except newspapers. They're a universal scapegoat for everyone else's evasions and inadequacies!
>
> (Brenton and Hare 1985: p. 55)

Other plays strongly critical of particular aspects of government policy included David Edgar's *Maydays* (1983) and Howard Brenton's *The Genius* (1983). These take nuclear weapons as their theme and feature the Greenham Common nuclear base in Britain. Louise Page's *Falkland Sound* (1983) deals with the Falklands War, and following the crisis over the publishing of Salman Rushdie's *Satanic Verses*, Howard Brenton wrote *Iranian Nights* (1989) with Tariq Ali, demanding greater freedom of expression in literature.

Throughout the decade the 'troubles' in Ireland continued without an obvious solution. In the past, Irish playwrights such as Brendan Behan demanded radical action to rid the country of the British, but towards the end of the 1980s writers were approaching the topic with more sensitivity. The Irish playwright Brian Friel has written several plays dealing with the 'troubles', such as *Freedom of the City* (1973) which depicts the occupation of Northern Ireland by British troops in the 1970s, and *Translations* (1980) which laments the process of anglicisation there. The latter is set in the imaginary town of Baile Beag/Ballybeg, County Donegal, in 1833. British forces arrive to make a map of the area, anglicising the place names and defining it in ways which are foreign to the Irish-speaking natives. Its critical position shows the British as an occupying power brutally robbing Ireland of its Celtic identity, and suggests that the British and Irish will always be separated by cultural differences. His *Making History* (1988) explores how history is written and order is imposed on disordered themes and subjects, while the nostalgic play *Dancing at Lughnasa* (1990) looks back to his childhood in Catholic rural Ireland, as well as to the internal troubles in the North. In 1998 it was made into a successful film.

By the 1980s the women's movement had already made considerable advances in law, and feminism was becoming a mainstream issue. Yet in the opinion of many women activists, much work remained to be done in sensitising society to the need for further reform. Building on their success in the 1970s several promising young women playwrights began to emerge with a varied body of work, such as Caryl Churchill, Shelagh Delaney, Ann Jellicoe, Joan Littlewood and Pam Gems, Sarah Daniels and Clare McIntyre. Their works are eclectic, from McIntyre's humorous, observant feminist plays such as *I've Been Waiting* (1986), which shows what she sees as the confusion, anxieties and obsessions of modern women, to more controversial works such as Sarah Daniels's *Masterpieces* (1984) which deals with pornography, violence and lesbianism.

Caryl Churchill

Since she began her career in 1958, Caryl Churchill has had sustained success. Some of her most notable works were performed in the 1980s and 1990s, and include plays for radio, television and the stage. They introduce themes of importance to women and to women's consciousness, and combine her feminist interests with socialist politics. She is also respected for her intelligence, wit and skill in presenting plays. She experiments with drama, but at the same time writes works which are popular and accessible to the general public and critics.

Vinegar Tom (1978) and *Light Shining in Buckinghamshire* (1978) are both feminist works which dealt with bodily abuse through alcohol, eating disorders and violence. *Cloud Nine* (1979) examines in role-plays how race and gender are socially constructed, and shocked the audience with its transvestite performers. But *Top Girls* (1982) is one of her best-known plays. Marlene, the protagonist, progresses from humble origins to become a successful career woman. She has left behind Angie, the child she had at the age of 17, and towards the end of the play she returns to visit her articulate but poor, unambitious sister Joyce, who has taken on the role of Angie's mother. Its feminist message is that if women simply copy men by adopting masculine behaviour, then the women's movement will achieve nothing. Instead, her message is that women must find another, more original path. This is a theme common to several of her works in the 1980s and echoes the arguments of modern feminism.

The dynamic *Serious Money* (1987) shows the loss of liberal values in society, and an increasing public amorality and selfishness. It looks at the ways in which London money dealers become morally corrupt following deregulation of the stock market; it became one of the most successful plays of the 1980s. *Mad Forest: A Play from Romania* (1990) has a quite different focus. It was written after a trip to Romania soon after the fall of President Ceauşescu, and considers the new realities of life following the revolution there. The play has received many accolades from drama critics and confirmed Caryl Churchill as Britain's leading female playwright.

Comedy

Despite the seriousness of many challenging new dramas of the time, there was also a rich vein of comedy writing, and during the 1970s and 1980s playwrights such as Alan Ayckbourn, Tom Stoppard, Neil Simon, Michael Frayn and Alan Bennett wrote some of the wittiest comedies of the British stage.

Alan Bennett began his career with Dudley Moore, Peter Cook and Jonathan Miller in 1960 at the Edinburgh Festival, and after a lifetime of highly praised work in theatre and television, he has come to be regarded as a leading dramatist of his generation. He has become known for his humorous use of language which often mixes provincial slang with the jargon of media and advertising. Like the poet Philip Larkin, his writing is often self-effacing, and focuses on dour, northern pretensions of an aspirational lower-middle-class, propriety and sexual repression. Bennett established his reputation with plays such as *Habeas Corpus* (1973), a complex comedy about social conventions and manners of the late 1950s. It includes a familiar range of comedy characters, such as a henpecked husband, a frustrated wife, a licentious vicar and a lowly tea-lady. A keen social observer, many of his works are inspired by his northern roots, and frequently portray traditional elderly northern characters and their domestic lives, such as the critically acclaimed series *Talking Heads*. Created for the stage and two television series in 1988 and 1998, *Talking Heads* are six character studies in which a single actress delivers a monologue directly to the camera, with minimal room decoration or scene changes.

Alan Ayckbourn

Alan Ayckbourn has been the most prolific and commercially successful playwright of the second half of the twentieth century. His sharp, satirical portrayals of the manners, behaviour and language of the lower-middle classes were easily appreciated at a time when individualism and bourgeois values were strongly expressed and encouraged in the politics of the Conservative government. His humorous plays also suggest a dislike of status-seekers and people who openly desire wealth, and some of the bleakest moments in his plays are reserved for these characters. Conflict set in a familiar domestic environment is another characteristic of his plays, as are pathetic, unreliable individuals, who are usually male.

One of his best-known works is *Absurd Person Singular* (1973), which shows three married couples in three different kitchens on three different Christmas Eves. *Joking Apart* (1979) is especially inventive, showing four scenes on four special occasions. These occasions are four years apart, and the couples are thus shown over twelve years, as the protagonists pass from their 20s to their 30s. In contrast, *It Could Be One of Us* (1983) is a comedy thriller with five different endings.

To comment more trenchantly on the politics and ideology of the time, during the 1980s Ayckbourn wrote several highly praised 'social' dramas, which contrasted with his familiar domestic comedies. The most admired of these was *A Small Family Business* (1987), in which a nation of shopkeepers becomes a nation of shoplifters in a family furniture firm of 'Ayres and Graces', whose members are implicated in drugs, murder and corruption.

Much of Ayckbourn's humour derives from the juxtaposition of tragedy and comedy, illustrated in the following extract from his play *Time of My Life* (1992). In this scene, a middle-aged married couple, Gerry and Laura, are celebrating Laura's birthday in an Italian restaurant. As the wine flows her tongue loosens, and she confesses to having had an affair. Her husband tries to discover the identity of the man, while the waiter snores in the background.

Gerry: Who is he then? Who is he?
Laura: Shhh, you'll wake up the waiter.
Gerry: Who is he? Laura!
Laura: There's no point in talking about it in here, is there?
Gerry: Now, I want to talk about it now!
Laura: Why do you want to talk about it now?
Gerry: Right, come on . . . we're going home.
Laura: I haven't finished my drink.
Gerry: You heard me. Home!
Laura: Don't you shout at me!
Gerry: I am not shouting at you, I wish to god I could . . .!
Laura: Calm down! calm down, will you. You'll drop dead in a minute.
Gerry: Don't worry I won't be the one who drops dead . . . have no fear about that. Whoever he is, he will be the one who drops dead because I'll murder the bastard! I'll kill him and thrash the daylights out of you!
Laura: Oh, shut up, big talk! Just shut up!
Gerry: I promise I will!
Laura: You can't murder him anyway.
Gerry: Why not?

> *Laura*: Because he is already dead, isn't he ... he's been dead since
>   1974 ... now, simmer down ... for God's sake ... that's better.
> *Gerry*: I still want to know who he was.
> *Laura*: What are you going to do? Go around and beat up his kids?
> *Gerry*: His kids? Do you mean he was married as well?
> *Laura*: You're getting warmer.
> *Gerry*: Now, who do we know who lost her husband in 1974?
>
>   (Ayckbourn 1992: p. 124)

In times of economic hardship and uncertainty, women are often those who suffer longest and hardest. This has been the theme of Ayckbourn's most critically acclaimed work of recent years, the *Damsels in Distress* trilogy of *Flatspin*, *Role Play* and *Game Plan* (2001), three plays connected by the theme of women in distress, told in a tragicomic series of events which affect all those involved. In *Game Plan*, for instance, a middle-aged woman has lost her husband, her job, and is about to lose her fashionable Docklands apartment, until her teenage daughter secretly uses the internet to advertise herself as an escort to affluent males, in order to raise money and save her mother from ruin.

Ayckbourn began his career at a provincial theatre in Scarborough on the north-east coast of England. Since then he has written over 50 plays which have been performed in London theatres, on television, in film and around the world. He currently holds a privileged position as director and playwright at the Steven Joseph Theatre in Scarborough, where the local young, old and disabled also make plays for its stages, as Ayckbourn believes that the theatre should belong to the entire community, not only to a small, privileged minority.

'Alternative' comedy

One of the most surprising developments of the early 1980s was the emergence of 'alternative' comedy. It has its origins in the Comedy Store, a small theatre in London's Soho, where members of the public were given the opportunity to tell jokes on stage until, in an intimidating, gladiatorial atmosphere, they were forced to leave either by a gong or by the jeers of a critical audience. 'Alternative' comedy began in 1979, the year Mrs Thatcher came to power, a time of high unemployment, economic recession and social conflict. It was a time of political polarisation, and the kind of things people laughed at indicated which 'side' they were on. For millions of young people the new comedy emerged as a powerful new 'weapon' to criticise the hypocrisy of Thatcherite society.

The audacious humour of the new comedians reflected the spirit of punk, and satirised stereotypical and hypocritical attitudes towards social, racial and sexual matters. It presented a powerful contrast to the sexist, racist jokes about Irishmen and mothers-in-law of some old-style comedians such as Jim Davidson and Bernard Manning. Comedians were both male and female, and cultivated an individual style in presentations which were energetic, urgent and explicit, and a way of performing which drew attention to its rawness and lack of sophistication, much as punk had done three years earlier.

The original Comedy Store also had a repertory company, known as Comic Strip. Members included actors and comedians such as Alexei Sayle, Rik Mayall, Robbie Coltrane, Ben Elton, Dawn French and Jennifer Saunders, many of whom had subsequent success writing and acting on television and in the cinema. By the 1990s many had become mainstream performers; indeed 'alternative' comedy had become an established form of entertainment, with frequent live shows on television and in small theatres around Britain. In 1999, there were some 88 comedy venues in London alone, and the sexist and racist comedy that had once been common was so marginalised it was almost extinct. By the twenty-first century the mainstream had become so varied that the term 'alternative comedy' had almost disappeared, with acts ranging from Shazia Mirza who entertains crowds with her tragicomic tales of life as a British Muslim teenager, to Al Murray, whose act as the 'Pub Landlord' parodies the pride and pettiness of the stereotypical, *Sun*-reading barman; two diverse acts which maintain a long British tradition of social satire.

Children's comedy: pantomime

One of the most traditional forms of entertainment for children around Britain is pantomime. It takes the form of a play performed during the Christmas period, and is based on *commedia dell'arte*, a style of comedy which flourished in Italy from the mid-sixteenth to the mid-eighteenth century. In Britain pantomime originated in the eighteenth century with John Weaver, a dance master at the Drury Lane Theatre in London, who began to present ballet-like entertainments in which the meaning was conveyed by gestures instead of dialogue.

In nineteenth-century England, pantomime began to acquire its present form, in which lively, colourful stories are told with music, singing, dancing and buffoonery. Fairy stories and Oriental tales are among the most common, and traditional titles include *Aladdin, Cinderella, Puss in Boots, Dick Whittington* and *Snow White*. A prominent role in the show is often taken by a guest star, a well-known 'celebrity' from television, sports or light entertainment, whose career is often 'on the rocks' (such as a former star of soap opera or faded glamour model), and the cast always features 'cross-dressing' – in which the role of the hero or 'Principal Boy' is usually played by a young woman, while the hero's mother – an older woman – is traditionally played by a man, known as a 'Dame'.

Pantomimes all include familiar routines, topical jokes, innuendo and double entendre, which provoke children and their parents to shout, cheer and boo. Audience participation is part of the tradition, and scenes are created to encourage the familiar cries of 'he's behind you' and 'oh yes it is' or 'oh no it isn't', in riotous, anarchic displays in theatres around the country.

Tom Stoppard

Tom Stoppard is one of the most consistently successful and critically acclaimed playwrights of British theatre. He was born in Czechoslovakia, but later settled in Britain where he worked as a journalist and drama critic, before starting to write plays. He is an eclectic writer who does not limit himself to one subject matter or style, and his plays have little in common with each other.

Rosencrantz and Guildenstern are Dead (1967) is his best-known work and became one of the most critically praised plays of the century. Its protagonists are two minor characters from Shakespeare's play *Hamlet*, whom Stoppard brings to the centre of the action. The play is like a series of sketches between two stand-up comedians. It shows how people try to make sense of a chaotic world, and how difficult this is when realities are always multiple, and truth always relative. In this well-known scene, Rosencrantz and Guildenstern play a game of verbal tennis. The players must hit questions across the net. Repetitions, statements and rhetoric all lose points, and the game is scored as in tennis:

> *Guildenstern*: What's your name?
> *Rosencrantz*: What's yours?
> G: I asked first.
> R: Statement. One-Love.
>
> G: What's your name when you're at home?
> R: What's yours?
> G: When I am at home?
> R: Is it different at home?
> G: What home?
> R: Haven't you got one?
> G: Why do you ask?
> R: What are you driving at?
> G: What's your name?!
> R: Repetition. Two-love. Match point to me.
>
> G: (*seizing him violently*): WHO DO YOU THINK YOU ARE?
> R: Rhetoric! Game and match. (*Pause*) Where's it going to end?
> G: That's the question?
> R: It's *all* a question.
> G: Do you think it matters?
> R: Doesn't it matter to you?
> G: Why should it matter?

R: What does it matter why?
G: (*Teasing R gently*) Doesn't it matter why it matters?
R: What's the *matter* with you?
G: It doesn't matter.
R: What's the game?
G: What are the rules?

(Stoppard [1967] 2000: 35–36)

Frivolity mixed with intellectual content is a hallmark of many of Stoppard's works. *The Real Inspector Hound* (1968) featured theatre critics who become part of the play. In *The Real Thing* (1982) there is a play within a play. In *Jumpers* (1972), *Travesties* (1974) and *Arcadia* (1993), Stoppard mixes playful verbal games with profound ideas.

Although he is sometimes criticised for being an apolitical and style-conscious writer, in the mid-1970s he turned his attention to political and human rights issues, in particular the situation of dissidents in Eastern Europe and the Soviet Union, subjects which inspired the production of some of his most critically acclaimed work. *Dirty Linen* (1977) is a critique of corruption in Parliament, while *Night and Day* (1978) considers the role of a free press and human rights in a totalitarian society. *Every Good Boy Deserves Favour* (1978) examines the related theme of free speech, in particular how during the Cold War, sane Soviet dissidents were routinely locked away in mental hospitals. In 1977 his interest in the theme led to him visiting Russia with a delegation from Amnesty International, and later Czechoslovakia where he met Vaclav Havel, the encounter leading to the stage play *Professional Foul* (1977) for Amnesty's Prisoner of Conscience Year in 1977, and later the TV play *Squaring the Circle: Poland, 1980–81* (1984) a fictional documentary about the history of the 'Solidarity' movement there.

As well as writing plays, Stoppard has also directed and written extensively for film, radio and television. His wide-ranging and ingenious works confirm him as a dramatist of world renown, and this was recognised in 1997 when he was awarded a knighthood.

Trends in theatre today

In Scotland, the 1990s began with a frenzy of activity following the decision in 1987 to make Glasgow the 1990 European City of Culture. The city invested heavily in the arts in order to develop a modern, progressive image. Experimental productions were among the chief beneficiaries and some were staged in unusual venues – such as a former tram shed – to house varied and eclectic works by John McGrath, Liz Lochhead, Tom McGrath and Bill Bryden. A short distance away in Edinburgh, the annual arts festival (which usually begins in August) continues to be the biggest, longest, and usually the wettest of its kind in Europe. Drama is its most important element and the festival 'fringe' offers a platform for alternative and more experimental types. There are no quality controls, and anyone can take part as long as there is somewhere to put the show on. The venues are diverse – from church halls to playgrounds – and plays are watched by audiences ranging from several thousand spectators to two men and a dog. Performances are often a mixture of comedy, caberet and low-budget theatre, characterised by surprise, excitement and originality. In 2002 there were 666 groups presenting 30,443 performances of 1,462 shows in the Fringe in 176 venues, and the smallest show took place in the back of a car!

The economic recession at the beginning of the 1990s created a feeling of caution and conservatism in the theatre, which extended throughout the decade. Already successful films and books were sometimes made into plays, such as Irvine Welsh's *Trainspotting* and Nick Hornby's *Fever Pitch*. But only 10 per cent of shows were of modern drama, and for the first time in 40 years it was virtually impossible to find a play with a political message on a London stage. Commercial theatre did not want to take risks with new productions, and preferred the established favourites such as musicals, which in 2005 constituted over half of West End shows. Several were from the 1970s and 1980s, such as *Guys and Dolls, Jesus Christ Superstar* and the rock musical *Tommy*. They were popular with tourists, for whom the music and spectacle may have been more important than the lyrics and themes. An exotic new addition was the new Lloyd-Webber produced musical *Bombay Dreams*, the West End's first Asian musical, which opened in 2002. Here was a flamboyant and melodramatic story of romance and murder in Bombay, which was expressed through dazzling choreography and a predictably happy ending. Music by A.R. Rahman and a script from Meera Syal ensured the success of this £4.5 million extravaganza, which subsequently transferred to New York's Broadway in 2003.

Although the role of the theatre as a forum for political debate had diminished, one exception was in December 2004, when *Behzti* (Dishonour) was shown at Birmingham Repertory Theatre. Its depiction of murder and rape in a Gurdwara (a Sikh temple), and an advertising poster showing an elderly woman carefully examining white bridal underwear, led to controversy, protest and a riot, when some 400 Sikhs broke theatre windows and stormed the doors. An audience of some 800 were evacuated, and the author Gurpreet Kaur Bhatti, a former Sikh actor who became a playwright, was forced to cancel the play, due to fears about her own safety. Although it was condemned by Sikh elders, some younger Sikhs spoke out in favour of the work. But the government refused to condemn the violence, and Salman Rushdie and other artists and authors criticised the authorities' unwillingness to challenge the Sikh community, who number around 300,000 in Britain.

During the 1990s, playwrights with Afro-Caribbean or Asian roots such as Caryl Phillips, Hanif Kureishi, Derek Walcott and Farrukh Dhondy continued to write new plays which reflected their experience of cultural change and racial identity. Many were adapted into successful television plays or screenplays for the cinema. But in 1998 there were only two London theatres which regularly staged plays written or performed by black artists. Critics believed this was not because black perspectives were being ignored, but because cultural differences were becoming increasingly unclear; more black actors were appearing in classical productions and musicals, in roles traditionally played by white actors, and works by black writers were becoming more mainstream, addressing themes other than race and marginalisation.

One of the greatest influences on theatre of recent years has been a growing financial pressure. Only around 70 per cent of productions make a profit, and this creates a tendency for writers and actors to work in television more than the stage, as television provides more creative possibilities and greater remuneration. Yet many writers are still keen to write for the theatre and, moreover, many major Hollywood names such as Kevin Spacey, Ralph Fiennes, Nicole Kidman, Madonna and Jerry Hall have been keen to work on small-scale productions in recent years, as appearances on the London stage seem to guarantee their professional credibility.

In general, however, the public has also been unwilling to buy expensive tickets without an assurance that it will enjoy the production, which in London is often held in a building lacking modern facilities and which cannot be modernised easily. Also, the associated costs of meals, drinks, car parking, the strict laws on drinking and driving, as well as the competition from television and other home entertainments, have all made the public only willing to pay high prices to see established works and fine acting.

In spite of the theatre's difficulties, there continues to be generous coverage of new developments in the form of reviews and comment on new plays. Critical opinion in the twenty-first century looks back not with anger at the last 40 years, but with positive feelings about drama's ability to capture the spirit of the times in theatre, film and television, and a hope that it can continue to build on the strengths of its heritage.

Discussion topics and activities

1   Identify some of the main themes and influences expressed by British playwrights since the mid-1950s. Which period or style do you find the most interesting and why?

2   Summarise some of the main differences between theatre in your country and theatre in Britain. Try to consider issues such as themes, movements, the representation of women and minorities, censorship, finance and audiences.

3   Could some of the new movements such as gay theatre and alternative comedy be successful in your country? Give reasons why/why not.

4   Do you think plays should be written to shock, or should they be written to entertain?

5   Should controversial plays be shown even though they could cause offence to some members of ethnic groups?

6   Imagine a particular dramatic situation, perhaps one you have experienced. Write a short summary of it, then a description of the scene, the characters, and a short piece of dramatic dialogue.

7   Write a review of a play with which you are familiar. What did you like and why? Compare your review with that of another student.

Suggested further reading

Books

Aldgate, A. (1995) *Censorship and the Permissive Society*, Oxford: Oxford University Press.

Beauman, S. (1982) *The Royal Shakespeare Company*, Oxford: Oxford University Press.

Berney, K.A. (ed.) (1994) *Contemporary British Dramatists*, Andover: St James Press.

Boose, L. and Burt, R. (eds) (1997) *Shakespeare, The Movie: Popularising the Plays on Film, Television and Video*, London: Routledge.

Brenton, H. and Hare, D. (1985) *Pravda*, London: Methuen.

Callow, S. (1995) *Being an Actor*, London: Penguin.

Cameron, A. (ed.) (1990) *Scot-free: New Scottish Plays*, London: Nick Hearn.

Churchill, C. (1990) *Shorts* (10 short plays), London: Nick Hearn.

De Jong, N. (1992) *Not in Front of the Audience: Homosexuality on Stage*, London: Routledge.

Hanna, G. (ed.) (1991) *Monstrous Regiment: A Collective Celebration* (5 plays), London: Nick Hearn.

Lacey, S. (1995) *British Realist Theatre: The New Wave in its Context 1956–65*, London: Routledge.

Morgan, F. (ed.) (1994) *The Years Between: Plays by Women on the London Stage 1900–1950*, (5 plays) London: Virago.

Osment, P. (ed.) (1989) *The Gay Sweatshop: Four Plays and a Company*, London: Methuen.

Pinter, H. (1965) *The Homecoming*, London: Faber, 1991.

Shank, T. (1994) *Contemporary British Theatre*, Basingstoke: Macmillan.

Shellard, D. (2000) *British Theatre Since the War*, New York: Yale University Press.

Shepherd, S. and Womack, P. (1996) *English Drama: A Cultural History*, London: Blackwell.

Sierz, A. (2001) *In-Yer-Face Theatre: British Drama Today*, London: Faber.

Stoppard, T. (2000 [1967]) *Rosencrantz and Guildenstern are Dead*, London: Faber.

Trussler, S. (1994) *The Cambridge Illustrated History of British Theatre*, Cambridge: Cambridge University Press.

Wickham, G. (1994) *A History of the Theatre*, Oxford: Phaidon Press.

There are also numerous anthologies of English literature which include chapters/ sections on British theatre. A. Sanders's *The Short Oxford History of English Literature* (Oxford: Oxford University Press, 1994) contains a very clear and well-written account.

Journals

For comment on earlier works, see *Plays and Players*, especially for the period 1950–80, which carries extensive post-war British theatre criticism. For more recent works, see *The London Theatre Record* (1981–91), a leading journal of theatre criticism, which carries reviews of all major works of the period. In 1991 it became *The Theatre Record* (1991–). *The Stage* (1880–) is a weekly newspaper for the performing arts industry, and carries news reviews and features of topical interest.

6

Cinema

Introduction

For over a century British film-makers have provided entertainment for audiences around the world. War films, Bond films, Ealing comedies and horror have been among the most popular genres, but the most highly praised and best loved are adaptations of classic novels, which have a reputation without equal for attention to details of dress, decor and setting. At the same time, film-makers have become powerful historians of the twentieth century, capable of influencing public knowledge and opinions, for example with propaganda films during wartime, and with idealistic representations of British rule overseas in 'heritage' films.

In contrast to the lavishness of 'costume dramas', the making of films in a simple, direct way about people's daily lives is perhaps the industry's greatest strength. The 'documentary' style was developed in Britain and has influenced film-making around the world, and naturalistic works by directors such as Ken Loach and Mike Leigh are among the most highly regarded by critics.

Film-making has become a fashionable, creative and influential area of cultural life, yet, in spite of its successes, the film industry has suffered from a lack of investment, and British film-makers have never been able to compete with the extravagant productions made by the wealthy Hollywood studios. The government does not invest large sums of money in film, and for many years film-makers were reliant on the success of popular commercial genres, such as spy thrillers, horror and comedy. Consequently, some professionals have preferred to work in America, with the world presence of the major studios, plus the promise of big film budgets and earnings. The actor Charlie Chaplin and director Alfred Hitchcock were among the first to work in Hollywood, and their careers flourished there.

Film-making in Britain is heavily centralised around the south-east of England, but its commercial heart is the central London district of Soho, where production companies, publicity agencies and related trades have their offices. The majority of studios are based in outer London. Pinewood and Shepperton are among the most established, and newer ones such as Leavesden and Three Mills are among the largest.

The majority of films are shown at cinema chains such as Warner, Virgin and Odeon, which are found all over Britain. They provide a total of approximately 2,200 screens and offer popular, well-publicised films to audiences of around 2.5 million per week. Productions of more limited interest are usually shown in 'art house' or repertory cinemas, or on Channel 4 television. These screens offer more specialised programmes, such as short 'seasons' on a particular topic, as well as older films and films in foreign languages.

A growing number of courses in many colleges and universities offer training for careers in film and television. The National Film and Television School is one of the most respected institutions and is financed by the government and the film, video and television industries. A related organisation is the British Film Institute, which was founded in 1933 to encourage the arts of film and television. It has some 35 regional film theatres and incorporates film councils for Scotland, Ireland and Wales, as well as the National Film and Television Archive and the National Film Theatre (NFT).

All public cinemas are licensed by the local authorities. These have powers to prevent the showing of a picture if they believe it would be unsuitable. However, they generally follow the recommendations of the British Board of Film Classification (BBFC). This is a government body, established in 1912 to examine and classify material for public entertainment. It currently classifies more than 4,000 films per year and attempts to reflect public opinion by following a 'line' between the traditional moralists on the political right and progressive libertarians on the left. But critics complain that the British Board is among the strictest in Europe and they demand that its secret reports be made available to the public.

The current system classifies cinema films, DVDs and videos as follows: 'U' films are open to everyone; those with 'PG' suggest parental guidance, as some scenes may be unsuitable for children; '12' – nobody under age 12 may rent or buy a '12' rated video or DVD; '12A' – nobody under age 12 may see a 12A film unless they are with an adult; '15' – nobody under age 15 may see a '15' film in a cinema, or rent or buy a '15' rated video/DVD; '18' – nobody under age '18' may see an 18 film in a cinema, or rent or buy the video/DVD. Video rental is common in Britain, where some 5 million are hired each week.

In a major ceremony, the British Academy of Film and Television Arts (BAFTA) makes awards each year to films from around the world. Two other important events are the London Film Festival in November and the Edinburgh Film Festival in August. Both take place annually and show some 250 films which are often complemented by talks and interviews from international specialists. There are also several smaller annual events around the country, such as the Celtic film festival, which takes place in a different town each year.

Pioneers

Making movies in Britain began towards the end of the nineteenth century. At that time, there were no commercial cinemas, and films were shown in fairgrounds, shops, theatres, schools and even in the open air. They were short, silent, and often presented by the people who made them. Many were of humorous incidents, or perhaps a brief record of some major event, such as a ship launch. But cinema of today has its origins in the mid-1920s when, after interruption during the First World War, a new generation of film-makers appeared. These included the directors Victor Saville and Alfred Hitchcock, producer Michael Balcon and stars such as Ivor Novello and Fay Compton. By the 1930s, the success of Hitchcock's thrillers had made him the most important director in Britain.

In 1929 Hitchcock directed the first British 'talkie', *Blackmail*. After the arrival of films with sound, cinema audiences grew fast and a small industry expanded to meet demand. But British productions were still relatively unknown abroad. This began to change with Alexander Korda's comedy *The Private Life of Henry VIII* (1933), which was a major success in America and became the first British picture to win an Oscar. Historical themes, together with adaptations of literary classics, soon became one of the most admired and respected styles of British film-making.

But the arrival of the Second World War interrupted progress. Most studios closed, while a few continued to make films for propaganda purposes. These aimed to encourage patriotic feeling and boost national morale in documentary films which emphasised community solidarity. Several were documentaries, such as *London Can Take It* (Harry Watts, 1940) and *Listen to Britain* (Humphrey Jennings, 1941). Others were feature films, such as *In Which We Serve* (Noel Coward and David Lean, 1943), *Millions Like Us* (Frank Launder, 1943) and *The Shipbuilders* (John Baxter, 1944). They reflect a hierarchical, stable and unified Britain, where everyone knows their place, respects authority and makes personal sacrifices.

In a similar vein, early representations of Britain at war, such as *The Cruel Sea* (Charles Frend, 1953), *The Dam Busters* (Michael Anderson, 1954) and *Reach for the Sky* (Lewis Gilbert, 1956), reassured the post-war public. They gave moral justification to combat, romanticised war heroism, and made audiences feel both proud and relieved. But they ignored the friction caused by women entering the labour market and the armed forces, which met with widespread disapproval.

The immediate post-war period was austere but peaceful, as government and all sections of society worked together for the common good. There were few popular diversions, and television was still an expensive novelty. The cinema became the main source of entertainment, in which the fantasy, romance and escapism of American films represented a post-war land of 'milk and honey'.

However, at Ealing Studios in west London, producer Michael Balcon preferred to ignore the influence of Hollywood and promote a characteristically British film industry, making films about ordinary communities and the drama and comedy of everyday life. One of the best-known films to emerge from Ealing was the police drama *The Blue Lamp* (Basil Dearden, 1949). It was a popular tribute to law, order and stability, which captured the mood of the era. It showed a paternal, protective police force and a calm, cohesive community, in which the chief character, PC George Dixon, was almost a sacred figure. The highly successful film led to its adaptation as a long-running television series, *Dixon of Dock Green*.

Ealing Studios became better known for their distinctive comedy films. These have entered film history as nostalgic, detailed portraits of post-war Britain: a genteel country of friendly policemen, maiden aunts, village shop-keepers and numerous eccentrics who challenge conventional society and ridicule pomposity. Titles include *Kind Hearts and Coronets* (1949), a satire of upper-class manners, and *Passport to Pimlico* (1949), a humorous critique of British bureaucracy. *The Lavender Hill Mob* (Charles Crichton, 1951) is one of the most famous. It features a mild-mannered bank clerk who plans a gold-bullion robbery, eventually disguising the loot as Eiffel Tower paperweights. The Ealing style is especially noted for its fine 'character' performances, clever scripts and empathy for individuals who oppose big business and challenge authority. It subsequently influenced numerous comedy films and television series, and is fondly remembered as a cosy celebration of English individuality.

Documentary film-making

One of the most characteristic types of British film is the documentary. It began in the 1930s, when Scottish film-maker John Grierson (1898–1972) pioneered new techniques. Grierson wanted to make authentic records of everyday life and was the first to use the term 'documentary' to describe a style of film.

Grierson strongly believed that film-makers had a duty to reveal and describe society in order to understand and improve it. To achieve his aim, he worked with the government, making dignified, creative studies of different industries and workers in Britain and the British Empire. These included *Coal Face* (1935) and *Night Mail* (1936), frank studies of the mining industry and postal service. His later work included examinations of unemployment, pollution, education, health and housing. He also pioneered the use of interviews in film, using the camera to record the words of those directly involved. Grierson's work quickly became influential, establishing objective, impartial techniques and the 'documentary' as a film genre.

Since the 1960s, documentary techniques have become more common in television, where journalists and news reporters use them as essential investigative tools. In film, realism and authenticity evolved into free cinema, whose pioneers Lindsay Anderson and Karel Reisz explored authentic, natural aspects of British society, for instance in Anderson's *O Dreamland* (1953), about a day in the seaside town of Margate, and Reisz's *We are the Lambeth Boys* (1958), about a south London youth club. At first the public was bemused, but enjoyed seeing themselves and their lives represented in film.

Social realism

Interest in making more honest and open representations of social life was also present in theatre and literature. Between 1956 and 1959 the works of many new playwrights and authors such as John Osborne, Colin Wilson and John Braine attracted critical interest. Between 1959 and 1963 several of their novels and plays were adapted for the cinema in a new wave of films which brought to cinema audiences fresh, raw portrayals of the British working class, their language, living conditions, aspirations and follies. In particular, they reveal the changing nature of society in those years: how increased affluence was leading to greater individuality, less idealism and a reduced sense of social responsibility.

The film adaptations are generally faithful to the novels, with films set in smoky, provincial, grey northern towns. They focus on the lives of ordinary working people set among small, sparsely furnished terraced houses, oppressive factories and grim pubs. To fill the roles, actors left behind their drama-school RP accents and spoke in the regional vernacular to convey a sense of life, energy and authenticity, and despite their drab surroundings, there is a spirited optimism in many of the characters, reflecting the freedom, consumerism and permissiveness which many young people of the time were beginning to experience. *Look Back in Anger* (Tony Richardson, 1959), *Room at the Top* (Jack Clayton, 1958), *Saturday Night and Sunday Morning* (Karel Reisz, 1960) and *A Kind of Loving* (John Schlesinger, 1962) were among the first and most highly praised of a body of work which became known as 'new cinema' or 'new wave'.

Richardson's *Saturday Night and Sunday Morning* was adapted from a novel by Alan Sillitoe and remains one of the most representative. It is set in a small Nottinghamshire town, where Arthur Seaton (played by

121

Albert Finney), a hard-drinking, hard-fighting, virile young man, rebels against the tedium and restrictions of his marriage and his work. But, unlike many older members of his community, he has no political beliefs or ideology and is shown as cynical and alienated, detached from his own people and disinterested in political ideas, wanting little more than Saturday night in the pub and the dream of retirement to a bungalow in the suburbs. The realist style was also used to reflect social problems, as anxiety grew over rising crime rates and a younger generation which was frequently portrayed by the mass media as 'out of control'. In *The Blue Lamp* (1949) a kind, community policeman is callously murdered, while *Victim* (1961) broke new ground with the theme of blackmail of homosexuals.

Films of the 'new wave' were usually shot in black and white, with little bright lighting. Modern jazz, pop music and long pauses were frequently used to support the action. It was also a style without theory or glamour, and therefore very different from the politicised film-making of communist countries, and from the mixture of glamour, escapism and Cold War politics which characterised film-making in the USA during the 1950s.

But the new styles were not popular with the older generation, who often found them worrying and confusing. Many stopped going to the cinema, especially given the popularity of commercial television. With declining audiences, competition from Hollywood and television, and little financial help from the government, the survival of the film industry depended on the profits from popular domestic genres, which were quickly and cheaply made to attract the new teenage market.

The magnetism of youth

From the mid-1950s a new generation of teenagers and young single adults was emerging with its own fantasies and desires in film. The industry responded with films made specifically for young audiences: comedy, horror, sex, violence and the occasional literary adaptation were all common. Filmmakers argued that their works reflected an increasingly liberal, permissive society. Increased affluence, the emergence of youth culture, the gradual emancipation of female sexuality and rising rates of crime and violence all supported their case.

Following its arrival in the mid-1950s, rock 'n' roll music was also heavily exploited in film. The explosive rhythms in the American *Rock Around the Clock* (Fred Sears, 1956) led to riots in the cinemas. There were media reports of violence and hysteria among the teenage public and a delirium previously only generated by certain types of religious experience. American films featuring Elvis Presley were enormously popular with teenage audiences, and British studios responded with musicals featuring English singers – Cliff Richard and Tommy Steele, among others. These were undistinguished except in commercial terms. But their popularity

ensured that films became important features in the career of many successful pop stars.

It was the Beatles who brought a measure of critical interest to the 'pop'
musical. *A Hard Day's Night* (Richard Lester, 1964) was an enormous
commercial and critical success, on which *Help!* (Richard Lester, 1965) and
the animated, surreal musical *Yellow Submarine* (George Dunning, 1968)
subsequently built. They helped to make popular music not just the 'property' of youth, but a kind of entertainment which was acceptable and
accessible to all the family.

The mid-1960s was a turbulent time in which old certainties were challenged and became eroded. Traditional ideas about class, politics, drugs,
sexuality and the place of women were all being interrogated in society and
the arts. The changing roles of women were depicted in a number of films,
which were set in a liberated, permissive, 'swinging' London. The new
image could be seen in the leading roles played by Rita Tushingham in
A Taste of Honey (Tony Richardson, 1961), Julie Christie in *Billy Liar*
(John Schlesinger, 1963) and *Darling* (John Schlesinger, 1965), and later
with Judy Geeson in *Here We Go Round the Mulberry Bush* (Clive
Donner, 1967). Their roles ignored the traditional roles of marriage and
childbearing, and instead emphasised freedom, fun, innocence and sex
appeal.

The traditional attitudes of the older generation and the ruling class were
being challenged on many fronts. *The Servant* (Joseph Losey, 1963) in
which a Cockney manservant changes roles with his effeminate, aristocratic
master dealt with issues of class and homosexuality in a subtle and indi-
rect manner, but much angrier and more direct was Lindsay Anderson's
If . . . (1968), which criticises the elitism, arrogance and cruelty of the
public-school system. It is set in an exclusive, old-fashioned private school,
where pupil Mick Travers (Malcolm MacDowell) leads a student rebellion
with machine-guns and hand-grenades against the school authorities, in a
film which often resembles the American *Rebel Without a Cause* (1955).

The speed and excitement of social change began to attract foreign film-
makers, such as Michelangelo Antonioni, Jean-Luc Godard and François
Truffaut. The public loved their extravagant, modish films which captured the mood of the moment. But the most successful film-makers were
those already resident, such as Roman Polanski with *Repulsion* (1965)
and *Cul de Sac* (1966), and Richard Lester with the Beatles films plus
The Knack . . . and How to Get It (1965), and Michelangelo Antonioni's
Blow Up (1966).

The American director Stanley Kubrick made numerous films in Britain,
and during the 1960s and 1970s his works were among the most varied
and stylish of their time. Several have since become classic works of
modern cinema, for example *Lolita* (1962) and *2001: A Space Odyssey*
(1968). But his most notorious work was *A Clockwork Orange* (1971),
in which violent, make-up-wearing gangs enjoy a disturbing life of crime,

sex, violence and Beethoven, whom the state attempts to correct by brain-washing techniques and thought-control. Although adapted from Anthony Burgess's 1962 novel, which recalled allegedly true events of twenty years previously, the time of the action remains unclear. In the words of the protagonist Alex (Malcolm MacDowell) it is 'just as soon as you could imagine it, but not too far ahead – it's just not today, that's all'. But in the turbulent times of the early 1970s, it appeared accurately to document England's present. One of the most disturbing and controversial films ever shown in or about Britain, Kubrick withdrew it soon afterwards, following alleged 'copycat' juvenile violence, and public demands that scenes be cut.

Popular genres

After the austerity of the post-war years, young audiences found the style, excitement and escapism in many 1960s films novel and thrilling. When mixed with the themes of spying and Cold War tension, the result was the

Figure 6.1
The classic Bond film, *Goldfinger*, starring Sean Connery

well-known James Bond films. Many are adaptations of the thirteen thrillers written by Ian Fleming, the first of which, *Casino Royale*, appeared in 1952. In literary terms the books were generally undistinguished, but the screen adaptations supplied a highly commercial combination of glamour, gadgets and faraway locations, in which the hero saved his exotic girlfriend and the world from evil despots with Russian accents.

The cocktail of ingredients was no more complicated than Bond's favourite Martini, and proved just as popular. Around half of the world's population has seen a James Bond film, a series which began in 1962 with *Dr No* (Terence Young), in which Sean Connery (a Scot) played the leading role. Since then the most famous secret agent in English fiction has been played by George Lazenby (Australian), Roger Moore (English), Timothy Dalton (Welsh) and Pierce Brosnan (Irish). But after some 25 years of the Bond formula, public interest began to decline. The disappearance of the Cold War, greater equality for women and greater public familiarity with exotic destinations left it looking tired, corny and old-fashioned. However, in the mid-1990s public interest began to revive, as Bond was reborn as a modern, progressive, 'new man' in *GoldenEye* (1995) and *Tomorrow Never Dies* (1997), which led to renewed interest and popularity.

In contrast to the big-budget Bond productions, the *Carry On* films were among the cheapest to produce yet were among the most commercially profitable of the 1960s and 1970s. They began in 1958 with *Carry On Sergeant*, and appeared almost annually until 1980, regularly finding

Figure 6.2 A scene from *Carry On Up the Khyber*

125

enthusiastic young audiences. Individual performances were usually carica-
tures: a fat, unattractive wife with a weak, mousy husband, a large-breasted
attractive young woman, an effeminate idiot, and an athletic young
bachelor. Early films were frequently set in state institutions, such as a
school, hospital or the army. Inside, bad puns, double entendres and innuendo were used to ridicule and subvert the official routine and its guardians.
The films are clear descendants of the Ealing tradition created under
Michael Balcon, and became some of the most popular films in the history
of British cinema.

Although they were ignored by critics for many years, the *Carry On*
films have recently been the subject of new evaluation by a generation of
public and critics who enjoy their irony and kitsch, elements which also
attracted young fans to the horror films made by the Hammer production
company. Many of the latter were directed by the hand of Terence Fisher
and starred Peter Cushing and Christopher Lee, such as *The Horror of
Dracula* (1958). Early pictures created an atmosphere with shadows and
suspense, but in the 1960s they became more explicit, with vivid depictions
of blood, sexuality and violence, such as *Frankenstein Must Be Destroyed*
(1969). Plots were typically set on dark nights in elaborate Gothic castles.
Common themes included a struggle between good and evil, the familiar
and the unknown, or involved a scientific discovery over which man had
lost control. But their repetitive and heavily commercial nature made them
unpopular with critics. However, an enthusiastic teenage public was
unworried about critical opinion and ensured their survival until the 1970s.

In spite of some isolated successes, the 1960s were rarely profitable for
British cinema, which was seen as creatively inferior to big-budget American productions and stylish European 'art' films. Low levels of finance
from central government meant a heavy dependence on commercial genres
and, by the end of the decade, many critics considered the industry almost
dead, sunk by the popularity of television and the glamour of Hollywood.

The 1970s: spectacle and show

Faced with difficult conditions at the beginning of the decade, and competition from video systems as well as television, the film industry continued
to make numerous safe, commercial productions. Many were historical
dramas, such as *Young Winston* (1972), *Cromwell* (1970) and *Mary Queen
of Scots* (1971), which were always popular with audiences overseas. There
was little attempt to engage critically with contemporary social issues or to
challenge the public, but a notable exception was Alan Parker's *Midnight
Express* (1978). Based on a true story of drug-smuggling and imprisonment
in Turkey, it became one of the most highly regarded works of its time and
won many international awards.

Advances in technology allowed the creation of dramatic new special
effects in movie-making, but these made production more complex,

specialised and expensive; consequently it was often shared among various companies of different nationalities. There were several British and American collaborations, which produced some of the most extravagant science fiction films of the time. One of the earliest came in 1968 with *2001: A Space Odyssey*, and continued through the 1970s and 1980s with films such as *Superman II* (1980), and the *Star Wars* trilogy (1977–83). Although cinema attendances had declined, youth was still a major audience segment, and was readily captivated by the spectacular new effects and storylines echoing some of the dominant themes of the time, such as space exploration, militarism, the threat of invasion and Cold War.

The trend towards sci-fi in the youth market was complemented by a growing number of films starring famous singers and rock bands. These had previously been light and populist, created to market the members and their music to family audiences. However, newer productions were created with the aim of appealing mainly to the band's followers, for example *Slade in Flame* (1975) about Slade (the Oasis of their time), which succeeded in capturing not just the band at its height, but also the sordid and declining atmosphere of Britain in the early 1970s. But the pop genre continued to evolve and gradually became more imaginative and substantial; the Who appeared in *Tommy* (Ken Russell, 1975) an adaptation of their 1969 album, and their music drives *Quadrophenia* (Franc Roddam, 1979), a colourful exploration of the life and times of a frustrated young mod, immersed in London's youth culture of 1964. With this film and *That'll Be the Day* (Claude Whatham, 1973), set in the 1950s, British pop began to explore its own history.

Some musicians later began to appear in non-musical feature films. The Rolling Stones' singer Mick Jagger appeared in *Performance* (Nicholas Roeg, Donald Cammell, 1970), an exploration of sexual, social and narcotic practices in the London of the late 1960s. David Bowie appeared in *The Man Who Fell to Earth* (Nicholas Roeg, 1976), playing an alien who travels to Earth, looking for a way to save his dying planet. This was a highly praised film which raised questions about corporate imperialism, as well as Britain's decline as a world power.

Alternative voices, new directions

Although audiences of the 1950s had been shocked by teenage attitudes and behaviour, by the early 1970s films about rebellious youth were part of the mainstream cinema. The new issues of racism, women's rights and the 'troubles' in Northern Ireland were considered provocative, dangerous, unprofitable topics, and in the tough economic climate it was left to the innovative and daring production companies in the independent sector to exploit them further.

In the mid-1960s students in the art schools and colleges had become interested in making challenging, critical and experimental productions.

127

New technology was cheaper and made costs lower, which helped co-operatives and collectives to be established. A network of independent cinemas emerged known as 'art house' cinemas which showed films of a less populist, more specialised nature. The freedom from commercial pressures was important: it allowed them to make films about subjects which larger organisations and production companies would not touch. Themes included the radical politics of the 'new left' which included new agendas of feminism and anti-racism.

Racial tension escalated in many British inner cities during the mid-1970s, but it still had not been addressed by black directors in full-length features until *Pressure* (Horace Ove, 1975). This was an independent production by two Trinidadians: Horace Ove and Samuel Selvon. The story showed the reality of being young and black in London during the 1970s, and chronicles the attempts of Tony, an intelligent black school-leaver, to find a job. It is set against a background of a failing education system, police brutality and black power. It also explores the growing differences between the West Indians who came to Britain during the 1950s and 1960s, and their British-born children.

By 1980 films about black British people were becoming much more angry, explicit and partisan. *Burning an Illusion* (Menelik Shabazz, 1981) explores black love and consciousness, as seen through the eyes of Pat, a black woman. *Babylon* (Franco Rosso and Martin Stellman, 1980) features young, British-born Afro-Caribbeans in London's East End. The film is rich in Jamaican creole and portrays an exotic world in which the thoughts and culture of young Rastafarians are expressed within a cloud of cannabis smoke and through a thunderous avalanche of reggae music. *Rude Boy* (Jack Hazan and David Mingay, 1980) angrily depicts two Englands: one of prosperity protected by large, corrupt police forces; the other of youth with no future, who participate in race riots, support neo-fascists and collapse after cocktails of drink and drugs at punk concerts.

As well as racial issues, films also began to express the new politics of feminism in works such as *Maeve* (Patricia Murphy and John Davies, 1981) and *Doll's Eye* (Jan Worth, 1982). They examined issues such as rape, violence, pornography and the representation of women in the media. These and many others of the time sharply depicted feminist issues and politics in a way that no other commercial medium dared to do.

During his lifetime, Derek Jarman was one of the most stylish avant-garde film-makers. His film *Jubilee* (1978) used the punk phenomenon to express a nightmarish reality of life in Britain during 1977, the year of Queen Elizabeth's Silver Jubilee celebrations (commemorating her reign of 25 years). The characters, music and film sets together project a horrific collage of shocking metaphors, which include the murder of a rich pop star, the use of Buckingham Palace as a recording studio, an orgy in Westminster Cathedral and the castration of a police officer. The film ignores the politics of left and right, of feminism or racial equality. Instead, it depicts anarchy, nihilism and British institutions in crisis, becoming one of the most important film documents of its time.

Although many independent productions were highly original and metaphorical, critics argued they were made by and for a predominantly educated, middle-class audience. They also argued that their stylistic diversity sometimes obscured the film-maker's message. However, their main achievement was to promote more open discussion and debate about issues which had once been considered minor and peripheral, particularly those of gender and race, which helped them become issues which the commercial mainstream was willing to tackle subsequently.

'The British are coming!': film-making and Thatcherism

The early 1980s were times of rapid change within the film industry. The introduction of video, cable and satellite services promoted a growth of topics and allowed audiences more choice. New technology allowed films to be made with relatively modest budgets. Agencies in advertising and pop music also began to use videos in product promotion, and many new production companies appeared.

The BBC began providing technical assistance and finance for a variety of projects. But the greatest impact was made by the new television company Channel 4, which between 1982 and 1997 became involved as producer or sponsor of over 200 adventurous, low-budget films. High levels of unemployment, social unrest, riots and a war all provided inspiration for directors who portrayed a politically, socially and ethnically divided country.

Heritage and harmony

The beginning of the 1980s saw a strong demand for 'heritage' films, which projected a nostalgic, rose-tinted view of the past. One of the most representative was *Chariots of Fire* (Hugh Hudson, 1981). Based on a true story, the film deals with a Scot and a Jew running for Britain in the 1924 Olympics. It features several unconventional, rebellious characters who become proud and nationalistic in victory. The attention to period details and the film's morally satisfying ending offered a rosy, comforting picture of British life and institutions at a time of increasing social hardship and unrest.

The arrival of *Chariots* in the market was timed to perfection. Its nostalgic theme of British superiority coincided with the wedding of Prince Charles to Diana in 1981, victory over Argentina in the Falkland Islands (Las Malvinas) in 1982 and the victory of the ruling Conservative Party in the election soon afterwards. It became the film of the moment and won four Oscars. At the Academy Awards ceremony in America, scriptwriter Colin Welland famously declared 'The British are coming!' anticipating a revival in the fortunes of the British film industry. His prediction was correct and 'heritage' films, exploiting popular interest in aristocratic life in imperialist Britain, were among the most commercially successful of the decade.

Some of the best-known productions were by the team of Merchant–Ivory. Ismail Merchant, James Ivory and Ruth Prawer Jhabvala worked as producer, director and scriptwriter successfully to create historical films of upper-class living. Some of their finest were adaptations of novels by E.M. Forster, including *A Room with a View* (1985), *Maurice* (1987) and *Howards End* (1992), while *Remains of the Day* (1993) was based on a Booker Prize-winning novel by Kazuo Ishiguro. Beautifully filmed, richly costumed and classically acted, they presented an idealised, romanticised image of English life, and received numerous international awards. These and other films, such as David Lean's *A Passage to India* (made in 1984, also from a novel by E.M. Forster), *Gandhi* (Richard Attenborough, 1982), *Another Country* (Marek Kanievska, 1984) and *Henry V* (Kenneth Branagh, 1989) were highly popular with audiences, and even tempted older members of the public back to the cinema.

However, critics said they projected an elitist, exclusive version of a culturally homogeneous past, which was heavily romanticised and fundamentally false. They argued that 'heritage' films were created simply for the pleasure of overseas audiences, and made quick, easy profits for the film-makers. Nevertheless, both traditional and modern interpretations of historical stories remain among the most popular film genres in Britain.

Peter Greenaway

One of the most stylish but unconventional of British film-makers to emerge in the 1980s was Peter Greenaway (b. 1942). Allegorical stories, symbols, romanticism and games feature in his films. The visual scenes are elaborate and carefully constructed, often with large familiar paintings, giving his work a characteristic style which he mixes with wit and charm.

He began his career in 1966 and, like Derek Jarman, his early work was highly experimental, featuring surreal fantasy, playful narrative and absurdist titles such as *Goole by Numbers* (1976) and *Dear Phone* (1976). But later in his career he began to make more conventional feature films. Several took a cynical look at the lives of the professional classes, such as cooks, architects and draughtsmen, which became fashionable professions in the 1980s. *The Draughtsman's Contract* (1982) is a humorous costume drama and one of his best-known films. Set in 1694, the comedy begins when aristocratic Mrs Herbert contracts the services of a draughtsman to make drawings of the house to present as a gift to her husband.

130

Modern-day Rome is the setting for *The Belly of an Architect* (1987), where Stourly Cracklite, a wealthy Chicago architect, supervises an exhibition of architecture with his young wife Louisa. Distracted by illness, he is unaware of a young Italian architect's jealousy of both his professional life and his wife. In contrast, *The Cook, the Thief, his Wife and her Lover* (1989) is set in a smart restaurant. Sex, food and love are mixed together in a critique of vulgar consumerism during the Thatcher years. More playful was *Drowning by Numbers* (1988) which made Greenaway popular with feminists. It is set in a Suffolk seaside village, in the east of England, where three generations of women aged 19, 34 and 60, each named Cissie Colpitts, murder their three unsatisfactory husbands. But in a humorous twist, the local coroner agrees to certify their deaths as natural in return for sexual favours.

Prospero's Books (1991), an interpretation of Shakespeare's final play *The Tempest*, signified Greenaway's return to more experimental film-making, and is built around the 24 magic books which Prospero's friend Gonzalo gives him to take with him on his final voyage back to Italy. Amid much nudity, the 87-year-old Sir John Gielgud reads most of the dialogue, in a role he has played many times on stage. In Greenaway's more recent film, *The Pillow Book* (1996), a young Japanese girl grows up with a fetish for calligraphy, demanding that her lovers paint Kanji on her flesh, as did her father. Its elaborate images, computer graphics and superimpositions made it one of the most individual films of its time.

In 2004 he completed a trilogy of films in his most ambitious project to date, *The Tulse Luper Suitcases*, which seeks to reconstruct the life of Tulse Luper, a professional writer. Like Greenaway, he was born in Newport, South Wales, and his life as a 'professional prisoner' (as Greenaway has called him) is reconstructed from the evidence of 92 suitcases found around the world. The project comprises *The Moab Story*, *Vaux to the Sea* and *From Sark to Finish*, and comprises 92 DVDs, CD-Roms, and books. A painter, writer and novelist, Greenaway remains one of the most enigmatic film-makers in Britain today, who constantly seeks to innovate and explore an eclectic variety of themes.

Propaganda and caricature

As British society's problems grew deeper in the early 1980s, Lindsay Anderson's *Britannia Hospital* (1982) offered a humorous tale of a hospital close to collapse, due to strikes, riots and terrorism. However, the lazy, incompetent staff and their disinterested, insensitive boss only begin to worry when preparations begin for a visit by the Queen Mother. The film is widely seen as a tragicomic allegory of Britain in chaos and a humorous critique of the Thatcherite society which Britain was becoming in the early 1980s.

Later in the decade, government economic policy led to deregulation, expansion and competition in numerous professions. The effects on media and broadcasting were critically examined in writer and director Richard Eyre's film *The Ploughman's Lunch* (1983). It focuses on the activities of a BBC journalist and presents a cynical view of news presentation and management of the 1956 Suez Crisis and the Falklands War of 1982, showing the hypocrisy and insincerity of the mass media.

A major issue of the 1980s was the Cold War, the subject of *Defence of the Realm* (David Drury, 1985). A highly critical film, it analyses the stationing of nuclear weapons in Britain, the dubious activities of the security forces and the role of the media in supporting the government. But in Chris Bernard's *A Letter to Brezhnev* (1985), the Cold War was given lighter, more humorous treatment in a story about two young women who meet two Russian sailors in a Liverpool discotheque. But unlike much of the British news media during the 1980s, the film avoids the stereotyping of Russians as monstrous and evil, instead casting them as ordinary folk looking for a peaceful life.

The conspicuous consumption of food and drink became fashionable during the decade and the theme of food was used to make social comment in several films. Malcolm Mowbray's *A Private Function* (1984) is a humorous caricature of ambitious middle classes. It is set in a small Yorkshire town in 1947 and, during a time of post-war rationing, an unlicensed pig is being fattened for a civic dinner to celebrate the royal wedding of Princess (later Queen) Elizabeth. More contemporary was *Eat the Rich* (Peter Richardson, 1987), a satire set in 'Bastards' – a smart London restaurant. When Alex – a black waiter – is fired, he returns to kill the staff, changes the restaurant name to 'Eat the Rich' and offers human flesh on the menu. Received by critics as cynical, bizarre and offensive, it was one of the most tasteless films of the decade.

During the 1970s a small but effective counter-culture and the initiatives of independent studios had done much to bring women's issues to the attention of mainstream, commercial cinema, and during the 1980s these issues were explored in a more populist manner. Several films examined the feelings and frustrations of women unable to experience life outside the home, such as *Another Time, Another Place* (Michael Radford, 1983), a bleak exploration of domestic repression. Set on an isolated Scottish farm during the Second World War, it focuses on a young woman's loveless marriage to a humourless Scot. But there were also several lighter attempts to portray similar themes, for example the humorous *Educating Rita* (1983). It tells the story of a young, married hairdresser who begins adult-education classes. Gradually she becomes divided between her oppressive domestic life and the attractions of academe. The director was Lewis Gilbert and the writer Willy Russell, the duo who, in 1989, made *Shirley Valentine*, a humorous tale about a Liverpudlian housewife and mother who shares with her neighbour a holiday on a Greek island, where she finds happiness with local fisherman Costas Caldes.

Northern Ireland

Frictions in social life and terrorism in politics were common during the 1980s, but nowhere were they felt more violently than in Ireland. In 1979, the governing Conservative Party and the Labour opposition both expressed their wish to continue defending the six counties there and the rights of the Protestant majority. In comparison with other issues, relatively few films dealt directly with Ireland's troubles. Their delicate nature, the difficulty of treating issues in a balanced and fair way, and their limited appeal to audiences outside the province has deterred many film-makers.

Early cinematic interest in Northern Irish politics developed during the 1930s with Brian Hurst's *Ourselves Alone* (1936), the title a translation of the Irish-Gaelic *Sinn Fein*, the Irish Republican Party. Since then, the majority of films have been thrillers, with spying, conspiracy, violence and murder, set amid guerrilla warfare and terrorism. These were generally made by American or English directors, but in 1982 Irish film-maker Neil Jordan made his directorial debut with *Angel*, the first of several highly praised works. It examines how a quiet, passive civilian becomes involved in murderous terrorist activities following the death of his friend. In 1992 Jordan returned to exploit a similar theme with *The Crying Game*, which examined the formation of political and national feelings in Britain and Ireland, and *Michael Collins* (1995), the story of a man whose belief in guerrilla violence against the British forces is changed into a desire for peace after he witnesses the horrors of civil war. Two years later John Boorman made *The General*, set in Northern Ireland and about the 'troubles'. Unlike many films about the province, it does not take sides. Instead, it illuminates the situation as seen through the eyes of Martin Cahill, a violent but humorous armed robber who hates not only the IRA, but also the Protestant Loyalists and all forms of authority.

However, films of the 1980s were much more partisan in their perspective on the role of the security forces. *Boy Soldier* (Karl Francis, 1986) argues against sending soldiers into the streets. And more explicit in its message is Ken Loach's *Hidden Agenda* (1990), which alleges conspiracy, corruption and 'dirty tricks' among the British forces in Ulster.

The role of women within the Republican movement is explored in several films and short documentaries, such as *Maeve* (Patricia Murphy, 1981), while Pat O'Connor's *Cal* (1984) considers the life events which lead a peaceful young Catholic man to become involved with the struggle of the Irish Republican movement. Yet not all films about the tension in Ireland were sombre in their treatment. In the tragicomic *No Surrender* (Peter Smith, 1986) Protestants and Catholics in fancy dress, bickering punk rockers, a camp comedian and an incompetent magician, all meet in an energetic and occasionally farcical scenario, set in a Liverpool nightclub on New Year's Eve.

Ken Loach

Realistic films dealing with social problems and issues have become one of the main strengths of British cinema. One of its leading exponents is Ken Loach (b. 1936), a critically admired director who has established a reputation for political awareness in his films. He was born in the English Midlands and began his career at Oxford University where he was president of the Drama Society. He later worked at the BBC, directing plays for the weekly drama series *The Wednesday Play* and *Z Cars*. These frequently dealt with some of the most controversial social problems of the period, such as *Up the Junction* (teenage pregnancies and abortion), *Cathy Come Home* (homelessness, drug abuse and domestic violence). Their frank, realistic portrayals challenged the complacent, literary and historical dramas which were then common in television drama.

The struggle of the underprivileged against an uninterested society is a theme common to many of his works. However, their seriousness is lightened by humorous incidents, witty scripts and a message of optimism about people's ability to conquer their problems. His early film *Poor Cow* (1968) is a sensitive exploration of an impoverished single mother's search for a decent life, and since then his work has critically commented upon varied social issues. One of the most highly regarded of his works is *Kes* (1969). Set among a coal-mining community in Yorkshire, it shows the aimless drifting of a young boy, the inadequate 'authorities' of his family and teachers, and how his pet bird – a kestrel – helps to bring meaning to his life.

In the 1980s and 1990s his films engaged more closely with the injustices of Thatcherism. *Looks and Smiles* (1982) considers the desperate choices open to two young school-leavers at a time when employment opportunities are few. For greater authenticity the cast members were all amateurs, drawn from the South Yorkshire community of Sheffield, the setting for the film. *Raining Stones* (1993) is a tragicomic view of the effects of unemployment on a Catholic family in Manchester, while *Ladybird, Ladybird* (1993) looks at the plight of a single mother. In *Riff Raff* (1991) Loach humorously depicts the different reactions of a gang of labourers from different regions of Britain when they are ordered to convert a much-needed hospital into a block of luxury flats.

However, Loach has not restricted his work to films about England. *Hidden Agenda* (1990) considers the role of the British army in Northern Ireland and in *Land and Freedom* (1995) he focuses his attention on the Spanish Civil War. This intelligent and powerful film looks at contemporary social issues through the experiences of unemployed Liverpudlian David Carne, who goes to Barcelona to fight for 'land and freedom' in

1936. *Carla's Song* (1996) also deals with political struggle. It is set in Nicaragua in the mid-1980s during the overthrow of the Sandinista government by the right-wing, US-supported Contras and tells the tragicomic tale of a Glaswegian bus driver and his Nicaraguan sweetheart.

Towards the end of the 1990s Loach made widely admired films, which brought him recognition as a major British director. Three were set in Glasgow: *My Name is Joe* (1998), *Sweet 16* (2002) and *Ae Fond Kiss* (2004). The last is named after a love poem by Robert Burns, and tells the story of a relationship which crosses cultural and religious dividing lines, in a story of Romeo and Juliet set on the River Clyde. Casim, a Muslim businessman and disc-jockey, meets Roisin, an Irish Catholic music teacher. The weight of family expectations is summed up in the following scene, in which Casim discusses the difficulty of his situation with his best friend Hassin:

> *Hassin*: There's so many birds out there and yet you've went daft over one bird.
> *Casim*: I've nae went daft over her.
> *Hassin*: Well, yer gonna drop you're own family? You're gonna split your own family?
> *Casim*: Am I supposed to marry someone I don't know?
> *Hassin*: You've got your family to think about, you've got your religion to think about.
> *Casim*: I'll lose her!
> *Hassin*: I don't give a fuck if you lose her. Who would you rather lose? Your family or this bird?
>
> (transcribed from the film)

Critics say Loach's vision is a pessimistic, austere one, but on the other hand he is admired by many for having always been a consistent, lone, politicised voice, speaking out in defence of the oppressed and disenfranchised. These are rare characteristics in modern British film-making and have made Loach into one of the most respected directors in Britain today.

Ethnicity and identity

During the 1970s and early 1980s the only films dealing with the experiences of ethnic minorities were low-budget productions by relatively unknown film-makers. Because their films did not have great commercial appeal, they could only be seen in small, independent cinemas, and not in large chains, which offer more commercial, mainstream productions. But between 1985 and 1991, grants became available to improve arts facilities following the riots of the 1980s. As a result, several black film co-operatives appeared, such as Sankofa, Black Audio and Ceddo, based mainly in London and the Midlands.

One of the founders of Sankofa was Isaac Julien, who made several films expressing the anger and frustration felt by many black Britons. These include *Territories* (1984), *Remembrance* (1986) and *Looking for Langston* (1989), based on the black American poet Langston Hughes (1902–67). Another notable work dealing with the experience of black Britons is *Handsworth Songs* (John Akomfrah, 1986), a critical examination of racial conflict in modern Britain, which was filmed in Handsworth, Birmingham, during the riots of 1985.

But black film-makers were few in number and their themes gradually became incorporated into the commercial mainstream. One example is *Playing Away* (1986) written by Caryl Phillips and directed by Horace Ove, a light, humorous observation of hypocrisy and prejudice in an English rural community, when a cricket team from Brixton visits a small country village for a friendly game as part of the village's 'Third World Week' celebrations, an encounter which has comical consequences both on and off the field.

Some of the most highly praised explorations of urban life came from Hanif Kureishi, in collaboration with a white British director, Stephen Frears. Born into a Pakistani family in south-eastern England, Kureishi has worked across several areas of popular culture, and his novels, theatre plays and screenplays brought to public attention the increasingly diverse nature of British society, and the problems experienced by marginal groups. His are sometimes described as 'condition of England' works, and deal with sexuality, politics and ethnicity.

Films by Kureishi offer a powerful critique of divisive Tory society, but at the same time provide an optimistic message about people's ability to triumph over adversity, for example the entertaining, exotic *My Beautiful Laundrette* (1985). The film tells the story of Omar, the nephew of an Asian businessman. He opens a launderette in a tough area of London, together with Johnny, a white friend from school. Both have their own problems, which intensify when they become lovers. The film explores themes of racial tension, youth, class and sex, in one of the most original and highly regarded films about Asian culture in Britain.

In 1987 Frears directed *Prick Up Your Ears*, telling the story of gay playwright Joe Orton. It shows a repressed nation, divided by hypocrisy and a rigid class system, tensions which inspired Orton's angry plays and mirrored those of Britain in the 1980s. Frears and Kureishi again collaborated on *Sammy and Rosie Get Laid* (1987), a satirical interrogation of Asian culture in British society, which features Sammy and Rosie, a mixed-race couple who live a bohemian lifestyle in a marginal area of London. Theirs is a happy, 'open' marriage, but when Sammy's father, a Pakistani gangster, appears, there is mutual disapproval of each other's lifestyle, politics, class and culture. A similar, critical exploration of growing up between cultures is offered by Hanif Kureishi in his warm, reflective and humorous film *My Son the Fanatic* (1998), about a dissolute Indian taxi-driver whose son becomes a fundamentalist Muslim, in a film that examines immigration, prostitution and adultery, as well as the growth of Islam in Britain.

Film-making towards the millennium

Historical films, realist films and films with a strongly regional flavour were among the most successful of a period when, 100 years after the first movies were shown, British film-making began to discover a new sense of its own abilities and achievements.

The influence of literary sources continued to be strong, but instead of idealised 'heritage' films, creative directing produced fresh, imaginative, simplified versions of classic stories. This approach was developed in the USA, where Franco Zeffirelli directed *Hamlet* (1990) and later *Jane Eyre* (1996). Creative, modern interpretations of classic novels were soon exploited by British directors. *Carrington* (Chris Hampton, 1995) focused on the Bloomsbury Group, a literary and artistic circle prominent during the 1930s. But instead of portraying its most prominent member, Virginia Woolf, his subject was Dora Carrington, an obscure painter. Similarly, Taiwanese director Ang Lee made a modern version of Jane Austen's novel *Sense and Sensibility* (1995) and Michael Winterbottom adopted a fresh, energetic approach to interpret Thomas Hardy's controversial novel *Jude the Obscure* with his film *Jude* (1996).

Several other notable films were inspired by true historical events and reflected contemporary demands for devolution and constitutional reform. Cinematic interest in Scotland was reflected in *Braveheart* (Mel Gibson, 1995), in which William Wallace fights to liberate the Scots from the tyranny of rule by the English during the thirteenth century. Its emotional approach to devolution was shared by *Rob Roy* (Michael Caton-Jones, 1995), the story of Rob Roy MacGregor. Set in Scotland during the early 1700s, beautiful scenery and tough action distinguish a film about a man who refuses to sacrifice his integrity to save himself or his family. The issue of the British monarchy in crisis was delicately explored in two films: *The Madness of King George* (Nicolas Hytner, 1995), set in 1788, and *Mrs Brown* (John Madden, 1997), set in Victorian England. Both were highly praised and used a historical perspective to examine the unpopularity of the monarch of the period: in the former George III and in the latter Queen Victoria.

Born into an Italian family living in Britain, Anthony Minghella directed one of the most outstanding films of the 1990s. *The English Patient* (1997) is based on a Booker Prize-winning novel by Michael Ondaatje, a Canadian writer. It tells the story of the Hungarian explorer Lazlo Almasy and his affair with the beautiful Catherine Clifton in pre-war Cairo, through to 1945 and the last weeks of his life, when he is a patient in an abandoned Italian monastery. Made with a modest budget of only

£2 million, it was nominated for Oscars in twelve categories and won nine, becoming the most highly regarded British picture for many years.

New realism

The economic decline of the 1990s was mirrored in a wide range of films. Many were made in a style known as 'naturalism' or 'new realism'. This kind of film-making was less overtly political and attempted to represent ordinary people's proud battles in difficult circumstances by showing situations from the viewpoint of the protagonists, and taking a non-judgemental view of their actions.

Realistic portraits and natural performances are predominant characteristics of the films of Mike Leigh (b. 1943), who became one of the most highly regarded directors of the 1990s. He began working in London's fringe theatres during the 1960s, where he earned a reputation for sharply observed social commentary. Since making his first major film *Bleak Moments* in 1971, he has worked extensively in theatre and television, for which *Abigail's Party*, an early 1970s comedy of social manners among the lower-middle class, was among his best-known works. In 1988 he made *High Hopes*, which considers the tensions between families of different social backgrounds in London during the mid-1980s. The film is both serious and funny, and sharply criticises the growing inequality, greed and selfishness into which society appeared to be descending.

In 1991 he made *Life is Sweet* and in 1993 the tragicomic *Naked*. These and others are revealing studies of class and manners which rely more on detailed characterisation than on plot and action. They are distinguished by convincing performances delivered through a natural style of acting, which Leigh encourages by creating scripts only after extensive improvisations by the actors. But his films are lightened by humorous incidents and perceptive remarks, as is well demonstrated in the acclaimed *Secrets and Lies* (1996). His ability accurately and sympathetically to chronicle the manners and lifestyle of Britain's lower classes has encouraged critical comparisons with Charles Dickens.

British screenwriter/director Alan Parker has directed numerous films for British and American companies, several of which were highly regarded musicals: *Bugsy Malone* (1976), *Fame* (1980), *Pink Floyd – The Wall* (1982) and *Evita* (1997). In 1991 he made *The Commitments*, based on Roddy Doyle's novel about a group of friends who form a soul band to sing their way out of an economically depressed Catholic area of Dublin. The style was typical of many popular films of the 1990s, which were accompanied by a lively pop soundtrack and showed their youthful protagonists dancing defiantly through the continuing economic recession.

The Full Monty (Peter Cattaneo, 1996) epitomised the trend towards 'new realism' in film-making, and became the most successful film of the

1990s. Set in the industrial city of Sheffield, it shows the impact of unemployment and the decline of the steel industry on a group of steelworkers, who become strippers to earn a living. Funny and highly metaphorical, this low-budget film was also successful in America, where it rivalled *Titanic* for many Academy Awards. Also set in south Yorkshire was Mark Herman's tragicomic *Brassed Off* (1996) with its humorous but sensitive depiction of Grimley, a declining mining community, and the passion and pride of the musicians in the colliery band. A similar tale of passion and pride was shown in *Billy Elliot* (Stephen Daldry, 2000), in which an 11-year-old becomes a ballet dancer, to the disgust of his father, a widowed miner, in an enjoyable, funny and uplifting film set in 1984 against a background of the miners' strike.

Humorous pictures in which the protagonists put on a brave face and assert their identity to combat the recession were popular in the mid-1990s. Two of the most successful were set in Scotland. Director Danny Boyle worked with producer Andrew Macdonald and writer John Hodge on the dark thriller *Shallow Grave* (1994), before the same team made *Trainspotting* (1995). Initially a best-selling novel and then a play, this succeeds in creating humour from the story of anti-hero Mark Renton, who struggles to kick his heroin habit in a world of drug dealers, AIDS and poverty. Unlike many films and plays about drug addiction, *Trainspotting* is told from the point of view of a drug addict, and is set in the poverty and squalor of the 'other' Edinburgh, a side rarely seen by visitors to Scotland's capital.

Films depicting the situation of British Asians and Afro-Caribbeans gradually became more mainstream, showing them not so much as marginal ethnic groups, but as having similar problems to many others in society, for example *Bhaji on the Beach* (Gurinder Chadha, 1993), *Babymother* (Julian Henriques, 1998) and *East is East* (Damien O' Donnell, 1999). In the latter, George is a Muslim immigrant who runs a fish and chip shop in Salford, near Manchester. His wife Ella is a white Briton, and their children grow up torn between the strict Islamic culture of their father and the modern attractions of short skirts, discos and pop culture of Britain of the early 1970s. However, the secular world allows them to shape their own identities rather than have them imposed by family, community and religion in a humorous story in which the family is shown as the cause of and solution to most kinds of problems.

The similarities rather than differences between people of different backgrounds and religions are also the theme of Gurinder Chadha's *Bend it Like Beckham* (2002). Set in the suburb of Hounslow near Heathrow airport, Jesminder (Jess) lives the life of a typical teenage Sikh girl except that she wants to be a professional footballer. Together with her best friend, a local white girl, she rebels against the traditional attitudes of her parents by running off to Germany with a girls' football team, in an amusing and characterful film. Although Chadha's later film *Bride and Prejudice* (2004) covered completely different territory, re-creating Jane Austen's *Pride and Prejudice* as an escapist 'Bollywood' musical, it also shows the similarities between romance in early nineteenth-century Britain and early twenty-first century India.

Fantasy and escapism

Some of the most commercially successful films of recent years have been romantic comedies. *Four Weddings and a Funeral* (1994) began a successful formula which was repeated with several later productions, for example *Notting Hill* (1999), *Bridget Jones's Diary* (2001), *Love Actually* (2003) and *Wimbledon* (2004). Many were made by the British production company Working Title, and have been enormously popular with audiences around the world. But critics said their representations of the country and people were exaggerated, and shamelessly exploited stereotypical imagery which would appeal to American and other overseas audiences, rather like expertly presented 'traditional' goods for export in a duty-free shop. However, *Bridget Jones's Diary* and the sequel *Bridget Jones: The Edge of Reason* (Beeban Kidron, 2004) were highly popular with many young British women, who readily identified with Bridget's image of a lonely, self-doubting young girl, seeking romantic fulfilment through marriage to a handsome, successful wealthy man. This led some critics to comment that, three decades after feminism, her attitude to sex was more permissive than her sexual politics, as with many women in Britain today.

The Harry Potter films have been the most successful, profitable and critically praised. They began with *Harry Potter and the Philosopher's Stone* (Chris Columbus, 2001) and a budget of some $125 million. The massive investment reflected the confidence the makers had in the films, which are based on the bestselling children's books of the same name. A simple story about a young boy destined to be a great wizard was followed by *Harry Potter and the Chamber of Secrets* (Chris Columbus 2002), *Harry Potter and the Prisoner of Azkaban* (Alfonso Cuaron 2004) and *Harry Potter and the Goblet of Fire* (Mike Newell, 2005). In the films, ordinary schoolboy Harry is taken out of his obscure, ordinary life to fight evil at the Hogwarts School of Witchcraft and Wizardry, where mysteries and strange happenings lead Harry and his friends into magical adventures, brought from the page to the screen with spellbinding special effects.

The films owe their popularity to the bestselling books of the same name, whose plots they follow closely. But the most surprising aspect of the stories is their popularity at a time when children's literature was seen to be in retreat from computer games and other high-tech entertainments.

The surge in demand for escapist fantasy was reflected in the popularity of the *Lord of the Rings* trilogy, based on J.R.R. Tolkien's bestselling classic. Filmed mainly in New Zealand and with an international cast, the trilogy comprises *The Fellowship of the Ring* (2001), *The Two Towers*

(2002) and *The Return of the King* (2003) and featured some 15,000 extras and 3,000 crew, with an estimated budget of £180 million, figures which seem even more fantastic than the story of elves, dwarves, hobbits and wizards, who are locked in a struggle to save Middle-earth.

Not fantasy but definitely escapist was the one notable music picture of the early years of the millennium, Michael Winterbottom's *24 Hour Party People* (2002), which charts the music scene in Manchester between 1976 and 1992, and the rise and fall of the local record label Factory Records. A nostalgic trip from punk and new wave to rave, as the city became one of the focal points for British counter-culture and anti-Thatcher sentiment, the film won much praise from fans and critics alike.

The new currents emerging in British film-making created and contributed to a new sense of optimism, and in 2003 there were record levels of film production in the UK, with 30 major feature films attracting inward investment of £729 million, compared with £266 million in 2002. International partnerships also increased, with 99 in 2003, compared with 66 in 2002, and 44 UK-produced films. In 2004 cinema box-offices took around 25 per cent per cent of their income from admissions to British films, the highest for many years.

However, Hollywood-produced films still generate more than 70 per cent of cinema revenues. The main difficulty is that US films are widely promoted and have a massive publicity budget, so more people want to see them. Moreover, most British cinemas are in the hands of a few small chains, such as the Warner and Virgin multiplexes, and these will only show films guaranteed to attract big audiences. As a consequence, it is much harder for British films to find exhibition outside the much smaller, 'art-house' cinemas, which specialise in less commercial, lower-budget productions.

However, despite its difficulties, in the new millennium London still provided the industry worldwide with film-makers, costume designers, production crew and technical specialists. It also became the world's leading centre outside Hollywood for the latest techniques of digital post-production, special effects and sound recordings, as well as for actors, studios and settings of world renown.

Discussion topics and activities

1 What do you consider to be the most distinctive characteristics of the British cinema since 1945? Which style do you prefer and why?

2 Should the state give funds to encourage the making of certain types of films to create a national cinema, or should the film industry be left to sink or swim in the free market, like any other industry?

3 If you were a film censor, what would you prohibit and why?

4   Choose one of the films mentioned in the chapter. After watching it, write a review for a 'quality' newspaper, saying what you liked about it and why. Alternatively, write a script of the review and read it on video camera to an imaginary television audience.

5   Imagine you are a film-maker. Decide what type of film you would like to make (e.g. crime, historical drama, thriller) and when and where it would be set. Then write a brief synopsis of the story and choose which actors you would like in the main roles.

Suggested further reading

Books

Aitken, I. (1990) *Film and Reform: John Grierson and the Documentary Film Movement*, London: Routledge.

Ashby, J. and Higson A. (2000) *British Cinema Past and Present*, London: Routledge.

Barr, C. (ed.) (1986) *All Our Yesterdays: 90 Years of British Cinema*, London: British Film Institute.

Boose, L. and Burt, R. (eds) (2003) *Shakespeare, The Movie: Popularising the Plays on Film, Television and Video*, London: Routledge.

Curran, J. and Porter, V. (eds) (1983) *British Cinema History*, London: Weidenfeld & Nicholson.

Dickenson, M. and Street, S. (1985) *Cinema and State: The Film Industry and the British Government 1927–84*, London: British Film Institute.

Dewe-Mathews, T. (1998) *Censored: The Story of Film Censorship in Britain*, London: Chatto & Windus.

Friedman, L. (ed.) (1996) *British Cinema and Thatcherism*, London: UCL Press.

Harper, S. and Porter, V. (2003) *British Cinema of the 1950s: The Decline of Deference*, Oxford: Oxford University Press.

Higson, A. (1995) *Waving the Flag: Constructing a National Cinema in Britain*, Oxford: Oxford University Press.

Higson, A. (2003) *English Heritage, English Cinema: Costume Drama Since 1980*, Oxford: Oxford University Press.

International Dictionary of Films and Film-makers (1997) Detroit: St James's Press.

Landy, M. (1991) *British Genres: Cinema and Society 1930–60*, Princeton: Princeton University Press.

Murphy, R. (2002) *British Cinema of the 90s*, London: British Film Institute.

Murphy, R. (ed.) (2002) *The British Cinema Book*, London: British Film Institute.

Park, J. (1990) *British Cinema*, London: Batsford.

Richards, J. and Aldgate, A. (1999) *Best of British: Cinema and Society from 1930 to the Present*, London: I.B. Tauris

Robertson, J.C. (1993) *The Hidden Cinema: British Film Censorship in Action 1913–1975*, London: Routledge.

Warren, P. (1993) *British Cinema in Pictures: The British Film Collection*, London: Batsford.

Walker, A. (1985) *National Heroes: British Cinema in the 1970s and 1980s*, London: Harrap.

Young, L. (1996) *Fear of the Dark: Race, Gender and Sexuality in the Cinema*, London: Routledge.

There are also numerous guides to film and video which contain details and synopses: *Halliwell's*, *The Time Out Film Guide* and the *Virgin Film Guide* are among the most comprehensive and are updated every year. In addition, the British Film Institute publishes the *British National Film and Video Catalogue* (annually since 1963, with video citations since 1984). A useful yearbook is also published annually by the BFI.

Journals

All the major newspapers and many monthly fashion magazines include regular articles on film. *Empire* is a monthly magazine which is less academic and more general than some of those mentioned below.

The *Journal of Popular British Cinema* appears four times each year, and began in 1996. Its articles reflect upon a new area of interest within film studies: that of popular genres.

Monthly Film Bulletin was published every month by the British Film Institute between 1934 and 1991, giving a synopsis and a critical review of every feature film released in Britain during that time. In 1991 it merged with *Sight and Sound*.

Sight and Sound appeared quarterly from 1932 and since 1991 has appeared monthly.

Screen has been the major journal of film theory since 1971. It first appeared in 1959 and is available quarterly.

Cineblitz International is also useful for those interested in the South Asian film industry.

Films

Many of the films mentioned in this chapter can be bought at some of the more specialised video/DVD stores in Britain. In addition, the BFI has an extensive public library of books, films and film scripts, and The British Council frequently lends films and organises film seasons at its centres around the world.

The National Film and Television Archive has over 300,000 titles from 1895 onwards, and provides detailed information and a viewing service for students and researchers.

7

Television and radio

Introduction

Everyone born in Britain since 1940 is part of a generation which grew up with television. Recent research has shown that in the UK the average television set is switched on for between five and six hours a day, and the average British adult watches for approximately three hours. Children are among the biggest consumers; a recent study found that 86 per cent of children aged 6 and below watch up to 6 hours per day. This means that the average child born in the mid-1990s, when 18 years of age, will have spent more time watching television than any other activity except sleep, and during a lifetime, the average Briton will spend more time watching television than doing paid work.

Programmes are broadcast 24 hours a day, and the most popular are the news, factual and drama programmes, while religious programmes have the least appeal. Although over 50 per cent of homes now have access to satellite and cable stations, the most popular are the five national terrestrial channels. Two of these are provided by the British Broadcasting Corporation (BBC), and three are provided by independent broadcasters. Additionally, there is Digital Terrestrial TV (DTT) and non-terrestrial TV, providing programmes from cable and satellite stations. DTT is available using a conventional aerial together with a special box or 'decoder'. It offers a service known as 'Freeview', a package of interactive television and radio stations, which was present in around 2 million homes in 2004.

The BBC

The BBC is based in London, but has regional television and radio studios around Britain. It was created by a Royal Charter which has to be periodically renewed, and is controlled by a board of governors appointed by the Queen on the advice of the government. Its daily work is supervised by a Director General, who is chosen by the governors in consultation with the Prime Minister. Although the Corporation has close ties to the government, direct political influence is not permitted, and in the past there have sometimes been complaints from Parliament that the BBC is unfairly critical.

The BBC controls two national terrestrial TV channels. BBC1 shows programmes which have a broad appeal, while those of BBC2 are often more specialised. These include leisure, lifestyle and documentary programmes, as well as the Open University broadcasts (which allow home study for university degrees) and other education programmes for schools and colleges. A range of BBC publications as well as a range of software audio and video material accompany many courses.

The BBC recently introduced two new channels which are available only on 'Freeview'. These are BBC3, which shows comedy, science, music, arts and education programmes, and BBC4 with deeper coverage of history, culture, business, the arts and current affairs. Up to 75 per cent of BBC programmes are made 'in house'. The rest are made externally by independent production companies such as Celador, RDF Media, Hat Trick and Endemol, which make programmes that are then sold to broadcasters in Britain and abroad.

The BBC also has five national radio stations. Radio 1 broadcasts current pop music, live concerts and news. Radio 2 plays a wider range of popular music and 'specialist' programmes. Radio 3 broadcasts almost exclusively classical music and occasionally jazz. Radio 4 offers news and current affairs, together with arts programmes, religious services and cricket commentary. Radio 5 broadcasts mainly live news and sports programmes, which are orientated towards younger listeners. The national stations are complemented by 39 regional and local BBC radio stations. These are mostly speech-based and increasingly broadcast in the languages of the local communities: Radio Cymru broadcasts in Welsh, Radio Nan Gaidheal broadcasts in Gaelic, and several others broadcast in Asian languages. BBC programmes are popular with the general public, and in 2003 the BBC took 54 per cent of the total UK radio audience.

A distinctive characteristic of the BBC is that, unlike most other television and radio stations, it does not broadcast advertisements, except those for its own programmes. It is funded by annual licence fees, paid by over 21 million households (99 per cent of the country) that own a television set. Penalties for non-payment can be severe, and even custodial for repeat offenders, which makes Britain the only country where members of the public can be sent to prison for watching television! In 2004 a colour licence cost £121, and black and white one £40.50. The absence of commercial pressures allows programme planners to be in direct contact with the needs and expectations of the general public. Programmes have traditionally been created not with a need to attract viewers for commercial publicity, but with a sense of responsibility towards the community. The BBC's documentaries, plays and current affairs series critically engage with society, and in this way television has come to occupy a cultural centrality which is unique to Britain.

In recent years the BBC has had to adapt to new technology and competition. In 1991 it began international television broadcasts with World Service Television. BBC World shows news and current affairs programmes to some 50 million homes worldwide, and BBC Prime shows a programme of light entertainment and drama to an audience of around 4 million in Europe. These stations do not receive any income from television licences or from government. Instead they generate income through voluntary subscription.

The BBC also broadcasts international radio. The World Service broadcasts in English and 42 other languages, and is funded by the Foreign and Commonwealth Office. It has a programme of current affairs, business, sport and the arts, and in 2004 had an audience of around 146 million worldwide. In recent years it has also made programmes available on FM, digital broadcasting and on the internet for improved reception quality.

Independent television

The commercial broadcasters try to emulate the high standards of quality and service set by the BBC. There are numerous commercial satellite stations, but only three commercial terrestrial ones. These are ITV, Channel 4 and Five, which all rely on income generated by advertising.

ITV is independent. A federation of companies broadcasts a broad range of popular programmes to 14 regions of Great Britain and Northern Ireland. GMTV provides a national morning service, and ITN provides a national news service.

Channel 4 is an independent national service which began broadcasting in 1982. It encourages innovation and the making of distinctive programmes for a diverse range of interests and preferences of audiences in a multicultural society. Unlike some other channels, it does not make its own programmes, but commissions them from independent companies. In Wales the service is known as Sianel Pedwar Cymru (S4C), which transmits many programmes in the Welsh language.

The newest terrestrial station is Five, a commercial station which began in 1997. It makes and shows popular programmes to a wide audience around the country. The majority of programmes shown on all channels are made in Britain, America, Australia, New Zealand and Canada; foreign-language films and programmes are rare.

Independent local radio began in 1973 and in recent years the number of stations has expanded greatly. There are currently around 270 that make their money from the sale of advertising time. Many serve local ethnic minorities and broadcast in the language of the community. They offer a general programme of entertainment, news, sport, consumer information and phone-ins. Although local radio is well established, national independent stations are still a novelty in Britain. There are only three: the first was the classical music station Classic FM which opened in 1992.

Broadcasting content is strictly controlled by OfCom, an independent government organisation which enforces a code of practice on violence, taste and decency, especially before 9 pm when young children may be watching. All tobacco advertising is prohibited on television and cigarette advertising on the radio. Political advertising is also banned, but each major party is allowed a number of broadcasts every year.

Journalism, communications and broadcasting are growth areas and there is no shortage of interest in careers. Training for posts in independent television or the BBC has become increasingly possible thanks to a growing number of courses in many colleges and universities. The National Film and Television School is one of the most respected training institutions. It is financed by the government, together with contributions from the film, video and television industries. Outstanding work in television is recognised each year by the National Television Awards at a prestigious ceremony in London.

The formative years

The British Broadcasting Corporation was founded in 1922 by a group of companies making radio equipment, and in November 1936 it transmitted the first television pictures. But for many years radio was considered the senior service. It was older, more established, and offered a better choice of programmes. Transmissions came from Broadcasting House in London, an impressive building built for the BBC which opened in 1932. Above its entrance the sculptor Eric Gill used a theme from Shakespeare's play *The Tempest* to symbolise radio: Prospero sending the spirit Ariel into the world. The classical theme continued with its motto 'Nation Shall Speak Peace Unto Nation', adapted from a line in the Old Testament 'Nation Shall Not Lift Up A Sword Against Nation' (Micah 4:3).

Life inside the BBC was formal, old-fashioned and badly paid. When appearing on camera, announcers wore traditional evening dress and spoke with a formal RP accent. But newsreaders were not televised, as it was believed that a change of facial expression could threaten impartiality. This was strengthened during the war when the BBC established a reputation for public responsibility and reporting the truth, and afterwards it occupied a role of cultural authority and importance. Under its first Director General, John (later Lord) Reith, there was a strong ethic of public service, and the BBC aimed to educate, inform and entertain. Television programmes carried an air of self-improvement and there were regular series on gardening, cooking, classical music and drama. In 1949 a regular weather forecast began for farmers and, no doubt, in recognition of the traditional British interest in the weather. *The Archers* (1950–) is a radio soap opera which was originally created to transmit useful information to the agricultural community. It is set on the imaginary Brookfield Farm in Ambridge, and has become the world's longest-running radio drama series. *Desert Island Discs* (1942–) mixes music with talk. A well-known 'personality' is interviewed and invited to choose eight records they would take to a desert island, together with one book (apart from the Bible and Shakespeare which are already there) and one luxury. Despite changing fashions in programming, in the twenty-first century both continue to be among the most popular programmes on BBC radio.

The post-war consensus in British politics created an environment in which political parties and institutions worked together for the good of the whole nation. There was a strong sense of a patrician society, where the leaders knew best what was in the nation's interests. The role of the BBC was central in transmitting patrician values, and between 1945 and 1955 it strengthened its reputation as the guardian of the nation's morals and the official provider of culture to the community. Programmes were broadcast only in the evenings, and even stopped between 6 and 7 pm to allow children to be put to bed. Perhaps unsurprisingly, the BBC's unofficial role as nanny to the nation earned it the nickname 'Auntie'.

With the coronation of Elizabeth II in 1953 demand for television sets increased, and the number of viewers grew. As ownership of a television set became more common, there was more interest in offering an independent, commercial channel, and in September 1955 Independent Television (ITV) began. News bulletins were read by men and women on camera. Regional accents could be heard in drama programmes, and the public began to appear in game shows. The diversity of material helped to break down class and regional prejudice, and the public were attracted by a range of openly populist programmes. But there was growing anxiety among the self-appointed moral guardians of the nation in the BBC and in the 'establishment' of Church, government and leading universities, who saw a link between the rise of popular culture, and the rise of crime, violence and teenage promiscuity. They believed that cheap, light entertainment such as popular music, game shows, westerns, crime dramas, and American sitcoms such as *I Love Lucy* would corrupt Britain's youth and hasten the decline of civilised society. The BBC believed that it was vulgar to be popular, and continued to broadcast its range of staid, conservative programmes. As a consequence, it lost many viewers.

Realism in television (1955–70)

Television was a vital component of the cultural revolution of the 1960s. In 1961, 75 per cent of homes had a television set. By 1969, the figure was 90 per cent. The educational reforms and the economic security which had been steadily incorporated into British society of the post-war period created a new cohort of youth who were keen to change the ideas of the older generation. A new wave of realism was breaking across cultural and artistic life, which in television and cinema featured open, frank portrayals of previously ignored groups such as women, blacks and the poor. For the first time, sensitive and even taboo subjects such as wife-beating, alcoholism, sex and drugs were represented in provocative new dramas. People were shocked and confused, and demanded documentary programmes which could clearly describe and explain the vertiginous social changes.

On both channels, news and documentary programmes began to examine daily life in Britain's provincial towns and cities. Reporting became more intimate and revealing, when for the first time ordinary people frankly described their experiences and problems to camera. Earlier in 1953 the BBC had created *Panorama*, a documentary programme dealing with current affairs. Since then, its reports from the British inner cities to war zones such as Suez, the Falklands, Libya, the Gulf, Afghanistan and Iraq were often impartial and usually argued against government policies of the time. This led to Parliamentary criticism that it was the propaganda work of traitors and communists. Nevertheless, its success has endured, and it continues to be the most respected and authoritative programme of its kind. It sets the standard for documentary journalism, in which the BBC has become a world leader.

In the 1950s the BBC had seemed old fashioned and stuffy, but in 1960 its new Director General Sir Hugh Carlton-Green wanted to introduce political satire which had become popular in the late 1950s. The public had more freedom to say what it wanted, and the impartiality of the BBC was further emphasised with the creation of satirical programmes such as *What the Papers Say* (1956–). This irreverent, anarchic bulletin is still presented each week by a different newspaper journalist, who indicates the bias, and sometimes hypocrisy shown in a variety of national newspapers. Later came several other shows with wide appeal, most notably *That Was the Week That Was* (1962–64), presented by David Frost, which openly mocked Labour and Conservative leaders of the time, and attracted millions of viewers before it was taken off the air before the 1964 election.

The freedom to comment and criticise spread throughout the arts, and some of the most notable new works were critical new dramas. Playwrights such as Harold Pinter, Dennis Potter and Alan Bennett flourished, as well as film directors such as Ken Loach and Tony Garnett, who made challenging, memorable dramas for *Armchair Theatre* (ITV, 1956–) and *The Wednesday Play* (BBC1, 1964–70). The plays evoked the hedonism and energy of youth, but they were also marked by the strength of their social concern. Jeremy Sandford's *Cathy Come Home* (1966) dealt with homelessness, and Nell Dunn's *Up the Junction* (1965) revealed the horrors of illegal abortion. The content of these dramas shocked people, but they also contributed to greater public understanding of serious social problems and stimulated parliamentary debate and action in the areas of abortion and the provision of social housing.

The influence of realism in television extended to even the most popular genres, such as police dramas and soap operas. Earlier, during the mid-1950s, the police were shown as almost sacred figures, symbolising the tradition, stability, and the conservative nature of British society. For many years the most popular police series had been *Dixon of Dock Green* (BBC, 1955–76), set in the imaginary police station of Dock Green in east London. Each episode resembled a moral tale, paternally delivered by the nation's best-known policeman, PC George Dixon, who was presented as an average British male of the 1950s: a gardener, a fisherman, a football fan, a darts player, a married man who preferred tea and beer to coffee and wine. This was not a realist series, but showed an idealised 'little England' in which everyone respected the police, and crime was seen as a temporary difficulty, an aberration caused by the disruption of war. Stories were written to reassure the public, in which order was always restored, and family life triumphed.

Currents of social realism flowing through the arts of the early 1960s led to more realistic television depictions of the police. Unlike the earlier *Dixon*, viewers often found Troy Kennedy-Martin's police drama *Z Cars* (BBC, 1962–78) uncomfortable to watch. It was set in the imaginary location of Newtown, a modern urban 'jungle' close to Liverpool. It showed policemen who looked, talked and behaved in a realistic way. They drank heavily, gambled and were sometimes violent. The series began to show crime as a threat to society, and as a social problem which needed a firm response, and was a critical and popular success, establishing a new style of writing and directing television drama.

Coronation Street

The enthusiasm for social realism on television led to the creation of *Coronation Street* (ITV, 1960–), ITV's most successful series ever broadcast. It is a serial drama or 'soap opera' and was created by Tony Warren, when he was only 23. It deals with the daily lives of ordinary folk in a short, grey, narrow street in the imaginary northern town of Weatherfield (based on Warren's home town of Salford). The slow, distinctive theme tune was played by Eric Spear, and remains largely as it was played in the first episode, drawing viewers to the television in a kind of secular call to prayer.

151

A programme featuring the daily lives of ordinary folk had never been seen on television before. Earlier drama series such as *The Grove Family* featured middle-class southerners with RP accents, and at first the public were shocked by the northerners' rough speech and manners. Many viewers found it disturbing, while some critics doubted it would be successful. Early episodes resembled the more serious social realism of *Look Back in Anger*, *Saturday Night and Sunday Morning*, the television plays of *Armchair Theatre* and *The Wednesday Play*, but they have gradually evolved into a lively series with surprise, tragedy, farce and conflict but unlike many other soap operas, much humour.

Although Ken Barlow (played by Bill Roache) is the only remaining member of the original cast, the characters have changed relatively little over the years. The dominant personalities are women, and stories are told with much humour, pace and the occasional moral lesson, in a mixture of drama and (often camp) comedy. The programme has a wide range of fans, and since the mid-1960s each episode has been regularly seen by an audience of 12–18+ million of all ages, in all parts of the country. Big storylines always increase the number of viewers, and over 27 million people watched the departure of Hilda Ogden (Jean Alexander) from the show in 1987. More recently, the remarriage between Ken Barlow and Deirdre (Anne Kirkbride) attracted 12.9 million viewers, beating the 8.9 million who watched Prince Charles marry Camilla Parker-Bowles.

In 2005 'Corrie', as it is affectionately known, won many awards at film and television's BAFTA awards. It was also voted Best Drama on ITV's *South Bank Show* awards, and in the twenty-first century continues to be the most popular programme on British television, watched and referred to by almost everyone.

Adventure and imagination: fantasy dramas (1960–70)

In contrast to the realism of many new dramas of the 1950s and 1960s were the later fantasy styles which emerged in the 1960s, influenced by space travel, spying, Cold War tension, as well as affluence and consumerism. Fashionable clothes, fast cars, exotic locations and memorable theme music were common features of several exciting and original series. For many fans and critics the imagination and creativity made it a 'golden age' of creative television. One of the most popular and enduring was *The Saint* (ITV, 1962–69, 1978–79, 1989–90), based on the stories of Leslie Charteris, who had been writing crime adventures since the 1920s. The protagonist was Simon Templar, a suave, sophisticated crime fighter, originally played by Roger Moore.

Exotic locations had strong appeal for a generation of Britons who had recently begun to experience foreign holidays and continental fashions for the first time, and several other series had a more international flavour. *Department S* (ITV, 1969) and the playboy author-adventurer *Jason King*

(ITV, 1971–72) all brought style, adventure and espionage into British homes. Other series were fantastic, imaginative and surreal, such as *The Champions* (ITV, 1969–71) and *The Avengers* (ITV, 1961–69, 1976–77). The latter featured two private detectives; the lead was played by Patrick MacNee as John Steed, who was accompanied by a variety of female assistants during the life of the series. The most popular was Diana Rigg as Emma Peel. Confident, chic and independent, she symbolised modern, youthful progressive attitudes and values opposite Steed's establishment conservatism. Wittier and brighter than her co-star, the elegant, attractive Peel regularly threw villains around with graceful, balletic ease, in performances which were clearly feminist in pre-feminist times.

Surrealism was also an element of *Randall and Hopkirk (Deceased)* (ITV, 1969–70), in which 'Marty' Hopkirk was the deceased partner in a firm of detectives, who returned as a white-suited 'ghost' invisible to everyone except Randall, his crime-fighting partner. As with *The Avengers*, distinctive period settings and imaginative plots contributed to the appeal of this short-lived but memorable detection drama.

The most long-lived of the fantasy dramas was *Dr Who* (BBC, 1963–90), which featured the adventures of a Time Lord, known only as 'The Doctor', an eccentric, anti-authoritarian loner. His home was the 'Tardis', which outside resembles a police call-box, but inside is an enormous craft, capable of travelling backwards and forwards through time and space. The Doctor and his crew had numerous enemies: the most famous were the Daleks. These were motorised, one-eyed robots who did not kill, but famously 'exterminated' the opposition, while a young generation of viewers at home watched from behind the sofa in terrified amazement. After seven different doctors and assorted adventures in time and space, the series finished, after it had begun to look dated against the special effects of modern science fiction films. Fans were outraged, but in 1996 the BBC made a successful Dr Who film for television and the series won an award for the best television drama of all time. In 2005 the series finally returned in a new, highly successful drama which retains all of its traditional elements. Like many contemporary television series it is also made using strong British imagery consisting of familiar urban locations, typical street scenes past and present, as well as the fashionable Doctor (Christopher Eccleston) and his pretty young assistant Rose (Billie Piper).

Fantasy and escapism were features of many popular and original programmes, not only with adults' series, but also with children's such as *Supercar, Fireball XL5, Stingray, Thunderbirds, Captain Scarlet* and *Joe 90*, which were first shown consecutively between 1961 and 1969 on ITV. Created by Gerry Anderson, they featured different teams of futuristic, international 'policemen' based in space, on land or at sea. With the exception of Joe 90 (a myopic 9-year-old) the main protagonist was a square-jawed, fair-skinned male with a mid-Atlantic accent. In each episode political imagery was to the fore in thinly disguised Cold War scenarios, which saw the Americanised hero and his team save the world from some external threat. Although the puppet series were intended for juvenile audiences, they were also enjoyed by many adults and successfully captured the imagination of a generation with sci-fi plots, distinctive theme tunes and an eccentric, exotic mixture of characters.

The Prisoner: 'I am not a number'

The Prisoner (ITV, 1967–68) is regarded by many critics as the most distinctive, original and enigmatic fantasy drama ever shown on television. It was created and written by Patrick McGoohan, who also played the leading role of 'Number Six'. It arrived at a time when around the world different political ideologies were fighting for supremacy, and questions of how best to organise society were dividing countries and causing riots, wars and revolutions around the globe.

Central to the drama is imprisonment of the main character in what superficially appears to be a paradise: beautiful, warm, sunny and relaxed. It appears to lack nothing in the material sense, but on the inside it is revealed as a sinister environment, inhabited by superficial, passive citizens who are afraid to think critically, talk politics or ask who rules. In the 'totalitarian' Village no one has a name, only a number. McGoohan is prisoner Number Six. He is interrogated about his professional past, but refuses to give any information, and repeatedly demands to know who is in charge of the mysterious society, the identity of Number One.

Each of the seventeen episodes deals with Number Six's attempts to escape, and with attempts by the leaders to discover why Number Six resigned from his job in the secret service in London, until in the last episode there is a suggestion that Number Six is the real Number One; that I = 1; and that man himself, not political ideology, holds the key to freedom.

Like many of its contemporaries *The Prisoner* was surreal, stylish and entertaining. But unlike most other programmes it also raised important political questions about totalitarian societies, democracy, liberty and the freedom of information. It has been the subject of much academic writing, and invites comparison with Aldous Huxley's *Brave New World* and George Orwell's *1984*. Each year, enthusiasts meet to discuss themes and re-enact scenes, sometimes in the original setting of Portmeirion, an eccentric Italianate 'folly' on the coast of North Wales near Harlech.

The golden age of popular television (1965–75)

'Youthquake'

By the mid-1960s, the BBC was beginning to recover the viewers it had lost to ITV ten years earlier. There was a general acceptance within the BBC that the new popular culture was here to stay, and that to function with a public mandate it needed to appeal to a larger segment of the population. But radio was still losing listeners. In spite of a growing variety of popular music made in Britain and America, BBC radio offered little more than a chance to hear the Top Twenty songs. Only Radio Luxembourg, a commercial European radio station, provided occasional relief. Many young people wanted to hear a wider choice of music and in 1964 a new station, Radio Caroline, began broadcasting from a ship in the North Sea. Its owner, Ronan O'Rahilly, had no official permission, but because the station was outside the territorial waters of the United Kingdom, the authorities were powerless to stop him.

In its maritime isolation Caroline played a mixture of popular and progressive music, and broadcast 'alternative' news about underground culture, drugs, politics and sexuality. There was a real hunger for news and discussion of such topics by British youth, who still had only two television and radio stations to rely on, none of which broadcast specifically to young people. Caroline was an immediate success, and other illegal stations soon appeared, such as Radio London in the estuary of the River Thames. They became known as 'pirate' stations, and after only one year they had an estimated audience of 15–20 million listeners. They broadcast a broad range of music and distinctive programming, such as John Peel's *The Perfumed Garden*, which provided an exotic mix of poetry, classical and folk music.

In 1967 the government introduced the Marine Broadcasting Act, forcing many stations to close down. But the Labour government had noted the need to improve the BBC's offering to the young people of Britain, and reorganised its output with four national stations and several regional ones. Radio 1 began broadcasting pop music and soon afterwards former 'pirates' Dave Lee Travis, Kenny Everett, John Peel and Tony Blackburn all joined the station, where they enjoyed long and successful careers.

The massive interest in 'pirate' radio had indicated the potential size of the audience if the right programmes for young people could be found. But the BBC appeared old-fashioned, out of touch, and still in denial about the existence of teenagers. Its only youth programmes were for children, such as *Andy Pandy* and *The Flowerpot Men*, both from 1946. But *Cool for Cats* (ITV, 1956–61) and *Six-Five Special* (ITV, 1957–58) indicated the way forward, as did *Ready Steady Go!* (ITV, 1963–66), which offered live music to a studio audience dressed in the latest 'mod' fashions, dancing the latest dances and speaking the latest slang, all within a studio adorned in the pop art style. Audience participation was part of the show and televising the 'party' helped to spread music and other elements of popular culture to audiences around Britain.

In 1964 the BBC launched *Top of the Pops* to compete with *Ready, Steady, Go!* The first show was broadcast from a converted church hall in Manchester, and gave special emphasis to the Top Twenty, a list of the bestselling records of the previous week in the UK, compiled from record

155

sales in a number of record shops throughout the country. The songs played on the show were usually those moving up the chart and it quickly became a magnet for young viewers. It was an immediate success and appearances rapidly became essential for any groups with a single to promote. In the artists' absence, a dance troupe known as Pan's People performed to the music. Their exposed flesh and sexually provocative choreography caused offence among the 'Clean Up Television Campaign', a puritanical pressure group organised by Mrs Mary Whitehouse in response to what she saw as the depravity and licentiousness of modern television.

Sitcoms: 'He's from Barcelona!'

In a decade when popular television was attracting mass audiences, some of the most popular and successful programmes were situation comedies, or 'sitcoms', which each week featured regular characters in some familiar setting. Together with crime series and soap operas, they are regarded by many critics as one of the richest forms of modern cultural expression, and are regularly among the most watched and analysed of popular programmes.

The late 1960s and early 1970s are often regarded by fans and critics as a 'golden age' of sitcom. Many reflected social changes of the time and some of the most highly praised exploited the tensions between those who were enthusiastic about the bright new world of freedom, opportunity, popular culture and consumerism, and those who were cynical about it. A good example is *The Likely Lads* (BBC, 1964–66, 1973–74) featuring Bob and Terry, two friends from the north of England, one slow, introverted and aspirational, the other knowing, extroverted and cynical. The successful comedy series *Steptoe and Son* (BBC, 1962–65, 1970, 1972, 1974) exploited similar tensions between an aspirational, optimistic middle-aged son and his traditional, pessimistic, elderly father, who together sold second-hand objects from their east London yard.

Some of the most highly regarded sitcoms of the 1960s were provocative and challenging, mirroring the society around them, and their characters were often rebels and misfits, such as *Till Death Us Do Part* (BBC, 1966–68, 1972, 1974–75), one of the most controversial sitcoms ever shown on television. Written by Johnny Speight and regularly watched by a large audience of some 15 million, it was set in London's East End and featured the younger generation arguing with the older one about topical issues of sex, politics and religion. The leading character was family-man Alf Garnett, a working-class Tory bigot, who rejected entirely the liberalism, tolerance and progressive social attitudes of the time. Alf was the epitome of political incorrectness and regularly delivered abusive, hypocritical tirades against blacks, Jews, Communists, gays and feminists, at a time when many minority groups were struggling for recognition and

156

equality. Many viewers could not understand why the BBC showed the series. But Speight argued that Alf exposed many common hypocrisies and prejudices of people in the pubs, factories and boardrooms of Britain, and in this way he was able to ridicule and shame them.

Although nostalgic programmes were out of fashion, a popular exception was *Dad's Army* (BBC, 1968–77). Set during wartime Britain in the fictitious, genteel south-coast village of Walmington-on-Sea, it featured the local Home Guard (a unit of part-time soldiers too old, young or unfit for active service based in their home towns and villages) and their preparations against a possible invasion by the German forces in 1940. Many episodes showed comical attempts by the traditional, authoritarian figure of Captain Mainwaring to impose his will on the rebels and eccentrics in his unit, and their subtle forms of resistance and disobedience. Its gentle critique of institutional power and attempts by individuals to subvert it exploited a tradition of British comedy famously pioneered by Ealing Studios in their films of the late 1940s. The repeat showings of *Dad's Army* were among the most popular programmes of the late 1990s.

In contrast to the 1960s, during the 1970s audiences looked for reassurance and familiarity in light entertainment, and sitcoms became increasingly cosy, comforting and bland. This often involved crude stereotyping, for example of blacks and Asians as figures of fun, in series such as *It Ain't Half Hot Mum* (BBC, 1974–81) which comically portrayed the British Army cheerfully oppressing the Indian natives during the last days of the Empire, while *Love Thy Neighbour* (ITV, 1972–76) depicted a white, racially prejudiced, proletarian couple and their easy-going West Indian neighbours. Yet despite its crudity and racially stereotyped humour, for four years it was among the most popular comedies of its time, watched by around 20 million people in 1975.

A frequent source of comedy featured the main characters trapped in a situation they could not escape from, such as *Rising Damp* (ITV, 1974–78) which created genteel humour from the tension between Rigsby, a tyrannical, nosy, racist landlord, and his impoverished tenants, at a time of housing shortages and high unemployment. *Porridge* (BBC, 1974–77) depicted the antics of a couple of prison inmates in a series that went on to become a classic of its time, while *Fawlty Towers* (BBC, 1975–79) featured John Cleese from the Monty Python team as Basil Fawlty, the neurotic and politically incorrect owner of a southern English seaside hotel. Basil is the typical 'little Englander': a middle-class, middle-aged male who is philistine, banal, socially awkward and self-satisfied. He fears his wife, but regularly insults and humiliates his guests, whom he sees as his social inferiors. Manuel, his long-suffering Spanish waiter, has to put up with Basil's impatience and eccentricity, yet is frequently humiliated with a slap and cheerily excused to guests with 'he's from Barcelona!', which became something of a catch-phrase. Despite initial reservations about the programme's success, the series went on to become one of the most popular and critically praised comedies of English manners ever made, and the subject of frequent nostalgic repeats.

Broadcasting: consolidation and conservatism (1970–90)

During the 1970s there was a clear trend towards more conservative and less adventurous programme-making, in which tradition, continuity and nostalgia were the dominant themes of many genres. Historical series had been largely neglected since the 1950s but twenty years later viewers looked for more comfort and reassurance in their programmes, faced with the turbulence and uncertainty outside.

The televising of the wedding of Princess Anne at Westminster Abbey in November 1973 and a selection of programmes about Queen Elizabeth's Silver Jubilee in June 1977 were two of the decade's biggest televisual events. In a time of uncertainty and change, the monarchy was still respected as Britain's most prestigious institution, and this reached a peak in 1981 with the royal wedding of Prince Charles, which had an estimated worldwide audience of 500 million, a record at the time.

Royalty was still a rallying point for British society, which was still highly traditional and deferential. This was exploited in several drama series which romanticised the lives and times of past monarchs, such as *The Six Wives of Henry the Eighth* (BBC, 1970), *Elizabeth R* (BBC, 1971) and *Edward VII* (ITV, 1975). These and other series, such as *Upstairs Downstairs* (ITV, 1971–75), about an upper-class Edwardian household and its servants, offered cosy, nostalgic evocations of past greatness and reminded viewers of the order and stability of a great nation. New series about the Second World War achieved a similar effect. *Colditz* (BBC, 1972–74) was a drama series set in a German prison camp, which at times resembled an austere English public school, while *Secret Army* (BBC, 1977–79), *Manhunt* (ITV, 1970) and *Enemy at the Door* (ITV, 1978–80) depicted the heroic efforts of the resistance movement in occupied Europe. Their theme of strength and solidarity in the face of adversity was a familiar, reassuring and inspirational one to people on both sides of the political divide during the strikes and industrial confrontations of the turbulent 1970s.

Britain seemed to long for a return to the certainties of the past and imperial greatness, and when Mrs Thatcher was elected in 1979 and Charles and Diana were married in 1981 it briefly seemed that the tide had turned. Tradition, deference to authority and conservative values were firmly in vogue, and were reflected in a growing popular interest in programmes about history, royalty and upper-class living. Significantly, the tone was not investigative or critical, but respectful and even elegiac. Some of the most popular were drama series adapted from classic novels to recreate the atmosphere and settings of an age of elegance. They provided an encyclopaedia of period style, capturing audiences' attention both in Britain and abroad. Epitomising the trend was *Brideshead Revisited* (ITV, 1981), dramatised by John Mortimer from Evelyn Waugh's novel and starring Jeremy Irons, John Gielgud and Laurence Olivier.

In spite of the legal reforms to ensure equal opportunities for women and ethnic groups in the 1960s and 1970s, in many popular television series, from the music show *Top of the Pops* to the sitcom of *Steptoe and Son*, working women were often shown as sexually provocative and available. The representation of immigrant groups and individuals also suffered from stereotyping. In television series such as *Till Death Us Do Part* and *Love Thy Neighbour*, Afro-Caribbean immigrants were the frequent target of racial jokes and clichés, in programmes that were among the most popular of their time.

During the years of Tory rule Britain became still more intolerant, divided and confrontational, with higher rates of unemployment, aggressive cuts in public spending, tough and brutal policing. However, there were signs that programme-making was finally getting to grips with more accurate representations of society, as several new soap operas appeared which attempted to more accurately represent life in Britain of the time. *Brookside* (C4, 1982–2003) was set in Liverpool and was the first soap to deal with major social issues of unemployment, crime, homosexuality and AIDS. The series was created by Phil Redmond, who earlier had created the soap opera *Grange Hill* (BBC, 1978–), which is set in a comprehensive school in the south of England. Another major arrival was *EastEnders* (BBC, 1985–). It was created by Tony Holland and Julia Smith, and is set in Albert Square, in the fictitious borough of Walford, in London's East End. The highly popular series often rivals *Coronation Street* in the ratings.

The presence of a new generation of British-Asians and black Britons led to a greater representation in television sitcoms and crime series. However, most scriptwriters were white Britons, and despite the trends towards more realistic depictions of society in other genres, their attempts to write about non-whites in series such as *The Fosters* (ITV, 1976–77) were frequently criticised as unrepresentative and stereotyped. However, authors argued that they needed to write in this way to attract the public, because more accurate, critically praised series such as *Empire Road* (BBC, 1978–79), written by West Indian writer Michael Abbensetts for a black cast, were not popular with viewers.

One of the most successful Asian writers of the time is Farrukh Dhondy, who was born in Poona, India, and later studied at Cambridge University. He has also written children's books about young black and Asian children in London, the cultural differences they encounter and the misunderstandings. In 1983 he wrote *No Problem* (C4 and LWT, 1983–85) with Mustapha Matura, a West Indian writer, which depicted a London household in which the parents had returned to Jamaica, leaving their five children in charge. However, like many other earlier series and the later *Tandoori Nights* (C4, 1984, 1987), with its 'star' Jimmy Sharma (a British-Asian curry-house owner), it was strongly criticised for producing stereotypes, and for its failure to represent any of the contemporary problems faced by black British youth. However, other critics argued that sitcoms could not and should not do this, as their purpose was simply to offer light entertainment to a mass audience.

Crime series

While many dramas and light entertainment programmes were cosy and reassuring, new crime series began to reflect social confrontation and breakdown more accurately; for example *The Sweeney* (ITV, 1975–76, 1978) and *The Professionals* (ITV, 1977–83) showed hard detectives with a cynical attitude towards rules and authority. This reflected the changing focus of British policing, which began using rough, tough methods in an attempt to stop the anarchy into which, for several years in the mid-1970s, the country appeared to be descending. But by the 1980s it was also becoming clear that with deep cuts in public spending, high levels of unemployment, drug addiction and racial discrimination, ordinary men and women sometimes found themselves in marginal situations where the law was broken unwillingly and often through necessity. These scenarios were often reflected in several realist crime series such as *The Bill* (ITV, 1984–), set in the imaginary area of Sun Hill in London's East End. It is a realistic, character-driven series, which takes a less judgemental attitude to criminal behaviour, and although it was initially criticised for sometimes showing officers of the law as liars, cheats and bullies, it was also regularly praised for its realistic representation of contemporary crime and police procedure.

As black and Asian ethnic groups became more established in society, their presence was reflected in several crime series, for example *Gangsters* (BBC, 1976, 1978), *Wolcott* (ITV, 1981) and *The Chinese Detective* (BBC1, 1981–82). Some critics welcomed the originality of the portrayals, but as with the representation of non-whites in sitcoms and soaps, many critics said they were unrealistic and unrepresentative, and heavily dependent on stereotypical imagery.

Following the advancements gained in equality before the law in the 1960s and 1970s, during the 1980s more and more women were entering traditional, male-dominated occupations such as the police force. *Juliet Bravo* (BBC, 1980–85) reflected these changes with its casting of Kate Longton as Inspector Jean Darblay, who is in charge of a provincial police station. Central to the series was her fight not only against crime, but also against the personal and professional pressures of being a woman in a macho, sexist profession. A similar context was also explored in *The Gentle*

160

Touch (ITV, 1980–84) but most notably in *Prime Suspect* (ITV, 1991–), the latter featuring Helen Mirren as Jane Tennyson, a tenacious, intelligent detective who leads murder investigations while also having to deal with an arrogant and corrupt police force.

This ground-breaking series was written by Linda La Plante who worked closely with one of the few high-ranking women officials in the London Metropolitan Police in order to understand the pressures on a woman with a high-profile role in a male-dominated profession. The result was a series critically acclaimed by the public and critics for the portrayal *not* of a strong woman who behaves like a man, but of a weak, untidy, messed-up woman who does her job well. The series reflected the problems experienced by women not just in traditional male-dominated fields such as the police, but in many other fields of employment too. Despite the equality achieved by women in the workplace and before the law in the 1970s, dramas like these were ground-breaking until the early 1990s, but nowadays there is often a leading female character driving contemporary, mainstream dramas.

Crime has always been a popular genre with British audiences, and in the 1980s and 1990s the new small camera technology facilitated the creation of new genres such as 'reality' programmes or 'fly-on-the-wall' series, in which filming took place discreetly in order not to influence events. *Police* (BBC1, 1982) recorded daily life in a Thames Valley police station, and was one of several documentary programmes on the police directed by Roger Graef. *Living in Styal* (ITV, 1982) recorded daily life in a Cheshire prison for women. In contrast, *Crimewatch* (BBC, 1984–) is a different type of series which continues to report unsolved real crimes using reconstructions, video films and phone-ins.

These and other programmes have helped to make the police more responsive to public expectations and demand, and in this way, it is argued, police accountability to the public is maintained. At the same time the public are also made aware of the variety of problems encountered by the police on a day-to-day basis, and the difficulty of resolving them to everyone's satisfaction.

Politics and television 1975–90

Throughout the 1980s numerous documentaries such as BBC's *Panorama* continued to examine critically the government's policies on major issues, such as the destruction of the coal, steel and manufacturing industries, the local communities which had depended on them, the war with Argentina in 1982 and the riots in the streets of many British cities. Previously, there had been a tradition of freedom to criticise the government of the time, which had always been honoured. But in the 1980s Mrs Thatcher tried, on several occasions, to silence the press. There was even an unsuccessful attempt to silence the satirical tone of *What the Papers Say*, followed by an attempt to ban *Secret Society* (BBC, 1987), which the journalist Duncan Campbell made about political and military secrecy. Two of the six programmes were initially withdrawn due to political pressure from the government: one relating to a secret military satellite named Zircon, the other to allegations of 'dirty tricks' which the government had played during an election. This provoked a public controversy as the government had no legal right to ban programmes in this way. However, one of the programmes was finally shown at a later date.

The Conservative government expected more patriotism and support from the national broadcasting media and was already preventing spokesmen for the Irish Republican organisation Sinn Fein from appearing normally on television. Their words had to be dubbed by actors, in the belief that if viewers heard their original voices, they could be persuaded to support the Republican movement.

Although it became more difficult to criticise government in the documentary format, drama still allowed critics to express truths in more subtle ways. The social costs of Conservative policies were sharply reflected in Alan Bleasdale's *Boys from the Blackstuff* (BBC, 1982). The series was set in Liverpool and showed the loss of the dignity of work in a tragicomic style, in a drama that was among the most critically admired of the decade. However, even if a Labour government was returned with a massive parliamentary majority, it would be powerless against the right-wing forces of the civil service and press. This was the theme of *A Very British Coup* (1988), a drama series adapted from the novel by Labour MP Chris Mullin. Cold War and government secrecy over nuclear defence were themes explored in Troy Kennedy-Martin's short series *Edge of Darkness* (1985). The story dealt with a police detective who investigates the murder of his daughter, a Green Party activist. But the drama also addresses wider issues connected with environmental exploitation and the dangers of nuclear weapons, issues which had become of increasing public concern during heightened tension between East and West at the beginning of the decade.

Political satire was also prominent, most notably in the memorable series *The New Statesman* (ITV, 1987), which starred Rick Mayall as Tory MP Alan B'stard, who gained his seat after arranging for his opponent to be injured in a car crash. *Yes, Minister* (BBC, 1980–82) and *Yes, Prime Minister* (BBC, 1986–88) similarly exposed comical attempts by officials to manipulate the democratic process to gain power and prestige in Westminster and Whitehall. On one occasion Mrs Thatcher appeared in the series, in a part written by her press secretary Bernard Ingham. In the sketch, civil servant Sir Humphrey and Tory MP Jim Hacker debate new Tory policy with the Prime Minister, played by herself.

> *Thatcher:* I want you to abolish economists!
> *Sir Humphry:* All of them, Prime Minister?

Thatcher: Yes, all of them. They never agree on anything. They just fill the heads of politicians with all sorts of curious notions, like 'the more you spend, the richer you get'.

Jim: Yes I . . . you're quite right Prime Minister. We can't have the nation's time wasted on curious notions, can we? No, no, no. . . .

Thatcher: Quite right Jim, an absolute waste of time. They've simply got to go!

Jim: Simply got to go!

Thatcher: Yes Jim, but don't worry if it all goes wrong – I shall get the blame. I always do!

It is sometimes said that such shows can influence how people vote; however, in 1987 political satire was allowed on television in the pre-election period for the first time since 1964. And in spite of series such as *Yes, Prime Minister,* the cruel mimicry of the grotesquely funny, animated puppets of *Spitting Image* (ITV, 1984–92) and the new 'alternative' comedy on television, the Conservatives still won the election with another huge majority.

Recent trends in broadcasting

Until the 1990s relatively few television and radio stations had been available to the British public, and what was available was closely controlled by the government. However, in 1991 the Broadcasting Act was introduced; its aim was to expose television more fully to market forces, as well as make it more responsive to local communities. It required BBC and ITV to commission 25 per cent of their programmes from independent programme-makers, instead of relying exclusively on those made 'in house'. Furthermore, each private broadcaster had to present programmes made in and about its region. A Gaelic broadcasting committee was appointed to ensure that a broad selection of television and radio programmes was broadcast in Gaelic for reception in Scotland. Gaelic television began broadcasting in 1993, and other local stations were encouraged to serve ethnic minorities.

The trend towards more diverse sources of broadcasting continued, and in March 1997 a new, privately owned channel, known simply as Channel 5, began broadcasting. It offers a complete service of news, sport and light entertainment, and is subject to the same programme requirements as ITV. This was followed in October 1998 by the introduction of digital television, providing access to many more channels.

In radio too there were developments, as pirate radio re-emerged as part of an anti-Thatcher counter-culture, as well as being a local initiative to help bind together a community at a time when in many areas, the sense of community was being weakened. But instead of broadcasting in the

163

North Sea as the 'pirates' of the 1960s had done, inner-city tower blocks were now the preferred location for Horizon, Dread Broadcasting Corporation, Kiss FM and others. Many broadcast only over a short distance, and played the kinds of black music that could not easily be found on the radio. However, when faced with prosecution some applied for a licence, such as Kiss FM, which eventually became a legal station. Now, however, as the officially recognised broadcasters play a wide range of music, there is currently less public interest in the estimated 150 pirate stations around Britain, and the authorities frequently regard them more as a nuisance than as a symbol of radical opposition.

Initial optimism about the new broadcasting freedoms was counterbalanced by public concerns about the lowering of standards in the struggle to win audiences, as well as the growing concentration of the broadcast media into fewer hands. With this in mind, in 2003, the Communications Act was introduced. The Office of Communications (OfCom) was created to manage the ownership and economic affairs of the independent broadcast media, as well as regulate programme standards, fairness and complaints in all types of broadcasting. The separate, public service obligations of the BBC continue to be managed by its Board of Governors, but a significant new regulation is that no individual or organisation controlling more than 20 per cent of the national newspaper market can hold an ITV licence to broadcast, or hold a 20 per cent stake in any ITV service. Similarly, an individual or organisation with an ITV licence may not hold more than 20 per cent of the local or regional newspaper market in the same region.

While the government was concerned about the concentration of ownership, the public was concerned about the proposed cessation of analogue TV transmissions. This will probably be in 2010, and will require viewers to buy either a digital decoder or a new television set with a decoder already built in, measures which so far have caused confusion and resentment. Moreover, some members of the public do not want more channels, believing that the existing standards of the BBC will be further lowered to compete with the bland populism of many satellite channels.

More general concerns from both the public and the government were expressed over the future of the BBC, in particular over its news reporting. This followed the broadcast in May 2003 of a news item on Radio 4 about the evidence relating to Iraq's alleged weapons of mass destruction. A serious allegation was made against the government, but was subsequently found to be untrue. The consequences were felt widely, as the alleged source of the information committed suicide, while the reporter involved together with the Chairman and the Director General of the BBC resigned, leaving its reputation as a provider of reliable news badly damaged.

Popular genres

The most popular programmes on British terrestrial channels are soap operas. They consistently attract the largest audiences, and their familiar storylines of romance, adultery, violence and death are common to the genre everywhere. However, unlike those in many other countries, the most popular British varieties feature not glamorous individuals such as young doctors, successful lawyers and wealthy businessmen, but scruffy, plain-talking people in old-fashioned pubs and cheap terraced houses in series such as *Coronation Street* (set in the north near Manchester), *EastEnders* (set in east London), while *Emmerdale* features a rural community in the Yorkshire Dales. This may be because there are many who live in similar communities around Britain, who like to watch characters with similar attitudes, values and sense of humour. This view is supported by the spectacular failure of *Eldorado* (BBC, 1992–93), a 'soap' about an affluent, leisured, expatriate community on the Costa del Sol in southern Spain. Despite the attractions of sun, sand and sangria it attracted negative reactions in the press and an audience of only 5 million, and the sun set on the series after only 12 months.

Together with the 'soaps', crime series continue to provide some of the most diverse, original and highly praised popular drama. But since the 1980s formats have evolved, and the characteristic elements of so many earlier series, such as violence and car chases, have become unfashionable and rarely seen in police dramas today. Instead, series have become more character-driven, such as in *The Bill*, where there is a greater exploration of what motivates the police and villains to act as they do.

In contrast to the crime series set in the inner cities are the classic murder mysteries in genteel country locations. Many new examples of the latter emerged in the 1990s and appeared to be heavily influenced by the rash of interior decorating programmes being shown at that time. Made with high production values, sets were lavishly constructed and often resembled advertisements for stylish country living, as programme-makers recognised their attraction not only to home audiences, but to overseas ones, fascinated by the British country lifestyle. *Pie in the Sky* (BBC, 1996–98) featured a semi-retired detective-chef who also manages a picturesque village restaurant. *Heartbeat* (ITV, 1992–), based on the books of retired policeman Nicholas Rhea and set in the late 1960s, is a nostalgic series showing the humorous side of policing in the rural northern area of the Yorkshire Dales. But the most popular and highly praised is *Midsomer Murders* (1997–), the creation of crime writer Caroline Graham, on whose books the early episodes are based. In the series, Chief Inspector Barnaby and his assistant work in Midsomer, a beautiful area of English countryside (filmed mainly around the home counties) that provides a setting of fêtes, cricket, cream teas and ideal country homes. However, behind the civilised, genteel façade there are characters found in the traditional 'whodunit' story, such as pathological spinsters and homosexual vicars, whose greed, jealousy and ancient local rivalry frequently result in decapitations, burning alive, drugs and incest, a litany of crimes to rival the worst inner-city areas. One of the most exported of British series, *Midsomer Murders* has been sold to over 200 countries.

This is my life: 'reality' television today

After the years of secrecy, artifice, exaggeration and hypocrisy associated with the Tory government of the 1980s and 1990s, in 1997 there was demand for more openness and a 'fresh start' at every level of society. Moreover, the Cold War had disappeared, and there was a feeling that ideology had gone out of politics. The impact was also starting to be felt of new disciplines like cultural studies, which often analysed how public images and perceptions were carefully constructed by governments and private organisations. Consequently, in the mid-1990s some of the most popular programmes on British television were concerned with depictions of what purported to be authenticity, realism and 'everyday' life.

Programmes such as *Secret Lives* (C4, 1997–) scrutinised the lives of famous individuals from politics, society and the arts, and frequently exposed a much darker side to their subjects' common public image. The demand for honesty and openness also allowed gay issues to find expression on the small screen. *Out* (BBC, 1996) was a weekly information and news programme for gay men and women, and three years later the first gay drama series *Queer as Folk* (C4, 1999–2003) arrived.

Public curiosity and demand for authenticity spread to more populist programming and produced a growing number of reality shows, or 'factual entertainment'. Documentaries focusing on the lives of ordinary people began in 1964, when an ITV series *7-Up* interviewed 14 children who were subsequently interviewed every seven years about different aspects of their lives. In 1974 a BBC series *The Family* showed the daily lives and routines of an ordinary family, and with it the ugliness and tedium of the surrounding reality. Since then, various shows have sought to reveal ordinary life in front of the camera, with only mild public and academic interest. However, in the late 1990s the number of formats expanded, as reality TV became one of the most popular genres.

Current 'reality' programmes can be divided into three groups. First, the relative affluence, prosperity and freedom enjoyed by Britons in recent years has seen an increasing trend for identity to be shaped through consumption; that is, people make statements about how they live through the goods and services they buy. Thus, for many people today, what they consume is a central part of who they are, and some of the most popular television and radio programmes today are about lifestyle and consumer issues, such as travel, food, cars and homes.

A different kind of 'reality' show is the 'docusoap' that mixes documentary with drama. In these programmes, discreet 'fly-on-the-wall' techniques are used to follow protagonists' experiences in a variety of contexts. The simplest kind often involve the public services, such as a hospital or a customs and excise department, as well as Heathrow airport, a driving school, a cruise ship, a large hotel and an animal hospital among many others.

Programme-makers recognised that personal identity was becoming increasingly negotiable and self-determined and shows were created wherein participants could adopt new identities and roles, such as *Faking It* (2002–) in which volunteers had to prepare themselves intensively for a completely new profession, and convince judges they were competent and experienced. Others such as *Wifeswap* (2003–) involved women with different social and educational backgrounds and outlooks exchanging houses, routines, work and children for two weeks, before meeting to share opinions over each other's domestic management.

A third variety of 'reality show' is the constructed documentary, in which non-actors are filmed interacting with each other in an artificial environment. As with the others, these have also been enormously popular in recent years, and seem to attract those who have little or no natural talent, but have a strong desire to appear on television and be 'famous'. The most successful of these shows is *Big Brother* which originated in Holland and became popular around the world. Twelve participants are chosen from some 5,000 applicants who send videos of themselves to get on the show. The show producers, known as 'Big Brother', set them tasks and provide rewards and punishments. The participants live together for nine weeks in a specially constructed house, where some 37 hidden cameras film their every move for 24 hours a day, the highlights being shown every night on television. Every week, the 'housemates' nominate two residents for eviction, and the viewing public vote to decide who it should be. The last surviving member wins a substantial cash prize, and a brief moment of fame as a minor celebrity. Since it first appeared in Britain in 2000, each show has had audiences of more than 10 million viewers, many of whom also go to their websites and read about the show in newspapers and magazines.

The programmes certainly found large audiences, and even briefly made celebrities of many of the people who appeared in them, but despite their popularity the shows are also controversial. Critics said that the 'reality' is not as real as the programme-makers say; it is contrived, and the protagonists are not ordinary members of the public, but exhibitionists with a desperate need to appear on television. It is also said that methods are sometimes not as authentic as they appear, as sensational, shocking behaviour is encouraged to excite viewers at home. Others complain that there is too much voyeurism, and that the shows are further proof of a 'dumbing down' of television standards. But in their defence, the makers of 'reality' programmes argue that their shows give much encouragement to those who want to change themselves, their circumstances or lifestyle, and provide simple, honest insights into the work, family and social lives of individuals and communities.

Humour and sitcoms continue to offer some of the most lively, original and subversive material on television, as innovative and award-winning series present parodies and satires of familiar formats. The solemnity of documentary programmes is frequently the basis of comedies featuring an assortment of characters, from estate agents, police officers and journalists, to eccentric villagers from remote parts of Britain, in shows such as *Little Britain, League of Gentlemen* and *People Like Us*. But it was *The Office*, a spoof documentary about the worthlessness of office work, set in an industrial estate in Slough, which won Ricky Gervais, its lead actor, a TV comedy acting award at the Golden Globes in America, where the show also won an award for best comedy.

Chat shows also became the frequent butt of popular humour; in recent years they had become little more than publicity pieces for the guests, but the new parodies broke with the conventions of deference and prepared questions, subverting the format by satirising their subjects in shows such as *I'm Alan Partridge, Mrs Merton* and *The Kumars at No 42*. The last is an Asian show and demonstrated how, as different cultures and ways of living become more mainstream in society, they also become acceptable material for satire. Its forerunner was *Goodness Gracious Me* (BBC, 1996–98) an Asian show composed of humorous radio sketches, and later won a prestigious Sony Award. It then transferred to BBC TV (1998–99) where, unlike the earlier Asian comedy *Tandoori Nights*, it began to compete with shows intended for a white audience. But the most successful show in recent times is *The Kumars at No 42* (BBC, 2001–04). The Kumars appear like any normal and moderately affluent family living in suburban north London, except for the studio behind their house where they host their own chat show. The son Sanjeev and other family members 'interview' their guests, prominent celebrities, in a mixture of scripted dialogue and improvised humour. The actress and comedy writer Meera Syal has been instrumental in the creating, writing and performing of this innovative series, and has helped to make Asian humour accessible to a wider audience.

As with the formats of many popular British programmes, *The Kumars* has also been copied abroad; the Australian version features a Greek family, the German version a Turkish family, the Israeli version a Moroccan Jewish family, and a Dutch version a Surinamese family.

The past four decades have seen increasing competition for viewers' attention. In the twenty-first century this became more intense as the public continued to watch approximately the same amount of television as ten years previously, while the number of channels greatly increased. But television remains a popular topic of conversation, and second only to the weather among many British people. This helps to maintain the popularity of the terrestrial stations, as it is more difficult to share opinions about programmes seen on satellite and cable, which attract much smaller audiences. However, unlike in previous decades, decisions about what to watch now rest not with the television companies, but with the viewers, who have their fingers on the button.

Discussion topics and activities

1   What do you consider to be the most distinctive characteristics of British television since the 1970s?

2   What similarities and differences can you see between British television of recent years and that of your country?

3   What are the advantages and disadvantages of having a state-run monopoly of television funded by a TV licence? Would you like to see it in your country?

4   Do you consider the television in your country politically to favour one party or another? How is this favouritism expressed?

5   The main kind of audiences for programmes can often be identified from the kind of products advertised during the breaks. What do you notice about adverts shown during the soap operas/game shows/sport/ documentary programmes/other genres on television and radio in your country?

6   Think about the representation of regional and ethnic identities in television dramas and soap operas in your country. Is their depiction realistic, is it stereotyped, or does it depend on the type of programme? Does it matter how they are represented?

7   In what ways does television affect your life?

8   Take an example of a soap opera or crime series with which you are familiar. Describe its main characteristics and say what you like or dislike about it. Write a review of a recent episode for the television section of a 'quality' newspaper.

9   Make a video of your own TV news bulletin. Divide into groups, with each one preparing a separate news story: international, national and local; crime, arts, sport, and so on. Choose a newsreader/'anchor' person from the class, and different 'reporters' to read stories to camera and carry out interviews, as with the news on television. The stories can be fictitious or real. Don't forget the weather forecast at the end! Your teacher should take the role of director/producer/news editor, and if possible, make copies of the video to hand out to students afterwards.

Suggested further reading

Books

Alvarado, M. and Stewart, J. (1985) *Made for Television: Euston Films Limited*, London: British Film Institute Publishing.

Ashby, J. and Higson A. (eds.) (2000) *British Cinema: Past and Present*, London: Routledge.

BBC Annual Report and Accounts (1997–98) London: BBC Publications.

Brandt, G. (ed.) (1981) *British Television Drama*, Cambridge: Cambridge University Press.

Briggs, A. (1995) *History of Broadcasting in the UK, 1922–75*, Oxford: Oxford University Press.

Bryant, S. (1989) *The Television Heritage*, London: British Film Institute Publishing.

Cain, J. (1992) *The BBC: Seventy Years of Broadcasting*, London: BBC Publications.

Catterall, P. (ed.) (1999) *The Making of Channel 4 (British Politics & Society)*, London: Frank Cass Publishers.

Chapman, G., Cleese, J., Jones, T., Gilliam, T. and Palin, M. (1989) *Monty Python's Flying Circus: Just the Words, Vols 1 and 2*, London: Methuen.

Chapman, J. (2002) *Saints and Avengers: British Adventure Series of the 1960s*, London: I.B. Tauris.

Cornell, P. and Day, M. (1993) *The Guinness Book of Classic British Television*, Enfield: Guinness Publishing.

Crisell, A. (2002) *An Introductory History of British Broadcasting*, London: Routledge.

Curran, J. and Seaton, J. (2003) *Power Without Responsibility: The Press and Broadcasting in Britain*, London: Routledge.

Daniels, T. (ed.) (1989) *The Colour Black: Black Images in British Television*, London: British Film Institute Publishing.

Fulton, R. (1990) *The Encyclopaedia of TV Science Fiction*, London: Boxtree.

Halliwell, L. and Purser, P. (1996) *Halliwell's Television Companion*, London: Collins.

Harbord, J. and Wright, J. (1995) *Forty Years of British Television*, London: Boxtree.

Hunter, A. (ed.) (1991) *Chambers Film and TV Handbook*, London: Chambers.

Kingsley, H. (1988) *The Papermac Guide to Soap Opera*, London: Papermac.

Lewisohn, M. (2003) Radio Times *Guide to TV Comedy*, London: BBC Books.

Lury, K. (2001) *British Youth Television: Cynicism and Enchantment*, Oxford: Oxford University Press.

Miller, T. (2003) *Spyscreen: Espionage on Film and TV from the 1930s to the 1960s*, Oxford: Oxford University Press.

Murphy, R. (ed.) (1999) *British Cinema of the 90s*, London: British Film Institute Publishing.

Selby, K. and Cowdray, R. (1995) *How to Study Television*, Basingstoke: Macmillan.

Sheridan, S. and Vegas, J. (2005) *Keeping the British End Up: Four Decades of Saucy Cinema*, London: Reynolds and Hearn.

Taylor, R. (1994) *The Guinness Book of Sitcoms*, Enfield: Guinness Publishing.

Tibballs, G. (1991) *The Golden Age of Children's Television*, London: Titan.

Vahimagi, T. (1994) *British Television: An Illustrated Guide*, London: British Film Institute Publishing.

Wright, P. and Cook, J.R. (ed.) (2005) *British Science Fiction Television: A Hitchhiker's Guide*, Cleveland: I.B. Tauris.

Journals

Many television series from the 1960s onwards are broadcast on the satellite channel UK Gold, and can also be found on other dedicated channels. Classic dramas and other series are also available in DVD/VHS formats from specialised retailers, for example, HMV, Amazon and the BBC shop.

Information on television and radio programmes can be found in all the national daily newspapers, which also carry reviews and comment on programmes shown earlier. The quality Sunday newspapers also carry reviews of the previous week's terrestrial television programmes. In addition, several other magazines such as *Time Out* also carry weekly listings. The *Radio Times* (BBC Magazines, 1923–) originated at a time when the BBC only transmitted radio programmes, but it now carries reviews and detailed listings of programmes on all channels. Similarly, *TV Times* (Independent Television Publications, 1955–) originally covered only commercial television programmes, but now covers BBC programmes too.

Until its demise in 1991, *The Listener* (Listener Publications Limited, 1929–91) carried reviews of radio programmes, while *Television – The Journal of the Royal Television Society* (Royal Television Society, 1927–) deals with more specialised matters in broadcasting.

8

Popular music and fashion

Introduction

For many young people in Britain popular music is an important element of youth culture. It is part of a world of fashion, image and style, which together express identity and individuality. But it is also one of Britain's most valuable creative industries; in 2003 over 236 million albums and 36 million singles were sold in the UK domestic market, and turnover was estimated at more than £2 billion.

As well as being a valuable commodity, music also forms part of a communal experience, and can be heard 'live' in a variety of settings, from small pubs to large fields and football stadiums. During the summer months music festivals of all kinds are held around Britain. Some take place over several days, such as the annual Glastonbury Festival in south-west England, while in London the Notting Hill Carnival is Britain's biggest street party. It is held by the Caribbean community each year, and features exotic types of dance music, from Caribbean steel bands to reggae and rap. Traditional music is also well supported around Britain, with Gaelic and Celtic music often being honoured at festivals in Scotland and Wales.

Music broadcasting is well established on national and local broadcasting services. BBC Radios 1 and 2, together with numerous independent radio stations, broadcast hundreds of hours of popular music each week. Jazz and classical music are widely appreciated; jazz can be heard on specialist radio and television programmes, as well as on Jazz FM in London and the north-west, while BBC Radio 3 and the independent station Classic FM broadcast classical music around Britain. Numerous newspapers, style magazines, fanzines and a flourishing specialised music press all carry regular columns of information, gossip and comment on music of all kinds. There are also many different types of music prizes awarded each year, among them the Brit Awards and the MoBOs (Music of Black Origin).

Many musicians begin without any formal training. Others learn at school and complete their studies at one of the prestigious London centres, such as the Royal College of Music, the Guildhall School of Music and Drama and Trinity College of Music. Outside London, the main centres are the Royal Scottish Academy of Music and Drama in Glasgow, and the Welsh College of Music and Drama in Cardiff; several other colleges and universities also offer degrees and diplomas in musical study.

For many years, jazz, classical and pop music were seen as very different types of music. But in recent years this has changed as pop musicians have increasingly recorded jazz, classical and classical-influenced 'crossover' music. At the same time, jazz and classically trained players have recorded songs written with mass audiences in mind: for example classical pieces are regularly used in advertising and film soundtracks, while recordings by singers such as Pavarotti have entered the British music charts. However, interest in more traditional recordings of classical music has declined. In 2000 classical music accounted for only 5 per cent of music CD sales. Full-length symphonies and operas did not sell easily, and new recordings tended to feature only selected extracts of classical works.

Early popular music

Until the nineteenth century, folk music was the most common musical style in Britain. Stories and information were communicated in folk songs, which often reflected the region and occupation of the author. But during the early 1800s the tradition declined in England, as people moved from the countryside to the towns and cities. There, music was made and heard in the park, the street and the public house. In the industrial areas of the north, community brass bands were numerous, and there were choral societies in many areas. Music-making was also a popular practice in the home, where for many years the piano and the voice were the principal sources of light entertainment.

As the Victorian cities grew in size, public entertainments became more extensive and varied. Large public houses and theatres known as music halls were built for 'variety' shows of singing and comedy. Soon afterwards, chains of music halls opened in cities around the country. Local and regional influences began to disappear, as London became the centre of musical activity for agents, songwriters, musicians and performers.

One of the most profitable activities was professional songwriting. Songwriters and music publishers got an agreed sum or 'royalty' from their published songs or 'sheet music'. These were frequently improved by the common but illegal practice of bribing famous singers to adopt their material, and by the end of the nineteenth century, popular entertainments and music-making were established commercial practices. The entertainments world was popularly known as 'Tin Pan Alley', and London's Denmark Street was its commercial heart.

During the early 1920s, traditional jazz and 'ragtime' music began to arrive from the USA. The dances which accompanied the music were more informal and easier to learn than the complicated European ones, and dancing became popular and fashionable. British hotels and restaurants provided ballrooms and dance-floors in imitation of the stylish New York establishments, and the BBC broadcast concerts from exclusive venues such as the Savoy, the Dorchester, and Grosvenor House, while couples at home rolled up the carpet and danced to the music.

The arrival of American musicals such as *Anything Goes* and *Porgy and Bess* during the 1930s brought the smoother, more sophisticated music of Cole Porter and George Gershwin to British ears. Their songs were relaxed and assured, glamorous and seductive, just like the singers who performed them. In Britain, many women singers became successful such as Gracie Fields and 'the forces' sweetheart' Vera Lynn. The liberated sound of modern jazz, or 'bebop', had also begun to arrive from America. But its anarchic, ironic, rebellious nature required concentration and dedication, and its popularity was largely confined to intellectual audiences.

After the Second World War demand was strong for cosy, comforting music which brought a sense of well-being and romance to a generation still recovering from the shock of war, and popular music consisted of slowly and sentimentally sung ballads, usually telling stories of unrequited love. This popular style of singing was known as 'crooning' and involved the intimate expression of private emotions to the audience, in songs sung slowly and sentimentally. In America, Italian-Americans such as Frank Sinatra, Perry Como, Mario Lanza and Dean Martin popularised this music, which later spread to Britain where local 'crooners' included Frankie Vaughn, Dickie Valentine and Ronnie Hilton. Theirs was relaxed and rhythmical music, created for refined, elegant dancing and romancing.

A gramophone and records were still expensive items, and popular music remained a mainly adult pastime. But with new technology, production costs soon fell. Radios became smaller, and with the invention of the transistor radio by Sony in 1955, the number of listeners grew quickly. A generation born in wartime wanted excitement and consumer goods, and in America new radio stations appeared everywhere, offering lively music shows to capture and seduce a generation of affluent young teenagers. Advertising was an important source of income, and to create more airtime for publicity, stations demanded songs of under three minutes, so musicians began to write short, catchy songs to capture the listeners' attention.

The sales of popular songs were increasing and from 1952 a list of the 12 top-selling singles was published in the British music journal the *New Musical Express*. It was compiled from the previous week's record sales at a number of shops and was initially used by the industry to provide information about the most popular kind of music. However, it was soon adopted for publicity purposes and was increasingly quoted in press releases and music company advertisements as endorsements of popularity, which in turn encouraged fans to buy the top-selling records. The 'hit parade' had arrived, which would soon expand to 20 top-selling records, with different charts in different papers and radio stations, all confusingly calculated in different ways.

Rock 'n' roll: the coming

By 1955 in America, the dream of a free, prosperous, consumer culture appeared to be coming true. There was full employment, and businesses were beginning to market their products to affluent teenagers. Their newly found independence was often expressed in the kind of clothes they wore, the kind of music they listened to and the heroes they idolised. But many young people felt a sense of dissatisfaction. In spite of their material success, America was almost at war with Russia, and the political situation was tense and confused. Many young men felt contemptuous of the world their parents had created, and initially found rebellious new heroes in the cinema. American stars such as Marlon Brando and James Dean were playing angry, anti-authoritarian roles in films such as *The Wild One* (1953) and *Rebel Without a Cause* (1955). However, it was during 1955, the year of Dean's death, that rebellion found sonorial expression in the soundtrack to *Blackboard Jungle*, a film about a group of aggressive young students. It was considered a turbulent and shocking movie, but its musical significance lies in the moment the unknown band of Bill Haley and the Comets assault the audience with the movie's title-music, *Rock Around The Clock*. This was rock 'n' roll music, vibrant, spirited and anarchic.

When the film came to Britain, its effect was electrifying. The youthful audience rose from their cinema seats to jump and dance. The title-music was released as a single, and for five months it was the most popular record in the country. When a quickly made movie of the same name was released in 1956, it led to vandalism and riots in many cinemas. Some municipal authorities banned it, while its effects on youth were discussed in Parliament, police stations, pulpits and the press. It was as if a Martian spaceship had crashed in London.

The term 'rock 'n' roll' was first used by an American DJ Alan Freed, to describe a cocktail of country music, blues, jazz and religious music known as gospel. This was largely exploited by black musicians such as Chuck Berry. Its name was derived from the frequent mention of 'rock' and 'roll' in the song titles and lyrics, which in black American-English meant 'have sex' or 'make love', but its significance was lost on the innocence of the British public.

As rock 'n' roll grew in popularity, white American musicians copied the sound. The alien music was often spoken in tongues and animal cries: A Wop Bop A Lu Bop, Be Bop A Lula, Oooooeeeee uh-uh oooooh yeah! Few could understand the lyrics, and the critics had no language with which to discuss it. There were no previous points of reference, nothing with which to compare it. But for white British youth beginning to achieve independence in the austerity of 1950s Britain, it contained the promise of freedom and excitement, a life without military service, war or demands for personal sacrifice.

The arrival of rock 'n' roll had a great effect on British youth culture. Among the early fans were 'New Edwardians', better known as 'Teddy Boys' or 'Teds'. Their long, elaborate jackets with velvet on the collar and pockets revived a style cultivated by young male aristocrats during the time of King Edward VII (1901–10). The jacket was worn with American country-style clothing: 'bootlace' ties, narrow 'drainpipe' trousers, brightly coloured socks, heavy suede shoes with thick rubber soles, the hair swept up and back, heavily greased with Brylcream. Their appearance was a florid sight in the drab high streets, coffee bars and cinemas of 1950s Britain.

The 'Teds' disliked conformity, austerity and authority, and sometimes there were fights and acts of vandalism. The media began to associate them with rebelliousness and saw them as a threat to society. Their differences in style, in tastes and opinions, and more visibly in music, clothes and behaviour began to mark what journalists described as the 'generation gap'. The popular newspapers were filled with lurid stories of Teddy Boy criminality, vandalism and stabbings. However, studies showed that in many cases the newspapers printed exaggerated stories to sell copies to a frightened, uncomprehending public.

British society was still deeply conformist and traditional, and while some were excited and enthusiastic about the changes taking place, many felt that the social order was breaking down, and their authority was in danger. The BBC did nothing to promote the new music, and at first the music press was almost as hostile as Parliament and the Church. In the early 1950s the *Melody Maker*, a leading music weekly, openly criticised rock 'n' roll, and defined quality popular music as jazz.

After Bill Haley there were other Americans who gained enormous fame in Britain and sold millions of records, such as Elvis Presley, Buddy Holly, Eddie Cochran and Jerry Lee Lewis, but few British singers could match their popularity. The most notable, such as Tommy Steele, Marty Wilde, and later Cliff Richard and Adam Faith, were not native speakers of this new musical language. They had little knowledge of the origins of rhythm and blues, country music and gospel. They had little understanding of how the cries and shouts were derived from communion with God. Instead, the demands of British show-business softened their song. They removed its

177

sexuality and fire, its drive and punch, but also made it more popular and commercially acceptable for British audiences. Yet by 1962 rock 'n' roll was in decline, and many critics wondered if popular music had a future.

Skiffle

Although the explosive, driving rhythms of rock 'n' roll were easy to compose, they were difficult to imitate, as electric instruments and amplification were still scarce in Britain. Around 1953 an acoustic type of music known as 'skiffle' emerged in and around the clubs of London's Soho. It was fast and rhythmical, and required a minimum of musical expertise. The instruments were few: a 'washboard' (a type of percussion instrument used to mark rhythm), two acoustic guitars and an acoustic bass, with the option of a kazoo, a banjo or a piano. Music was played with few keys and few chords, but the vigorous rhythmic support for the vocals made it distinctive and infectious.

Like rock 'n' roll its origins were black and American, and almost anyone could play it. A DIY musical revolution began, as youths without any musical knowledge or training picked up an instrument and taught themselves to play. It was especially popular with young, left-wing intellectuals in the art schools, who found its authentic, uncommercial sound an attractive, classless one. The new music appealed to youths trapped in a rigidly hierarchical Britain, and seemed perfectly in tune with the postwar plan of both Labour and Conservative governments to create a more open, equal society.

Its popular influence spread, and stars emerged, such as Lonnie Donegan and Ken Colyer. Donegan's *Rock Island Line* (1956) was the first British record to sell well in America, reaching number 6 in the US charts. At home, the BBC's Religious Department authorised a Twentieth Century Folk Mass which included skiffle music. The Salvation Army had the Hallelujah Skiffle Group, and the breakfast cereal Rice Crispies offered a free 'skiffle whistle'. But proposing the washboard as a new route to the future of rock 'n' roll was never taken seriously, and by 1958 the acoustic music began to disappear in favour of a more exciting, amplified sound.

The Beatles

It was the cosmopolitan port of Liverpool that provided the focus for an international revolution in pop. Its clubs, coffee bars and dance halls were already venues for poetry and jazz, and there was even a local pop paper *Mersey Beat*. There, between 1962 and 1964, hundreds of local groups began competing for attention, playing a mixture of black-influenced pop songs with faster, more aggressive rock 'n' roll, in a sound which became known as 'Mersey Beat'. Few bands survived or progressed, but one became the most famous in the world – the Beatles.

The history of the Beatles begins with a little-known Liverpool skiffle band – the Quarrymen – who would later compose and play the most successful music in the history of pop: John Lennon (1940–80), Paul McCartney (b. 1942), George Harrison (1943–2001) and, by 1962, Ringo Starr (b. Richard Starkey, 1940). Earlier the group had played under different names with different personnel, but inspired by their new manager Brian Epstein, their fortunes changed. *Love Me Do* (1962) was highly successful, and over the next two years they had numerous fresh, exciting singles which reached number one in the British music charts, such as *She Loves You*, *I Want To Hold Your Hand* and *Can't Buy Me Love*.

With their distinctive long hair, white shirts, narrow ties and dark suits, they mixed charm with cheek. Because they looked and spoke like their fans, many people identified with them, and they quickly became popular around Britain. Previously, most pop groups copied well-known American hits, or used the material of a professional songwriter. However, most Beatles' hits were written by Lennon and McCartney, with the main contributor on each song providing the lead vocals. They sang short, sentimental and nostalgic songs, often using slang and imagery from everyday life, which were combined with folk harmonies in the rhythm and blues style, from *Got to Get You into My Life*, to the music-hall of *When I'm Sixty Four*.

In 1963 they were described in the *Sunday Times* newspaper as 'the greatest composers since Beethoven', and in 1965 they were awarded the MBE by Harold Wilson, the Labour Prime Minister. Their intense popularity became known as 'Beatlemania', which in the USA was even more fanatical than in Britain. But in 1966 the intense hysteria which accompanied their appearances everywhere led the Beatles to stop touring.

As the group matured, their music became more eclectic. In 1967 the group released *Sergeant Pepper's Lonely Hearts Club Band*, a radical departure from their earlier material, but also a highly accomplished and varied recording. Songs took an affectionate look at an almost disappeared English popular culture of northern brass bands, music hall entertainers and travelling circus acts. In a pioneering style which influenced the recording and packaging of subsequent popular music, one song flowed into the next, and various styles were inventively combined to produce something new. The lyrics also appeared in print with the music, and the cover was attractively designed by the pop-artist Peter Blake. But the music also indicated the band's interest in drugs and mysticism, and they lost many of their former fans. However, the album's sophistication also found them a new, more intellectual audience, and marked the arrival of pop music as an object of serious comment.

The band were still popular and famous, but they were also under pressure. They began to look for more independence, both creatively and personally, and when their manager died in 1967 the band members began to work separately, but financial and musical problems started to have a

179

greater importance. By 1970 all members of the group had made solo albums, and in the same year the Beatles officially broke up, after 15 US and 13 UK number one albums, and 21 US and 17 UK number one singles.

During their eight years together they created the best-loved body of songwriting and music in the whole of post-war pop, but after splitting up they never enjoyed the same level of success in their varied solo projects. McCartney was the most successful, notably with the band Wings, and subsequently with numerous varied solo projects. The author of *Yesterday* – one of the most played songs of the twentieth century – he is possibly the most honoured musician alive, and was knighted in 1997.

British rhythm and blues

In the 1960s there were no videos, computers or mobile phones, and there were only two television channels. Young people were more reliant on creating their own entertainment, and this usually demanded innovation in sport, music or fashion. With relatively few material distractions, it is perhaps unsurprising that many cultural innovators of the era were aged under 25.

Many British musicians were attracted to black American music: the energy and emotion of black soul singers such as James Brown, the rhythmic, soul-blues of Ray Charles, and the harder, more energetic urban blues of Muddy Waters, John Lee Hooker, and Howlin' Wolf. Several composers began to incorporate different elements of the black musicians into their own musical repertoires, mixing them with other influences to produce a new kind of music.

The principal British exponent was Alexis Korner and his band Blues Incorporated. His was the world's first noted white blues group. Between 1962 and 1967 they influenced many other emerging British bands, such as the Animals, the Yardbirds with Eric Clapton and Jeff Beck, the Spencer Davies Group with Steve Winwood, Fleetwood Mac, and the Rolling Stones. Their style became known as British 'rhythm and blues' (R & B). At first they were seen as exotic musical acts playing a strange kind of music, but they soon found enthusiastic audiences in a network of new clubs around the country, the most famous being the 'Marquee' in London's Wardour Street.

The Rolling Stones

The most successful and long-lived of the early British R & B groups is the Rolling Stones. They were formed in 1962 by Mick Jagger (b. 1943), who abandoned his studies at the London School of Economics to focus on a more colourful career in music. Keith Richard (later Richards, b. 1943), Brian Jones, Bill Wyman and Charlie Watts joined soon after, replacing other musicians. They began making regular appearances at clubs in west

Figure 8.1 The Rolling Stones in concert

London, in and around the suburb of Richmond. Andrew Loog Oldham began to manage them, and in contrast to the more conservative image of the Beatles and other groups of the time, developed their image as wild, sexy and bohemian. Oldham encouraged them to wear long hair and exotic clothes at a time when most people wore short hair and dressed modestly. Their appearance and behaviour seemed daring and provocative in 1964, and shocked many of the older generation, but Oldham was shrewd enough to realise this would ensure their appeal to a younger audience.

Their musical influences are various, but have been largely based around rhythm 'n' blues, supplied from Richards' guitar and Jagger's blues-inspired vocals. Their early material consisted of cover-versions of well-known blues and rock 'n' roll songs, and were immediately popular. Their first two albums – both entitled *The Rolling Stones* – went to the top of the music charts.

To compete with the Beatles they began writing their own songs, with Jagger usually composing the lyrics and Richards the music. The disturbing

181

themes and neurotic rhythms of their early songs (notably on the album *Aftermath* in 1966) mixed with Jagger's grimacing, shaking and eroticism provided an explosive combination. In 1965 their first number one single in both the UK and America was *(I Can't Get No) Satisfaction*, which expresses dissatisfaction with consumer culture and sexual frustration, the song which has since become their signature tune. The success was repeated with *Jumpin' Jack Flash* in 1968. Both showed the power and energy of the group at their best, and established them as an exotic, potent, musical force.

In 1969 Brian Jones left the group, and shortly afterwards was found dead in his swimming pool. Mick Taylor joined the band, but left in 1975 to be replaced by Ron Wood. In 1993 Bill Wyman left, and was replaced by Daryl Jones. The success continued; no other group has had more British or US album hits, and 30 years after their formation, their live shows continue to break box-office records around the world.

Since the late 1970s spectacular concerts in huge sports stadiums around the world have become a central part of their career. They have continued to release a steady succession of singles and LPs in addition to their own solo projects. Their most critically praised albums were those of the late 1960s and *Exile on Main Street* (1972), although *Emotional Rescue* (1980) and *Voodoo Lounge* (1994) were also critically admired, the latter being number one in the UK and many other countries, and winning a Grammy award in the USA as best album of the year. Public interest in the band has also been sustained by the colourful private lives of its members, with Jagger's first marriage to the Nicaraguan model Bianca Perez-Mora, and subsequently to the American model Jerry Hall, while Richards' earlier problems with drugs and the police have become the stuff of legend.

In the new millennium their ability still to tour the world and to produce some of the most memorable stage shows ever seen, while relying largely on a back catalogue of powerful, resonant, nostalgic songs, is regarded by most critics and members of the public as an admirable achievement, and in 2003 Jagger received a knighthood for services to the music industry.

Mods!

While the Beatles and the Stones were seducing British audiences with their shows, soul music (especially from the Tamla Motown label) and Jamaican ska or 'bluebeat' were the main musical styles of black America and the Caribbean. They all had a strong, regular rhythm and were good records for dancing. In the affluence and excitement of London in the early 1960s, their popularity grew in parallel with pop. Few bands could play live dance music, so clubs offered recorded music from 'discs' and became 'discothèques', one of the first being 'La Discothèque', which opened in 1964 in London's Wardour Street.

Dance music was also heavily promoted on the television programme *Ready, Steady, Go!* (ITV, 1963–66). A 'club' atmosphere was created in the studio, in which the audience was part of the show. New dances such as the 'Bunny Hop', the 'Locomotion' and the 'Twist' were performed by fashionably dressed fans in a programme that transmitted visual messages around the country about music, dance and fashion in the metropolis.

The popular music and fashion industries saw that a numerically significant section of the population had money to spend on 'pop' culture, and there was a boom in spending on music and clothes. In fashion, the 'canon' of the couturier was challenged by the arrival of the ready-to-wear industry, mass-producing clothes in fashionable new styles, for example the mini-skirt, which seemed to affirm the new confidence of women in their sexuality. The skinny model known simply as 'Twiggy' became the fashion yardstick and promoted a new look, as a girl who was both very thin *and* desirable.

London of the mid-1960s was the centre of art, fashion and pop music, in which the most popular style was minimal and modernist. For some years a clearly defined, sartorial 'look' had been developing among some young, aspirational, fashion-conscious metropolitans known popularly as 'mods'. The male interpretation typically included a lightweight, continental suit with a three-button, two-vent jacket, narrow trousers, button-collar shirt, narrow tie, zip boots and short hair, with a long green military-style anorak known as a 'parka' to protect the clothes. The female style of mini-skirt, heavy, bright make-up, thick mascara, and short, straight hair imitated that worn by leading models such as Twiggy and Jean Shrimpton and designer Mary Quant. For the first time a fashionable look allowed girls to resemble boys, and vice versa; it seemed that *being shocking* to the older generation had became fashionable.

Consumerism was a central element of mod style and one of its most distinctive features was the Vespa or Lambretta scooter, typically adorned with an abundance of lights and mirrors. By 1964 it provided many London mods with a way to reach Brighton, a popular coastal resort that briefly became the location for confrontations with groups of 'rockers', a more traditional manifestation of working-class subculture. With their characteristic symbols of identity: motorcycles, leather jackets, denim jeans and long hair, the 'rockers' resembled American motorcycle gangs of the early 1950s, as in the American films *The Wild One* (1953) and *Rebel Without a Cause* (1955). Mod style, however, was less traditional and more aspirational, and seemed to challenge the rockers' defiance, helping to create sensational press reports about clashes between the two groups, headlines that seemed to anticipate civil war. However, studies showed the confrontations to be minor, and that reports were exaggerated to sell copies to older members of the public, who were anxious about the behaviour of young people in a rapidly changing society. Nevertheless, it marked the beginning of a tribalism among British youth, a fragmenting into different

183

groups with different preferences in music, clothes, hairstyles and other aspects of consumption, in what became one of the most distinctive characteristics of British society between 1950 and 1990.

Mod style soon became fashionable in rock music through the influence of groups such as The Who and The Small Faces. The Who had a reputation as arrogant, angry and unpredictable, and to the delight of their fans, the band spectacularly smashed their instruments at the end of their shows. *My Generation* (1965) is one of their most famous songs, a violent musical declaration about the inability of a younger generation to communicate with an older one.

Bands were still predominantly male, and there were still few female singers in British pop. Those who did manage to develop a career, such as Lulu, Dusty Springfield and Cilla Black, sang sentimental songs in the jazz and cabaret style, before working elsewhere in show-business where their talents were more appreciated.

Skinheads and soul

During the late 1960s black dance music continued to grow in popularity. There were several points of access. The light, amateurish but highly rhythmical reggae music of the time, and a faster, less vocal version 'ska' both established their popularity. In ska, the rhythms and melodies of reggae were mixed with the indigenous dance music styles of West Africa and the Caribbean. Toots and the Maytals, Desmond Dekka, Prince Buster and Judge Dread were among the most representative groups.

The music became fashionable among a minor subculture known as 'skinheads', who were known for their racism and violence. They quickly earned a reputation for attacking blacks and Asians, as well as other minority groups such as hippies and gays. With their characteristic shaven heads, and a 'uniform' of button-collar shirts, tight, short Levi jeans, heavy boots (ideally 27-hole Doctor Martens) or 'loafer' shoes, their displays of stylised aggression in the football stadiums of Britain marked the start of large-scale soccer hooliganism.

Skinheads seemed to embody the aggressive attitudes becoming more prevalent in British society as the optimism of the 1960s began to give way to political polarisation and confrontation. It was a time when the wrong skin colour, the wrong type of haircut or even liking the wrong type of music or football team could get a young person into serious trouble with gangs of juvenile delinquents at a football match, a pub, a shopping centre or a night club.

Skinheads gradually disappeared from both the football terraces and streets until the early 1980s when a brief revival saw 'neo-skinhead' bands such as the 4 Skins, Cock Sparrer and Sham 69 playing punk-inspired rock music. This was part of the 'Oi' movement, an anti-authoritarian, loose alliance of varied groups in Britain and abroad. But their crude political message of racism, hooliganism and street violence was much louder than its artistic one, and as a musical force they quickly disappeared.

'Northern soul' was another important point of access to the black American dance scene. During the late 1960s fans began to meet in the clubs of towns in the north of England to collect and dance to black American soul music. However, the most popular songs were not the latest, but those by obscure artists from earlier in the decade. These were songs recorded before major record companies signed the artists and changed their style. Interest in the music was heightened by the rarity of the records, which often reached Britain in the belongings of American servicemen and students before passing to specialist record shops. Fans believed these recordings were more original, and authentically expressive than later, more commercial material, as the songs were written and sung 'from the heart' and not coached and doctored by the major record labels in order to make them popular with a wider audience, and thus more commercially acceptable.

Some soul clubs founded their own record labels to reissue rare records. Special all-night sessions were organised in which distinctive, acrobatic dancing in stylish baggy clothing was standard. In 1970 the term 'northern soul' was first heard to describe this scene of DJs, collectors and dance fans, which reflected its origins in northern towns such as Wolverhampton, Stoke, Leeds and Nottingham. Wigan Casino became the best-known club, its name synonymous with the music of obscure artists such as the Pioneers and the Prophets.

In subsequent decades 'northern' remained highly popular in the Midlands and north. The heartfelt lyrics of the romantic, aspirational, oppressed black American singers seemed to resonate with the culture of the northern British working class. However, its records were old and rare so there was no major investment by the record industry. Consequently it has remained isolated and uninfluential, even though an enthusiastic group of fans continue to 'keep the faith' and maintain the tradition.

Progressive music

During the mid-1960s popular music began to change and diversify. Some musicians stopped writing short, popular songs for the radio and the charts, preferring instead the freedom to write longer songs, to experiment with new sounds and demonstrate musical virtuosity. The period was characterised by artistic freedom and experimentalism, and the Beatles had already begun to play with lyrics, sound and song length in progressive albums such as *Rubber Soul* (1965), *Revolver* (1966) and *Sergeant Pepper* (1967). Following their example, many others began rejecting the limitations of the traditional three-minute pop song, writing longer pieces for release on LPs, for example Pink Floyd and Soft Machine, followed by Yes, Genesis (later with Phil Collins), and Emerson Lake and

185

Palmer. They found a keen and loyal following among a largely middle-class public in colleges, art schools and universities, and many went on to become highly successful in Britain and America, with music characterised by lengthy guitar and drum solos, pompous lyrics, grand orchestration, extravagant costumes and 'concept' albums. Meanwhile, other musicians who had started playing R & B progressed into blues and rock music. Groups such as Cream, Led Zeppelin, Deep Purple and Black Sabbath founded a related style of 'heavy' rock. Its elements of fantasy, the repetitive guitar 'riffs', the screaming vocals and thunderous bass and drums quickly proved popular and influential.

Heavy bands were popular with 'hippies': young, mainly middle-class Americans who conspicuously rejected conventional ideas and lifestyles, and instead experimented with alternative ways of living based on peace and love. By 1967 this trend had spread to London where a hippy dress-style was characterised by exotic, Asian clothing, often mixed nostalgically with items of dress from the nineteenth century. Long hair, sandals and faded jeans were also common elements of a unisex 'look', which many older people found decadent and provocative.

Hippies were attracted by the simplicity and purity of folk music, which represented an attractive alternative to the increasingly commercial nature of rock. But in Britain folk had a reputation for being an earnest musical form, which during the 1950s and 1960s had been popular with left-wing students, bohemians and Irish expatriates. In the USA folk was combined with radical protest, and widened its appeal in songs by Joan Baez, Bob Dylan and others. In Britain too they were idolised and imitated by singers such as Donovan and others who sang a mixture of folk and rock. Later in the 1970s, folk-rock became established with the success of British groups such as Fairport Convention, Steeleye Span and the Albion Country Band. They played numerous small festivals and events, held quietly and discreetly by a growing alternative 'underground' culture functioning outside the commercial mainstream. They rarely appealed to a mass audience, and for many of their fans this helped to maintain their attraction.

All that glitters . . .

By 1970 a musical 'third way' had been proposed which involved combining elements of folk music and electric pop. Some of the earliest exponents were Marc Bolan and David Bowie. In 1971 Bolan formed the rock group T. Rex and began wearing glitter and make-up, while singing songs with childish rhymes and sexually suggestive lyrics, which hinted at both innocence and subversiveness. The public found him daring and provocative, ensuring maximum publicity for the band. Between 1971 and 1973 they had a succession of hit singles, such as *Ride a White Swan*, *Get it On*, and *Jeepster*. Their music had an exotic, exciting electric sound, and was delivered in a brash celebration of hedonism and sexuality, perfectly in tune with the tenor of the times.

The new influences reflected the changes taking place in society, where the women's liberation movement and the gay liberation movement were making people more aware of sexual difference and the need for more tolerance. For the first time it seemed possible to choose a new identity both on the stage and the street. At first this shocked many people, and the music industry quickly realised that dressing and behaving in a sexually ambiguous manner was an easy way to get publicity. Although the trends had begun in the non-commercial underground scene, the highly commercial 'music machine' soon realised big profits could be made by 'packaging' the style and selling it to gullible teenagers. In a pattern that has been repeated many times since, the popularity of T. Rex and David Bowie influenced many others to adopt a similar stage image. The Sweet, Mud and the Bay City Rollers were among the first to cultivate a theatrical, sexually androgynous 'look'. Many fans began to imitate their heroes, wearing make-up, glitter, velvet and ludicrously high platform shoes, and concerts began to resemble fashion shows.

The glamorous, theatrical style (or lumpen fad, depending on the point of view) was popularly known as 'glam' rock. Although there was little musical unity among its exponents, the strong, rhythmic beat and the 'sing-along' football-chant choruses of Gary Glitter and Slade, the lyrical simplicity of Elton John, the heavy metal pop-androgyny of Queen, and the avant-garde pop-rock experimentalism of Roxy Music, were all received enthusiastically by millions of fans.

Although Queen later became one of the most successful bands of its time, Roxy Music was immediately respected and influential. The band was led by Brian Ferry, who had been taught by the pop artist Richard Hamilton. Ferry brought wit, intelligence and pop-art style into their music, into their own theatrical stage act, and into their stylish album sleeves of statuesque models. For both groups and fans, style was becoming as important as musical ability. Many music critics, however, were less enthusiastic. They saw the new trends as vulgar, ostentatious and highly commercial: a victory of artifice over art.

David Bowie

'T.S. Eliot with a rock n roll beat'[1]

One of the most enduring and influential performers to emerge from the early 1970s is David Bowie (b. David Jones, 1947), a singer, songwriter and guitarist who has become one of the most successful, controversial and influential of British singers. He came into music from dance and drama, and after leading several modest rock bands, he began as a solo artist. In 1969, when the world was fascinated by the Apollo moon mission, he had

187

his first major success with the single and album *Space Oddity*, a dreamy, folk-inspired mixture of singer/songwriting about a mission to escape from Earth. It also marked the projection of his songs through different stage characters, beginning with the astronaut Major Tom.

Bowie became interested in the music of American singers Lou Reed and Iggy Pop, and at the same time began to introduce more shocking and theatrical elements into his own performances. In 1971 he changed to a heavier rock sound for the album *The Man Who Sold the World*. To publicise it he wore glitter, make-up and even a dress, to create a theatrical new identity. Shortly afterwards he made *The Rise and Fall of Ziggy Stardust and the Spiders from Mars* (1972), a sequence of songs about a mythical pop star. Ironically, it was the record which made Bowie himself famous, and marked the first of many high points in his career.

His performances were also significant for their incorporation of theatre and costume. In 1973/74 his controversial stage shows were the most elaborate ever seen on a British stage, with the artist appearing in concert with a painted face, with florid, provocative costumes, and publicly admitting his bisexuality. This was followed by *Aladdin Sane* (1974), an album which suggested imminent nuclear war. Soon after came *Diamond Dogs* (1975), a dark album about an Orwellian nightmare future, released at a time of high unemployment, strikes and inflation.

Since the mid-1970s Bowie has worked with numerous different bands and backing musicians, and has consistently made stylish and highly varied albums, becoming involved with soul, funk and rock bands. He also began a career as an actor, playing the leading role of John Merrick in the Broadway play *The Elephant Man* (1980) and making several films, the most critically acclaimed being Nicolas Roeg's *The Man Who Fell to Earth* (1976). As well as acting, Bowie also developed his interests in painting. He also set up the internet ISP BowieNet, before opening a bank, BowieBanc.com.

His more recent work has been received with only lukewarm enthusiasm by critics, but like many modern celebrities, although he has become marginalised as a musical force, he has also grown more famous than ever, and is critically respected as an original and influential performer, who during the past 30 years has changed the style of British pop.

The roots of rebellion

During the mid-1970s the major bands in the world were all British. Pink Floyd, Led Zeppelin, Genesis, Yes, Emerson Lake and Palmer, the Moody Blues and the Rolling Stones had all become wealthy, yet they rarely visited Britain, and recent lengthy 'concept' albums and experiments with classical music were seen by many fans as pompous, excessive and extravagant. Moreover, writing about popular music had become serious and deferential, and few journalists dared to criticise the pop and rock 'establishment'.

Articles appearing in the music press such as *Sounds*, the *New Musical Express*, *Melody Maker*, *Time Out* and the American *Rolling Stone* began to resemble sycophantic literary reviews, and there was boredom with their elevation of popular music into a 'high' art form.

In response, some British musicians began to revive the honest simplicity of styles from the 1950s and 1960s. They played short, direct, three-minute songs in a mixture of R & B, rock 'n' roll and American country music. This fundamentalist revival began in the south of England, in small pubs and clubs in London, such as the Hope and Anchor, and the Greyhound. The public liked the simple, home-made but professional sound of these groups, and many established a strong local following. Fans and business people often combined to create their own independent recording companies such as Stiff and Chiswick, where they recorded the music of artists they liked. These initiatives encouraged many others to start bands, and soon there was a DIY movement of young groups such as the Stranglers, and Eddie and the Hot Rods. Their enthusiasm, energy and attitude made many established groups appear even more tired and decadent.

Ian Dury's Kilburn and the High Roads, and Brinsley Schwarz were two respected and influential bands, but the most successful and long-lived was Dr Feelgood. Wearing sharp 'mod' suits from the 1960s, they played a mixture of blues, R & B and rock 'n' roll. Their music was elemental and electrifying, with the manic Wilko Johnson supplying the current and Lee Brilleaux connecting with the audience. *Down by the Jetty* (1975) was the first of many albums in a consistent catalogue that extended into the 1990s.

But reinterpretations of songs from the 1950s and 1960s were not enough to satisfy many fans. There was a deepening social and economic crisis, strikes, inflation and high youth unemployment. Violence and poltical polarisation were increasing and many young people were bored and frustrated, not only with their prospects, but with the music scene in general. There was anger at the complacency of an older generation, not only in government, but also in pop. This frustration was about to be expressed in a defiant, primitive musical language.

The Sex Pistols

In 1975 a British businessman, Malcolm McLaren, returned to Britain after working in America, where he had briefly managed several American bands including the New York Dolls. They seemed not to care about the music, but were more interested in shocking their audiences. McLaren's idea was to create a band not with talent, but with a potential to shock and disgust. In this way, they would become so notorious that people would pay to see them. Soon he was to unleash the Sex Pistols onto a bored, grey music scene that seemed to have lost its potential to shock.

There were four founder members: Johnny Rotten (b. John Lydon, 1956) on vocals, Steve Jones on guitar, Glen Matlock on bass and Paul Cook on drums. The band was created to attract attention and publicity on stage, off stage, everywhere they went. At the same time, McLaren's partner Vivienne Westwood was producing parallel items of clothing, such as dyed T-shirts with black, red or brown stripes, stencilled-in slogans such as 'Only Anarchists are Pretty', and featuring swastika symbols and an armband with the word 'chaos' emblazoned. Together they created a foreign message using familiar iconography, which simultaneously confused and fascinated.

The mid-1970s was a time when people were still largely defined by the clothes they wore, and even just a leather motorbike jacket was often enough to suggest deviancy. Dressed in tatty leather jackets, torn clothing, safety-pins, swastikas, zips, clips, studs and chains, with spiked, brightly dyed hair, and an occasional regimental tie, the punk 'look' was unique and provocative, simultaneously suggesting eccentricity and perversion. It was quickly adopted as a unisex fashion by fans around the country, but for many older citizens, the punk 'look' was deeply disturbing, and aroused feelings of hostility and sympathy in equal measure.

In 1976 the Sex Pistols had their first recording contract with EMI, one of Britain's oldest and most conservative record labels, and released their debut single, *Anarchy in the UK*. Their music was loud, primal and hostile. It consisted of simple guitar solos, repeated chords, a heavily distorted sound, and defiant, abrupt endings. Songs were delivered with energy and fire, in a Cockney accent infused with insults and rejections, volcanically released in a tone of bored sarcasm.

The band soon became notorious, and stories of their confrontational behaviour began appearing in the tabloid press. Then, following a television appearance in which the band swore and abused the presenter, EMI sacked the band. A tour followed, but many municipal authorities cancelled concerts to 'protect' local people. A new bass player Sid Vicious (b. John Ritchie, 1957) arrived to replace Matlock. Vicious was a disturbed youth whose anti-social behaviour of vomiting, drug taking and assaults were encouraged to gain publicity.

The group found a new recording contract with A and M Records, and planned a new single *God Save the Queen*, a satire on the Silver Jubilee celebrations of Queen Elizabeth II in 1977. To ensure maximum attention and promote record sales, the group signed for the company outside Buckingham Palace, the publicity depicting an image of the Queen with a safety pin through her nose. The BBC refused to play the song on the grounds of 'gross bad taste' (although DJ John Peel played it twice) while the IBA instructed all commercial radio and television stations not to broadcast the single, as it was in contravention of Section 4 (10) (A) of the IBA Act, being 'against good taste or decency, likely to encourage or incite crime, or lead to disorder'. Today, the song sounds cheeky and irreverent, but in Britain of the mid-1970s it was incendiary.

The Sex Pistols' songs and attitude regularly drew them into fights and confrontations with the authorities, and soon after they were sacked by their record company. But *God Save the Queen* reached number two in the music charts, and was followed by *Holidays in the Sun*, *Pretty Vacant*, and the album *Never Mind the Bollocks*, which went to number one in the album charts in 1977. This was a major achievement after the BBC and London's Capital Radio had banned every single except *Pretty Vacant*, and the negative media attention following an unsuccessful prosecution for the use of the word 'bollocks' on their LP cover.

Next came a tour of the USA, but internal problems saw Rotten and Vicious leave the group. This was followed by tragedy in 1979, when Vicious died of a heroin overdose following the alleged murder of his girl-friend. The group was finished and never recorded again. McLaren subsequently organised a biographical feature film *The Great Rock 'n' Roll Swindle* (Julian Temple, 1980) which featured the infamous Ronnie Biggs, who had escaped from prison in the 1960s and fled to Brazil. Rotten went on to a new musical career with the band Public Image Limited (PIL), while the other members disappeared from the music scene, as punk became mainstream and lost its power to shock.

During their brief period of fame they recorded only 25 songs which appeared on just five singles and one album in the United Kingdom. But their infamy led to the appearance of around 50 illegal recordings on various albums. During their time together the Sex Pistols illuminated the face of white pop, and their influence has been enduring.

Pop music: just do it (yourself)

During 1976 the Damned, the Clash, the Jam, the Stranglers, the Buzzcocks and others played with speed, energy, and a raw, untutored sound in deliberately off-key songs, sung loud and short. The punk philosphy was anti-superstar and anti-establishment, generating an increase in amateur music-making, as youth around Britain embraced its DIY ethic, and often without any musical training began to form and play in bands, taking comic, self-deprecating stage-names, such as Captain Sensible and Gaye Advert. At concerts fans did not dance, but jumped up and down in a style known as 'pogoing', and in an inverted gesture of appreciation enthusias-tically spat on the bands. Mainstream society was uncomprehending and shocked by the punk style and attitude; as with the arrival of rock 'n' roll, there was nothing to compare it with, no previous points of reference. The signs and symbols of punk did not speak a familiar language. But to many bored, unemployed teenagers leading dull suburban lives, it was a call to arms. The world outside watched with horrified fascination.

In the mid-1970s young people were living in a very different way to the older generation, having grown up with levels of freedom, independence and consumerism which their parents had never known. There was not only a gap between the generations but also a divide within the younger one. Despite the women's liberation movement and a trend towards greater equality in the work place, popular music was still male dominated, even though a few punk bands had female singers, such as Siouxsie and the Banshees, and X-ray Spex. There was also one all-girl band: the Slits. Although they were not openly feminist, their music was not aggressive, macho punk, but more complex in sound and rhythm. In 1977 this was considered brave and shocking, and just as women were beginning to compete with men in many other male-dominated fields, their intimidating stage presence challenged the traditional role of women in pop as background vocalists or suave, seductive temptresses.

For a short time it seemed as if the fans were in charge of music and the music industry, as the DIY ethic of punk helped to create a new, alternative pop culture. This consisted of small independent record companies and distributors, graphics companies, magazines, fanzines, fashion designers and journalists, who supported the kinds of music which the commercial mainstream would not consider. However, the major record companies soon realised the potential of punk and began to sign bands while softening their style to make them more commercially acceptable. Marketing also became more sophisticated, with coloured vinyl, picture discs, extra tracks and numbered, limited, editions. Moreover, the arrival of the music video channel MTV early in the 1980s brought the requirement for the band to 'look good' in front of the camera.

However, as the 'music machine' began to organise the scene, the values and demands of business and commerce all combined to weaken the communal ethos of punk, and by the early 1980s many bands had lost their originality and power to shock. Punk was becoming mainstream, the total antithesis of everything it stood for. Moreover, in the late 1970s the scene was becoming clouded by new political questions, such as the politics of racism, as Afro-Caribbean communities struggled for acceptance and racial equality. Punk was losing its potency, and reggae music became the new symbol of political defiance and alterity. Like punk, it expressed a symbolic challenge to the politics of the new Tory government, and a rejection of the right-wing racism of the National Front (NF), and as Thatcher came to power and the NF and other fascists battled with the political left and the police for control of the streets, bands including the Clash, the Police, led by 'Sting', PIL and the Gang of Four all recorded reggae songs, while reggae icon Bob Marley wrote a tribute to punk with *Punky Reggae Party*.

Several mixed-race bands formed to play the popular mixture of pop and reggae, known as 'ska'. This was the Two-Tone movement, a political pop whose message was anti-racism and anti-Thatcher. Between 1979 and 1982, mixed race bands such as the Selecter, the Specials, the Beat, Madness and UB40 expressed a defiant manifesto and gave their support to the Rock Against Racism movement. They appeared in numerous free, public carnivals, often encouraging the audience to join them onstage in a demonstration of left-wing populism which embraced black and white musicians and subcultures, and helped different forms of black music to become established in Britain.

It was not the first time music had been used in this way. In 1976 the movement Rock Against Racism was organised with the Socialist Workers' Party to fight racism and make the public more aware of the tactics of the National Front. From 1978 large concerts were periodically held to raise consciousness, raise funds and promote the cause of third world aid, for example the Live Aid shows of July 1985 – held simultaneously in London and in Philadelphia in the USA – and Live 8 in 2005. They were organised by the singer Bob Geldof to raise awareness and funds for famine relief.

A desire for honesty and authenticity in music saw renewed interest in folk music. An Irish band, the Pogues, brought a mixture of Irish folk and punk to new audiences in open-air festivals, clubs and concerts. Clannad fused Irish folk with New Age music to create a new musical form. British audiences began to discover New Age music, which was arriving from the USA, and whose repetitive and relaxing rhythms found appreciative audiences at the World of Music and Dance (WOMAD) Festival, started in 1982 by the rock musician Peter Gabriel to promote Anglo-Celtic and world music. During the 1980s and 1990s the WOMAD Festival grew in size and popularity, becoming a mainstream event from a small, marginal one, as world music embracing such diverse forms as Gregorian chants, African drums and Mayan humming began to represent authentic alternatives to the dominant commercial forms of dance and pop.

Club and street mix

In the mid-1970s the popular music scene was dominated by the presence of several different musical 'tribes'. The 'heavy' and progressive bands were still followed by a large audience of middle-class students, while dance music was still bought mostly by working-class audiences. Punk and reggae had broken the mould briefly, forming an alliance between working-class youth, middle-class students and art-school bohemians. However, the top-selling music was still dance. The venue for dancing was still the conservative atmosphere of the discothèque, amid an excess of chrome and spotlights and an enforced dress code of 'ties and collars' and 'no training shoes'. Inside, the mainly proletarian clubbers still ignored the musical rebellion taking place elsewhere in pop, preferring instead the aspiration and romance of American soul and Tamla Motown songs, which had dominated the scene since the 1960s.

However, record companies were marketing new bands such as the Bee Gees, a British group, who worked in America, and who had phenomenal success around the world with the soundtrack to the American film *Saturday Night Fever* (1977). The film featured John Travolta as Tony Manero, a young man who is a shop assistant by day, but 'king of the dancefloor' by night. With sales of over 30 million, it became the biggest selling film soundtrack of all time.

But technology was advancing, and new recording and mixing techniques were utilised to create clean, hard, repetitive drum beats, which were ideal rhythms for dance. This made record producers more influential, and in 1976 the German producer Giorgio Moroder popularised an infectious 'disco beat' in the music of the American singer Donna Summer. The creation of larger, 12-inch singles also allowed longer recordings, which were more suitable for disco dancing than the shorter, 3-minute ones preferred by the radio stations. A new electronic keyboard instrument, the synthesiser, also offered a wide spectrum of electronic sounds, and during the late 1970s and early 1980s the new techniques were assimilated into British pop by Gary Numan, Heaven 17, Spandau Ballet, Human League, Visage, OMD, Depeche Mode and others, who used synthesisers and tapes to make restrained, refined, futuristic pop and dance music.

In the hands of the new romantics, a new scene evolved in which glamour replaced the grubbiness of punk. Heavy, pale make-up, baroque, decadent dressing, and cool, detached posing were central elements of style for bands and their fans. The 'look' was camp and androgynous, epitomised by the style of Boy George, but despite its air of elitism, it was a scene accessible to all, not just art-school insiders, and while Bowie looked like he had arrived from Mars, Boy George was always the safe and ordinary 'boy next door'.

The new romantics seemed perfectly in tune with the politics of the time, which was slick, confident and new, but unlike other recent pop movements there was no anger or political message, just a chilly entrepreneurial elitism, made even cooler by the cold electronic neutrality of synthesised sound. They also made it more acceptable for the openly gay bands who were to follow later in the decade, such as Frankie Goes to Hollywood and Bronski Beat. However, their exuberance, pride and self-confidence was tempered by a growing awareness of the potential seriousness of AIDS among the gay community, which was becoming apparent by 1982 when Terrence Higgins became the first person to die from what was then called 'gay-related immune deficiency'. Even though many 'new-ro' bands were short-lived, their impact on popular music was influential. They created a fusion between the music and fashions of disco, pop and rock, which changed the character of British popular music, particularly between 1979 and 1983.

The democratisation of dance

By 1984, the year of the miners' strike, what people read, watched and listened to gave clear indications about their political inclinations, and whose side they were on. For many British teenagers and twenty-some-things, popular anthems from Bill Haley to the Sex Pistols had been a call to arms, the soundtrack of freedom and change. For the National Front, gigs by the Two-Tone bands were an invitation to riot. The music scene was still divided and tribal. Dance and club culture was in the ascendant, and George Michael, Spandau Ballet, Duran Duran and others made songs and videos that celebrated aspirations, status and success. In contrast, an alliance of left-wing musicians 'Red Wedge' loudly voiced its opposition to Thatcherism. Billy Bragg, the Style Council, along with ska and reggae bands such as the Specials, and those working with independent record labels, for example, Rough Trade (a workers' co-operative), all promoted an anti-Thatcher message. British arts, culture and society were still sharply polarised, and the thunderous armageddon of the pop tune *Two Tribes* by Frankie Goes to Hollywood was number one for nine weeks.

Although dance music was essentially aspirational and conformist, new technology allowed the creation of original and challenging new forms. In America, the energetic new sounds of 'rap' (a form of public poetry/ oratory) came up from the streets of New York and Chicago, in which performers loudly declaimed their angry messages over music that had often been taken from another record. Music compact discs were still some years away, but vinyl permitted a technique known as 'scratching', with DJs manually turning the disc to and fro, to create amplified sounds, which were then used to make new musical mixes. Rap and 'scratching' were soon followed by 'sampling', which involved the use of a sampler machine to record and mix musical extracts from different records to produce new sonic collages.

The new developments marked the beginnings of a major shift in dance music, in which professional songwriters and musicians were becoming marginalised. Instead, those with the technical knowledge to mix and manipulate diverse musical sounds and sources had authority. Some critics called them 'sonic outlaws' who stole and copied other people's music, while others defended their right to make 'fair use' of existing material.

The new developments allowed dance music to move away from its commercial, conformist origins to an altogether more underground and subversive musical style. Creative techniques allowed for a wider range of possibilities, particularly in 'house' music, which mixed 1970s disco-funk with a minimal, gospel-style vocal, together with a heavy bass and drum sound. The absence of any clear lyrics removed any clear musical or polit-ical message, leaving it functional and perfectly suited for wild, high-energy (Hi-NRG) dancing by a hedonistic, apolitical youth, disenchanted with the politics of Thatcherism.

195

'House' music took its name from the 'Wharehouse' (sic), a Chicago gay club, popularly believed to be its place of origin. Its wild bohemian sound was quickly adopted in British clubs of all types, particularly in Manchester, where counter-culture was particularly strong with the independent record label Factory Records, and bands such as The Smiths (with the singer Morrissey), Joy Division (who subsequently became New Order), the Buzzcocks and later the Happy Mondays and the Stone Roses, whose African and European influences heard in songs such as *Fool's Gold* helped to establish Acid House and rave culture before their export to Spain.

Since the 1960s the Spanish island of Ibiza in the Mediterranean Sea has been a popular destination for British tourists. But in the summer of 1988 its fine historic buildings and sandy beaches became the venue for large improvised parties featuring ecstatic, non-stop dancing *en masse*. It became popularly known as the 'Summer of Love', as thousands attended the open-air parties. The events marked the beginning of the so-called 'Acid House' movement, created after the coming together of 'house' music and the drug ecstasy, a type of amphetamine commonly known as 'acid' (not LSD). For many fans they were central elements in an emergent subculture of hedonism, dance and communality, which had not been seen since the late 1960s. Revellers favoured the more relaxed dress code of baggy clothes, dungarees and informal beach wear, often adorned with a 'smiley' motif. The music was equally eclectic, and included dub, rap, rock and house music, together with electronic influences from diverse parts of Europe. Among the most representative were the techno-anthems of Cabaret Voltaire, Kraftwerk and Tangerine Dream, Adamski and 2-Unlimited, which were enjoyed in a dancing frenzy of apolitical hedonism.

The new possibilities of electronic music permitted a rapid multiplication into varied sub-genres, with 'techno' one of the most common. Intense, hypnotic and ear-splitting, it was the 'punk rock' of dance, whose hard, repetitive, electronic sounds featured futuristic electronic 'bleeps' and an industrial-strength bass. The mix involved sampling, hip-hop, rap and other styles, but the most distinctive feature was its rhythm, supplied at a break-neck 124–35 bpm (beats per minute), compared with the usual 120 bpm or less for house and other kinds of dance music.

During the late 1980s the new sounds and styles were imported and developed in Britain by amateur producers and DJs who wanted to recreate the atmosphere of the parties in Ibiza, and in 1991 the Ministry of Sound, a south London club, became involved in their promotion. It was an inversion of the capitalist ethos promoted by the Tory government, as an oppositional counter-culture began to use business methods to promote itself. But official permission was impossible to obtain for such large, informal gatherings, and illegal events were held instead, often in huge venues such as empty warehouses and other buildings near London's M25 orbital road. They were known as 'warehouse parties' or 'raves', where crowds danced for several days and nights until they were raided by

the police. But in 1994 raves were prohibited amid a raft of new legislation contained in an attempt to secure the government's dwindling
authority, namely the Criminal Justice Act. However, its effect was to unite
thousands of young people against the government, as alternative lifestyles
of all kinds came under legal attack or were made criminal. In effect,
dancing became a political act, a gesture of protest and defiance which
united millions against the Tories.

In spite of the opposition, and perhaps because of it, dance music
continued to dominate the mid-1990s in a range of diverse styles, including
the speed and darkness of 'hard-core', the emphatic drums and bass of
'jungle', the dreamy, New Age spiritual sound of 'Goa Trance', and the
soulful sensuality of 'garage'. Even the American 'easy listening' music was
rediscovered, as the mellow, relaxed sounds of Burt Bacharach, Dionne
Warwick and others became fashionable again, as an antidote to the aggression of house and its many varieties.

There was also growing interest in Asian dance music known as
Bhangra, which originated in the late 1980s and fused Asian folk music
from the Punjab region of India with the synthesisers and bass of western
hip-hop, reggae and 'techno' music. The mixture of influences in Bhangra
seemed to reflect the dual identity felt by British Asians, many of whom
have grown up within two cultures. But it also found an audience among
young, white British, who were attracted by its exotic and mystical nature.
A decade later, the new British-Asian music, like house before it, had begun
to fragment into different styles, with its own specialist labels such as
Outcaste and Nation, and with established bands such as Apache Indian
and Cornershop, and by the mid-1990s British music reflected the cultural
scene as a whole: fragmented, diverse and international.

Britpop

The 1990s saw very little pop music carrying explicit political messages.
Instead, white British pop-rock and the Acid House scene were brought
together in the music of Primal Scream, the Happy Mondays and the Stone
Roses. The exceptions were the punk-inspired bands such as Crass and
the Levellers, who continued loudly to express their opposition to authority
in general and the Tory Party in particular, while Billy Bragg and Paul
Weller publicised and supported numerous socialist causes with 'benefit'
concerts and fund-raising projects, both within popular music and around
the country.

But in the pubs and clubs of London a new scene was developing, with
a more distinctively English sound. This was led by Suede and Blur, two
bands who were clearly influenced by popular British groups of the 1960s
such as the Small Faces, the Kinks and early songs by David Bowie.
Meanwhile in Manchester, the Gallagher brothers Noel and Liam were
writing lively, catchy songs, combining the sound of the Beatles with the

Figure 8.2 Oasis in concert

attitude of the Sex Pistols for a band called Oasis. In 1994 Blur's *Parklife* and Oasis's first album *Definitely Maybe* were released. Blur's album and their earlier *Modern Life is Rubbish* outlined the territory which would soon be known as 'Britpop', and at first enjoyed only a small cult following based in Camden Town. Their doggedly British character and cartoonish depictions of familiar aspects of suburban life were sung in a satirical cockney drawl, most notably on *Parklife*'s title track (the spoken verses of which were inspired by the Martin Amis novel *London Fields)*. In contrast to the excess of Acid House, it was an honest expression of the modest, everyday and home grown, from guitar bands who acknowledged their musical roots.

In 1995 Oasis released the album *(What's the Story) Morning Glory* which became the defining sound of Britpop, and by 1996 the successful exploitation of the new bands had created a mainstream movement, which was covered on a daily basis by the mass media, fuelled by the north–south rivalry between Oasis and Blur, and the adoption of celebrated, iconic images, such as the 'mod' target design, the parka coat, the finely cut suit, Fred Perry sportswear and long-collared Ben Sherman shirts. Even the Union flag was appropriated as a style statement, in fashion shoots and clothing, and to decorate guitars.

The mass appeal of football also contributed to a renewal of interest in British popular culture, with the staging of Euro '96 in England and one of the most characterful national teams for some years.

Britpop featured in adverts for football matches, as well as in pubs, clubs and on the radio. It seemed to be popular with everyone. When Oasis played at Knebworth in 1996, 2.5 million people, or around 5 per cent of the population, applied for tickets. It was the year that football was coming home, the film industry looked buoyant, pop and fashion were celebrating Britishness, and the press and style magazines began to talk of 'Cool Britannia'.

There was also a political dimension which contributed to the changing mood of the country. Thatcherism was still deeply unpopular, but now it seemed unlikely ever to return. The decline of John Major's Tory Party in a cloud of sleaze and incompetence had been spectacular, but at the same time the economy was slowly improving, and importantly, there was the emergence of a credible new opposition leader with Tony Blair. It seemed political consensus was re-emerging, as the Labour Party appeared to be in close touch with the mood of the country and a large swathe of political opinion, which demanded a return to honest government and a fairer, more caring society.

Britain's new-found cultural confidence came to be expressed across the arts. In pop, the new music seemed to offer a soundtrack for change by a new wave of bands mainly from London and Manchester. Developments in pop were accompanied by new trends in fashion, film and other popular arts. Fashion designers such as Paul Smith, Oswald Boateng, Wayne Hemingway, Alexander McQueen and Vivienne Westwood became household names, as smartly dressed men began stylishly to sport the best of British labels, often encouraged by newly launched men's magazines such as *Loaded*.

Other bands were inspired towards celebrations of the familiar, and soon afterwards groups such as Supergrass, Pulp, Menswear, the Verve and Radiohead, among others, helped to shape the sound of British pop, as a new wave of British music became popularly known as 'Britpop', even though most of the prominent bands were *English*, from either London or Manchester. The new bands were helped by small independent record labels which had proliferated in the counter-culture of the 1980s. But significantly, the attitude towards commercial success had changed. While it had once seemed to dilute or spoil the purity of the music, financial success now seemed achievable, and even desirable.

But critical opinion was divided. Some remarked that at its best, the music of the period sounded like all the greatest British rock music produced during the past 40 years, while others were less generous, criticising the 'nostalgic reworkings' of earlier bands as shameless imitations, and Britpop as a branch of the heritage industry. They also described it as conservative, insular, parochial, self-conscious and derived. However, the public loved it, and it became a musical soundtrack to the cultural and political renewal of the late 1990s, a time when the USA had ceased to be a significant influence, and Britain stood proud in splendid isolation musically, creatively and culturally.

As the new music became established and popular, many new bands entered the scene, but their music had become more formulaic and familiar, and began to decline in popularity with the public. Some bands continued to evolve, for example the music of the Verve, the Manic Street Preachers, Prodigy and Radiohead, and as disillusionment spread with New Labour, their music grew darker, more introspective and less celebratory.

By the mid-1990s the kind of music people listened to had ceased to give an indication about their politics and outlook, and the role of popular music was reduced to a conveyor of light entertainment. It also became even more competitive and commercial, symbolised by the 'production' of the Spice Girls, an all-female singing quintet. 'Scary', 'Sporty', 'Baby', 'Posh' and 'Ginger' were selected after mass auditions to create a group popular with children aged 8–12. Their first album *Spice* sold 16 million copies, and from 1996 they had two-and-a-half years of success not matched since the Beatles. Some said they proposed a new ethos of equality with sexuality, or 'girl power'. Many others believed their success was not built on substance or ability and predicted a swift decline in their fortunes, although they made four albums until 2001, before embarking on solo projects with varying degrees of success.

The success of the Spice Girls encouraged promoters to try similar experiments. A new TV series *Popstars* was launched, in which singers were auditioned, and later formed the band Hear'say. Their eponymous album was released five months later and sold 250,000 copies, becoming the fastest selling British debut album ever. It was fame at the speed of light, and several more groups appeared, such as Backstreet Boys, Boyzone, A1 and NSync, all created with the intention of making them commercially attractive to teenage girls. However, their decline was equally rapid, and many broke up soon afterwards.

Access all eras

Manufactured bands were nothing new. In America of the mid-1960s the Monkees had been created by pop promoters to imitate the Beatles and appeal to young audiences, but the latest generation were commercially successful for a much shorter period. One exception was the growth in tribute bands, created as facsimiles of earlier groups. In the new millennium almost every major group from the 1960s and 1970s had been revived, for example by the Bootleg Beatles (the Beatles), Bjorn Again (Abba) and the Counterfeit Stones (Rolling Stones), whose nostalgic popularity, especially with student audiences, seems likely to continue.

But there was still evolution and innovation in the ethnically mixed club scene, which continued to make records grounded in Britain's ethnic diversity. In this fertile ground, new genres of music such as hard-core, jungle, drum 'n' bass and garage appeared, with their characteristic quick, light beats, deep, plunging basslines and melodic vocals sung in a modern soul style, for example by Craig David and Wookie.

Britain was becoming the creative hub of a worldwide market for a diverse range of music from the Asian underground, which typically mixed samples of Indian classical music and 'Bollywood' films with breakbeat, dance music, jazz and electronica. Talvin Singh, Nitin Sawhney and Asian Dub Foundation were among some of its most highly regarded exponents. Drum 'n' bass beats, swirling guitars, and Bollywood samples could be heard on ADB's *Community Music* (2000), while Sawhney's *Prophesy* (2001) featured Euro-Arabic singing, string sections from London and Madras, flamenco guitars, drum 'n' bass beats, and Indian chanting by the London Community Gospel Choir.

Meanwhile, long-established musicians such as Elton John, David Bowie, Sting, Paul McCartney and the Rolling Stones were all writing and performing new material around the world, and winning awards for their contribution to, and influence on music. Among the newer acts, Robbie Williams's achievements in successive Brit Awards have made him one of the most popular and honoured British singers for many years, while teenage jazz singers Jamie Cullum, Natasha Beddingfield and Joss Stone also enjoyed a sudden surge of popularity.

Britain continues to be a leader in pop and rock music, and its fragmented, diverse and highly commercial nature reflects the current state of the arts and indeed of society, where the most innovative and inspiring work is frequently the product of a creative fusion among British, Asian and Afro-Caribbean influences.

Discussion topics and activities

1   Which performers and movements do you consider the most interesting in British pop since the 1960s, and why?

2   Research online to find out about: Teds/mods/skinheads/hippies/punks/raves/subcultures and their respective tastes in music and style.

3   What differences do you notice between popular music in your country and British pop? Why do you think these differences exist?

4   Taking several well-known figures in pop music in your country, discuss who listens to them, what sort of audiences they are popular with and the reasons for their fame.

5   'Rhythm crazed teenagers terrorised a city last night.' This was an authentic newspaper headline following a rock 'n' roll concert. Imagine you were in the audience. Write an article describing the experience either for a traditional right-wing newspaper which does not approve, or for a lively music magazine with an enthusiastic young readership.

6   Choose a record with which you are familiar. Write a review of it for a music magazine read by teenagers.

7   Does your town/region have its own musical identity? What kind of music do people listen to? What do people traditionally sing about/write songs about? What are the origins of the music?

8   Could music without lyrics ever be considered political?

Suggested further reading

Books

Barnes, R. (1979) *Mods!* London: Eel Pie.

Burchill, J. (1978) *The Boy Looked at Johnny: The Obituary of Rock 'n' Roll*, London: Pluto.

Chambers, I. (1985) *Urban Rhythms*, London: Macmillan.

Chapman, R. (1991) *Selling the Sixties: The Pirates and Pop Music Radio*, London: Routledge.

Clarke, D. (1995) *The Rise and Fall of Popular Music*, Harmondsworth: Penguin.

Coon, C. (1982) *The New Wave Punk Rock Explosion*, London: Omnibus.

Dewe, M. (1998) *The Skiffle Craze*, London: Planet.

Gambaccini, P., Rice, T. and Rice, J. (1994) *The Guinness Book of British Hit Albums*, 6th edn, Enfield: Guinness Publishing.

Garratt, S. (1998) *Adventures in Wonderland: A Decade of Club Culture*, London: Headline.

Harris, J. (2003) *The Last Party: Britpop, Blair and the Demise of English Rock*, London: Fourth Estate.

Hebdige, D. (1979) *Subculture: The Meaning of Style*, London: Methuen.

Jasper, T. (1991) *The Top Twenty Book*, London: Blandford Press.

Knight, N. (1982) *Skinhead*, London: Omnibus.

Kureishi, H. and Savage, J. (1995) *The Faber Book of Pop*, London: Faber & Faber.

MacRobbie, A. (ed.) (1989) *Zoot Suits and Second Hand Dresses*, London: Macmillan.

Polhemus, T. (1994) *Streetstyle*, London: Thames & Hudson.

Savage, J. (1991) *England's Dreaming*, London: Faber & Faber.

Savage, J. (1996) *Time Travel*, London: Chatto & Windus.

Stuart, J. (1987) *Rockers!* London: Plexus.

Yorke, P. (1980) *Style Wars*, London: Sidgewick & Jackson.

Encyclopaedias of different popular musical genres – e.g. rock, reggae etc. – are also available from Virgin Books.

Journals

The weekly music press, in particular the *New Musical Express* (NME), provide a valuable source of information and commentary on the changing music scene, record reviews, concerts, interviews and so on. Their advertising sections also give interesting details about fashions of the period. Press archives can usually be consulted with prior appointment.

Recordings

The National Sound Archive of the British Library in London holds most British musical recordings, and has facilities for their inspection.

Note

1 *Daily Mail* 20 November 1996: 28.

9

Sport

Introduction

Sport is part of mass culture, and an estimated 3 million people take part in some sort of sporting activity every week, with walking (including rambling and hiking), swimming, snooker, pool, billiards, keep-fit, yoga, cycling, football and angling among the most popular. Watching sport, listening to it and reading about it are also major leisure time activities and important areas of economic activity in which over 400,000 people are currently employed. Live broadcasts and recorded highlights can be seen on most of the terrestrial television channels, while BBC Radio Five Live and other stations bring commentary and comment on events around the world.

For many spectators sport is not just leisure – it is a way of expressing personal and group identity, through supporting a team, chanting the club songs, wearing club colours and clothing, as well as bearing tattoos, face paint, flags and other adornments. Habitual attendance and taking part in its rituals provide many fans with a sense of community, with the most fanatical choosing to get married in their club's ground, and even to have their ashes scattered there.

Although most sports are played in urban centres, many also take place in the countryside, where until the late twentieth century the field sports of fox-hunting, shooting and fishing dominated. However, it has now become an area for more popular, organised recreation with activities such as mountain biking, hiking, running, mountaineering and off-road motor events. These are most popular not with wealthy country dwellers, but with an urban population that makes frequent trips out of the city to a cleaner, safer, more natural environment. It has sometimes led to conflict between rural landowners and urban dwellers over rights of access, as well as arguments over the need to develop the countryside as a leisure and sporting amenity, and exactly where, how and for whom this should be done.

Throughout the nineteenth and into the twentieth century most sports were played by narrowly defined social groups. Horse racing and fox-hunting, for example, were the preserve of aristocrats and wealthy landowners, while the origins of football and rugby lie in the English public schools such as Eton, Harrow and Rugby, where masters and alumni wrote the rules and took responsibility for the games' organisation and development. Outside this narrow social sphere, the masses in town and country enjoyed sports such as boxing and dog and pigeon racing, which were widely practised around Britain.

But the latter half of the twentieth century saw a greater openness and democratisation in British society, and many sports were transformed from the narrow preserve of affluent white males into a mass leisure and entertainment industry for urban consumers. Accordingly, women began taking part not only in most sports, but also in their administration, journalism, promotion and so on. Rates of participation among black and Asian sportspeople have also risen sharply, particularly in football, athletics and boxing. There is also more opportunity for disabled people, who now play a far more active and equal role in sport. As a consequence, there is now less elitism and snobbery over who plays what, where and how, which has allowed more people to practise freely sports that were once closed to them.

The cost of running a professional club in almost any sport is extremely expensive, but advertising, sponsorship and the sale of broadcasting rights to satellite media, such as Sky, have brought much-needed finance, investment and prize money. Television coverage has also helped to revive many declining sports, such as snooker and darts. However, critics argue that professional sport's transformation into a branch of the entertainment industry has brought many disadvantages. They argue that it has become too expensive: supporters are now treated as customers, whose loyalty is exploited and needs ignored. Moreover, media coverage influences whom spectators support, and how and where they spend their money. The result is that sport has been largely removed from its roots, and in the case of football and rugby, what was once an expression of a local identity has become a commercial 'good' for marketing, purchase and sale, just like any other.

Origins

Arguments over the origin of sport frequently relate it to an instinctive need to play. One of the functions of play in children is to improve co-ordination between the hand and eye, skills once necessary for fighting opponents and hunting prey, and it is generally agreed that physical games provide an outlet for these instincts. However, when human beings began living in small communities, keeping animals and cultivating crops, hunting and fighting were no longer necessary, and instead became recreational. Later, when people lived in towns and cities, the excitement of hunting was vicariously recreated for spectators with crude contests involving animals against animals, and animals against humans, which were organised for mass spectacle in large stadiums or arenas (in Latin, '*arena*' = 'sand').

A similar pattern of development took place in many countries. In Britain, bear baiting, cock-fighting and bull running were common; the latter was practised as recently as 1825 in Birmingham (the site is now 'the Bullring' shopping centre). But the games were dangerous – injuries and even death were common, and many people began to see them as cruel and old-fashioned. Ball games gradually became more popular, with rules and referees to control the action and avoid injury.

Country sports such as horse racing, hunting and shooting first became organised activities in the eighteenth century. At that time, many English landowners forced their tenants out of the countryside to create space for sheep farming. Wool was a highly profitable commodity and was used mainly for clothing, especially in uniforms for officials in Britain and the expanding British Empire. The poor and landless left their rural communities and sought work in the expanding industrial centres, often in textile factories. Meanwhile, the open spaces of the depopulated countryside became a place of pleasure for a privileged, leisured class, a 'country club' for the growing British establishment of landowners, government members, civil servants and other wealthy professionals.

The remaining country folk with no land and little money raced dogs and birds. In the mining villages of the north and Midlands there was a strong tradition of sports such as dog racing with greyhounds and whippets, hare coursing, pigeon racing and fishing. Many of these sports are still practised in parts of rural England today. In many country areas there was also a tradition of primitive activities involving throwing, chasing and animal baiting, but most disappeared in the nineteenth century. There was also a primitive form of football, which had been practised for many centuries in the countryside, in which vast crowds of drunken young men from neighbouring villages would fight each other for the ball, in a scene resembling a riot. A re-enactment of such an event takes place near Ashbourne in Derbyshire on Shrove Tuesday each year. There are few rules, but the most important is that participants 'may not commit manslaughter or murder'!

Some bloodsports are still practised in the countryside, but a huge majority now believe them to be cruel, unnecessary and outdated. There is a widespread anger and disgust at them, which has become a distinguishing feature of British life. Fox-hunting is the most controversial, in which huntsmen and women dress in the traditional eighteenth-century hunting clothes, and ride with dogs, often killing the fox after a long chase. The event has frequently been represented in popular artworks of the 'traditional' English countryside, which often hang in rural pubs and houses. But in recent years there have been many protests by the Hunt Saboteurs Association and others, who obstruct the hunters and sabotage the hunt. In 2004 after much public pressure, fox-hunting was banned by the government. Although it remains legal in parts of Northern Ireland, much of the countryside is unsuitable and the sport is rarely practised.

Horse racing has its origins in hunting. It is well established in Britain, with 59 courses, and some 12,000 horses currently in training. There are two main forms: flat racing in which the horses race around a flat course, and National Hunt racing in which horses jump over fences. The latter is also known as a 'steeplechase'. It originated in the eighteenth century, when wealthy aristocrats and landowners raced their horses around the countryside. Riders jumped over hedges, walls and ditches in preparation for hunting trips, navigating the area using the pointed steeples of village churches as landmarks.

The flat racing season is held during the drier weather from March to early November, while National Hunt races take place throughout the year. Some of the most popular events are the Derby, held at Epsom near London, a flat race named after the Earl of Derby who first organised the event in 1780. Royal Ascot, held near Windsor in June, lasts four days, and is traditionally attended by extravagantly dressed spectators, while the English Grand National is the best-known steeplechase in the world. This is largely due to its length, its difficult and dangerous fences, its history and its unpredictability. It has been held every spring since 1839 at Aintree near Liverpool.

Gentlemen and players

The development of organised sport in Britain cannot be separated from the social context in which it emerged. Thus, many team sports have their origins in the mid-nineteenth century, a period when there was increasing official concern over public health. The uncontrolled, unplanned expansion of British cities had created smog, disease and illness. Many of the wealthy had noticed the benefits of the sea air and bathing, and bought second and retirement homes in coastal towns such as Brighton, Blackpool and Bournemouth. Inland, spa towns such as Bath, Cheltenham and Leamington developed as health resorts where the affluent could enjoy clean air and warm spring waters surrounded by elegant, white Regency terraces and mansions. For the poorer classes, public parks were built in the larger cities, based on the original example of Victoria Park in east London, while in the countryside hill walking and mountaineering became popular with academics and intellectuals who appreciated the benefits of fresh air, exercise, nature and simplicity in remote and romantic natural beauty.

208

The fashion for exercise set by the rich and leisured began to affect the curriculum of leading public schools such as Eton, Harrow and Rugby. Masters believed that a healthy body created a healthy mind, and this was central to their mission of instilling discipline and building character in a new cadre of future officials for industry, government and Empire. To achieve their aims, they set about creating games with clearly defined sets of rules. At first, each school had its own, for example 'rugby football' (as rugby is formally known) referred to the game of football played according to the rules of Rugby School in Warwickshire. Similarly, the game of badminton took its name from the Duke of Beaufort's country home Badminton House, where the sport was first played in the nineteenth century. However, the different codes caused confusion when schools wanted to play each other, but this changed in 1863 when teams of former students or 'old boys' from the football-playing public schools met in London to agree a set of common rules. They wanted the game to be played more widely, and founded the Football Association (FA) to regulate the sport in England. To distinguish it from other forms of football and rugby, the game was nicknamed 'soccer' (abbreviated from 'association'). In 1871 the FA Cup was introduced, a knock-out competition for 15 teams. Today, over 600 amateur and professional teams compete for the trophy, the most historic football tournament in the world.

The early sportsmen were amateurs who did not want or need to play for money. For 'gentlemen', the truly sporting aim was not simply to beat the opponent, but to play the game as well as they could, displaying effortless style and superiority. Hard training was bad form; sweat wasn't necessary to achieve a moral victory, and there was no set list of fixtures. This was the 'Corinthian spirit', named after the Corinthian Casuals, a team formed in 1882 by England's best public school footballers for occasional matches against continental sides.

A similar pattern of development was followed in other sports, with rules made by elite bodies and games organised between private clubs which often had connections with public schools. Racing had the Jockey Club; cricket the Marylebone Cricket Club; golfers formed the Royal and Ancient Club at St Andrews. But the new games were also popular with the general public, and spectators would pay to see a good standard. Consequently, there were opportunities for the best sportsmen to play for money, and in 1884–85 a competitive football league with professional players began, the same league which continues in England today.

Meanwhile, in the Victorian cities official concern grew about social disorganisation. Drinking and fighting were widespread, especially among Irish immigrants, such as the notorious Hooligan family, whose behaviour added a new word to the language in the 1890s. Bare-knuckle boxing (without gloves) was illegal but frequent, especially on Boxing Day, 26 December, when open-air prize fights were held around the country. In an attempt to limit disorder, the middle-class authorities interfered in the lives of the urban poor, abolishing cock-fighting, bull running and other amusements. They hoped that with the opportunities to play and watch organised sports, aggression would be channelled, and the masses would be distracted from riotous behaviour, which, it was feared, could even lead to a proletarian uprising, as it had done earlier in France.

Sectarian rivalry

In the late nineteenth century the popularity of football, rugby and cricket rapidly spread across the industrialised urban areas, and by 1880 the city of Birmingham alone could boast 214 football teams. People felt close to their local clubs which were based around the neighbourhood pitch or stadium, some of which seemed to grow organically from row upon row of small terraced houses. Here were the new twentieth-century theatres for the working man. They held a sense of excitement, and were a focal point for local pride, tribal loyalty and identity,

The football team became a focal point for community solidarity, particularly for dislocated economic migrants from the poor rural areas of Ireland and England. Scotland had become the new home for thousands of Irish who migrated there following the potato famine of the mid-nineteenth century, and who by 1900 numbered around 250,000. The majority were from Northern Ireland, and the deeply rooted political and religious divisions between Catholics and Protestants, which had developed as a consequence of British rule there, came to be expressed in Scottish football. Glasgow Celtic was founded in the late nineteenth century by an Irish Catholic priest, and over the years the club has maintained its links with the Irish Republic, which is predominantly Catholic. In contrast, Protestant Irish immigrants in Glasgow adopted Rangers as their team, but still maintained their loyalties to Ulster (Northern Ireland) and the British crown. These often complex divisions were also expressed at many other clubs, but throughout the twentieth century they gradually disappeared. However, at Rangers they endured, and the club did not sign Catholic players until 1989 when manager Graham Souness brought in Maurice Johnston, a Catholic, amid great controversy and protest from most of their supporters.

Today, an intense rivalry still exists between Celtic and Rangers, and Glasgow 'derbies' always resemble a passionate international battle. Celtic loyalties are often demonstrated through the bearing of the Irish 'tricolour' flag, and while Rangers fans sport the flag of Ulster, depicting a red hand in the centre. Violent clashes are common, but such rivalry is not confined to Glasgow. In Northern Ireland too, similar tensions still persist between clubs which have strong sectarian traditions; for example it was not until 2005 that Derry City (Catholic) and Linfield (Protestant) agreed to play each other in a fixture which had been suspended since the 'troubles' of the 1970s.

210

In England, sectarian divisions disappeared many years ago, and never became a prominent feature of English football, and in the nineteenth century some teams took the name 'United', to show they represented the whole of the city, including professionals and amateurs, Catholics and Protestants. Other clubs took names such as 'Rovers', 'Rangers' or 'Wanderers'. In Victorian England, the freedom to rove and wander meant freedom from the clock, factory and field, which conferred on them a liberated, bohemian, exciting character.

Organised games helped promote a sense of solidarity, shared aims and respect for the law. Abroad in the countries of the British Empire, sport was used to similar effect and British officials played together with natives in games organised by the ruling class. Consequently, cricket, rugby and polo became well established overseas, for example in Australia, New Zealand, South Africa, India and Pakistan. The Empire Games were later organised for member countries (later becoming the Commonwealth Games), as well as overseas 'test' matches by the England cricket team, and rugby tours by all the home nations, all in an attempt to unite diverse peoples and colonies throughout the Empire.

Sport and the home nations

Sport was also used to help to unite the home countries of England, Northern Ireland, Scotland and Wales, but it has also fostered independent identities through the creation of separate national leagues and governing bodies. The differences can be seen clearly at international matches, with colourful displays of flags, tattoos, face painting, clothing, songs and rituals. England fans traditionally waved the red, white and blue of the 'Union Jack' – the flag of the Union between England, Northern Ireland, Scotland and Wales. However, as the UK has been restructured through devolution in the 1990s, the flags of the home countries have gradually been adopted by many fans. England's supporters now usually carry the flag of St George (a red cross on a white background), while Scottish fans bear St Andrew's cross (two diagonal white stripes on a blue background, also known as 'the Saltire'). Welsh flags carry a red dragon on a field of white and green. This dates from the fifteenth century and is widely used throughout the Principality. In Northern Ireland there are several different flags, and supporters carry the one which most closely reflects their political loyalties, for example to the Irish Nationalists, to the Ulster Loyalists or to other sectarian groups. To avoid creating further tension among the community, there has been no official decision on which flag should be flown but many fans carry the flag of St Patrick (two diagonal red stripes on a white background).

National identity is also reflected in music. In the UK the national anthem is *God Save the Queen*, which originated in 1745, and was played at sporting occasions involving all the home countries until the 1990s.

Figure 9.1 Soccer players during the World Cup Final, 30 July 1966

However, with the gradual trend towards devolution, other more representative hymns are now played and sung at national events outside England. For example, at football and rugby games in Scotland, the preferred tune is *Flower of Scotland*, a song written in the 1960s by Roy Williamson of the Scottish folk band the Corries. It celebrates the defeat of the English at the Battle of Bannockburn in 1314 in Scotland. In Wales, the preferred anthem is *Land of My Fathers*, an elegy to Wales written in the nineteenth century. In Northern Ireland *A Londonderry Air* is sung, a traditional Irish folk song of the 1850s, which in 1913 was given different words and gained sudden popularity as the tune *Danny Boy*. As with the flags, to avoid upsetting local sentiments the decision about which anthem to play at an event is generally left to the relevant local authorities.

Community singing and military bands were a traditional part of the pre-match entertainment at football games, but are now rare, with the exception of *Abide with Me*, a slow, mournful hymn about the approach of death, which has been sung at every English FA Cup Final since 1927. But at most games today the crowd can often be heard chanting and singing to encourage their team, as well as to insult and demoralise the opposition. Traditional club songs are often based on folk music, especially in Scotland where Protestant tunes are often sung by Rangers fans in derby matches with Celtic. But well-known pop songs with altered lyrics are often preferred, and were common in the 1970s when huge crowds of spectators, for example at Old Trafford, Anfield, Ibrox and Celtic Park, would sing and shout their team to victory, effectively acting as a 'twelfth man'.

Despite the mass popularity of major sports such as football, smaller, traditional sports and games are still practised in remote areas of Britain. In Scotland the Highland Games are held every year, and include events such as running, cycling and dancing. The games have a long history, and first began in Celtic times when clans gathered and held competitions to find the fastest runners and strongest men, who would be chosen by the clan leaders as messengers and bodyguards. But the event was largely un-noticed outside Scotland until 1866 when Queen Victoria began to attend in order to encourage closer ties with Scotland. That year, the small, traditional summer athletics event at Braemar was transformed into the Royal Highland Gathering. It opened with marching, kilted clansmen, accompanied by pipers playing the bagpipes, in a cultural and sporting event which some critics consider to have been a political 'show' contrived to please an English as well as an Anglicised Scottish aristocracy.

Today, the games in the north-east are based around athletics events, while the Highlands and Islands in the west of Scotland are better known for musical events featuring pipes. But visitors to the Highland Games at Braemar can usually see a varied programme of highland dancing and contests for players of the bagpipes, as well as 'heavyweight' contests such as 'throwing the hammer' – flinging an iron ball and chain as far as possible – and 'tossing the caber' – tossing a long wooden pole similar to a tree trunk – and 'putting the shot' – throwing a heavy metal ball. Shinty, a game similar to hockey, is also played in the Highlands by enthusiastic teams of male players.

But the traditional events and dress style, such as kilts and clan tartans, have had little or no impact in Scotland's big industrial conurbations, and remain virtually unknown. Similarly the games of rugby and cricket tend to be confined to the prestigious public schools, and are rarely played elsewhere. In contrast, golf is a game which originated in Scotland and has since travelled the world. Since 1897 the rules have been administered worldwide by the Royal and Ancient Golf Club, situated near St Andrews. But the sport which most people watch and play is football. Hampden Park in Glasgow was the first national stadium in Britain, and opened in 1893. Its massive capacity of 150,000 and the 'Hampden Roar' of the passionate Scottish fans in full cry was said to be unique. Matches with England have always been fast, furious affairs but ceased in 1989, officially because of the pressure of international features but also because of violence on and off the field.

Like Scotland, Northern Ireland retains a distinct sporting identity. The Gaelic games are a central part, and are widely played. They include Gaelic football, handball, hurling, camogie (women's hurling) and rounders, but are very different to the varieties played on the British mainland. Their popularity is illustrated by the fact that there are over 700 clubs in Northern Ireland affiliated to the Gaelic Athletics Association (GAA) and the Camogie Council, the official governing bodies. Rugby is also played, but as in Scotland it tends to be centred around public schools. Its ruling body is all-Irish, as it is for boxing, and recognises players on both sides of the border.

Many of the different sports played in Northern Ireland are played along sectarian lines, with the Gaelic games being played mainly among the Catholic population, and rugby by the Protestant community. In the past there has been strong resistance to the sports played by the English; for example in the nineteenth century many in the Catholic community refused to play English sports. Members of the Royal Ulster Constabulary or the British Army were seen as part of an occupying force, and could not join the GAA, and in the past at times of internal tension games were suspended amid fears of violence between teams composed mainly of Protestants or Catholics.

Although rugby is not widely played in Northern Ireland, in Wales it is popular with people from all social and religious backgrounds, and over the years it has become a major cultural force, one closely linked with national identity. In the 1970s Wales was recognised as a world-beating rugby team, but since then changes in the school system have led to a reduction in the number of young players who go on to play in the major clubs, and consequently there are fewer players to replace those retiring. Moreover, many good players leave Wales to earn big salaries at the top professional teams in Australia, New Zealand and South Africa. To prevent this, in 1995 the amateur game of rugby union became a professional one. Costs escalated, and some clubs disappeared, while others were forced to move and play elsewhere. But in general, the standards of play and facilities have improved, and the publicity generated by tournaments such as the Rugby World Cup and the Six Nations Championship have helped make rugby popular with spectators not only in Wales but in all the home countries.

Thus, England, Ireland, Scotland and Wales not only have their own distinctive sports, but also have independent associations which were originally founded to respect political, national and religious sensitivities. For historical and cultural reasons they have remained separate, and this is occasionally problematic, for example in Olympic football a British team has not competed since 1972. This is because the four countries of the United Kingdom wish to maintain separate national teams, and under Olympic rules only one team can compete. On the other hand, in some sports there are teams which represent not only the whole of the UK, but sometimes more. For example, the British Lions rugby union team is composed of players from the United Kingdom and Ireland brought together to play against the strong southern hemisphere teams of New

Zealand and South Africa. Similarly, the Barbarians are also a mixed team of rugby players from Britain, France and the Commonwealth countries. And in golf, the Ryder Cup team, which plays against the USA, used to be British but is now European. The main problem with such combined teams is that they do not offer a platform for the expression of national sentiment or identity, and consequently there is little spectator interest or demand for them. This may be one reason why British Olympic teams are not given funding and facilities equal to those of Russia, China and America, whose teams are followed keenly, and whose performance and victories are important symbols of national prestige.

Sport, leisure and government

National prestige is linked to sporting achievement in many countries, and governments frequently invest large sums of money to improve national facilities, standards and performance on the international stage. However, until the late 1950s the British government was not interested in promoting sport as the financial cost of the war years had left the country with other priorities. It was considered an area of private life with which the authorities had little concern. Local government provided swimming pools, parks and playing fields, but there was little effort made to encourage their use.

However, in the late 1950s and coinciding with a rise in crime and general anxiety about the nation's youth, attitudes began to change, and the government began using sport to promote social harmony, self-discipline, self-reliance, mixing across the classes, and indirectly to reduce crime rates. Two important enquiries, the Albermarle Report and the Wolfenden Report, were both published in 1960. The former emphasised the important role played by sport in the community, while Wolfenden examined how government bodies could act together to promote sport around Britain. One result was the Sports Council, set up in 1966 to select where money should be spent. It was a significant moment, as it was the first time the government had allocated funds specifically for the development of British sport!

The recognition of the social role of sport led to an improvement in facilities, and compared with 27 sports centres in 1972, there were 770 by 1981, with many boasting new materials, all-weather surfaces, floodlights and running tracks. By the 1970s many state secondary schools were also offering a range of team sports which usually included football, rugby, cricket and athletics, as well as a range of outdoor pursuits, such as hiking, rock-climbing, caving and pot-holing, and rivalled the private sector in terms of facilities and opportunities. The 1980s saw another period of expansion, mainly in response to a growing number of unemployed with free time and little money. Rather than indirectly affecting crime rates, which had motivated the promotion of sport in the 1950s, it was now seen as a genuine deterrent to large-scale social disorder. For example, in Belfast, 14 centres were built, rather than the 8 warranted by its population size.

In 1997 the new Labour government set up the Department of Culture, Media and Sport which works to promote and co-ordinate sport at all levels in the home nations. However, despite the efforts to promote sport among all sections of the community since the 1950s, those who participate belong usually to the more active and affluent sections of the community – most are male, aged 25–40, skilled and professional – while the 15–18 year olds, whom the government tries hard to target, are the most resistant – in 1999 the organisation Sport England found that only 21 per cent of 15–18 year olds had two or more hours of physical education (PE) a week.

Declining participation in sport has contributed to increasing concerns over declining public health and obesity. In earlier times, being obese was a symbol of wealth, but in the Britain of the new millennium it was most prevalent among the poorest socio-economic groups. There are several reasons why obesity has increased, beginning with reduced opportunities to cultivate the habit of playing sports when young. This began in the 1980s when many secondary schools sold their sports fields to provide extra cash to compensate for smaller education budgets given by the Tory governments of that era. Moreover, in the 1990s a new national curriculum for schools was introduced which did not give priority to sport, and a generation of young people who had been unaccustomed to taking exercise became a generation of adults seduced by home entertainments and computer screens, who also had a tendency to drive (or be driven) more and walk less. People were also eating more instant meals than 25 years previously, which contained more fat and sugar to provide 'taste', and further contributed to obesity. To reduce the future burden on the national health, the government began campaigning to alert the public to the risks of smoking, the need to avoid 'junk' food, to eat a balanced diet, and to take regular exercise. The results remain to be seen.

Gender issues in sport

Women's participation in sport has its origins in the nineteenth-century public schools. Just as boys' schools introduced organised games, newly established girls' schools encouraged their students to practise sports. Sporting ability was encouraged in public schools as it was seen as a desirable social attribute, which in the future would help girls to mix in the circles frequented by boys from a similar social background. When the elite Roedean School near Brighton opened in 1885, girls were encouraged to practise athletics, swimming, gymnastics, hockey and tennis – all games which were becoming fashionable among upper-class young men and women. However, a strict dress code was enforced, as arms, legs, ankles and throats had to be covered up, especially at major public events such as Wimbledon, where the first women's singles tennis champion was Miss Maud Watson in 1884.

Sports were not practised by women outside the wealthy and educated social classes until after the First World War. While men were serving overseas, many traditional male occupations in factories, mills and workshops were taken up by women. After the war, equality in the workplace created demands for equality in society, and while more wealthy, educated women were playing individual sports such as tennis, the less privileged played football.

In 1921 there were 150 women's teams playing regular matches in front of thousands of spectators. But the spectacles were not popular with traditional, male-dominated bodies such as the Football Association, which banned women's football from being played on grounds affiliated to the FA until 1971. Other energetic sports such as cycling, riding, rowing and shooting were also discouraged as they were said to demand 'indecorous posture'. And although tennis, golf, badminton and croquet were seen as more acceptable, the dress code was another obstacle, and persisted until the 1930s when trousers became fashionable for women, especially in golf. Consequently, from the 1920s until the 1970s women's participation in sports clubs was largely limited to roles as helpers and assistants for social events. There were some exceptions, which saw, for example, Mary Rand's success in the 1964 Olympic Games, and Ann Jones and Virginia Wade in women's tennis of the 1960s and 1970s, but the majority of female athletes were from a narrow social background, being white, middle-class graduates from university athletics clubs.

In the 1970s women's sport became less exclusive. Freedoms won by women, such as the introduction of the Equal Opportunities Act, the contraceptive pill and the trend towards smaller families, plus greater expectations of personal fulfilment, all contributed to increased leisure time. The construction of more municipal sports centres also provided further opportunities, and it was no longer necessary to apply for membership to an expensive, elitist club. In the 1980s women's participation further increased when exercise became fashionable. Fitness became linked with beauty and fame, and sport linked with dance. Public figures, pop stars and role models such as Princess Diana and Madonna led by example, while gyms and health clubs opened around the country to meet demand.

By the 1980s women were taking up employment in most areas of the economy, including newly developing areas of broadcast journalism and sports administration. In the 1990s women began producing sports programmes for radio and television, and the numbers of female sports writers, commentators and presenters increased. The popular football magazine *Four-Four-Two* was founded by Karen Buchanan, while the current managing director of Birmingham City Football Club is Karen Brady, and the well-known TV chef and broadcaster Delia Smith is a director of Norwich City. Influenced by the competitive spirit of the times, sport became a fashionable lifestyle for everyone, and sports clothes such as tracksuits and running shoes were worn by almost all young people, even among those whose idea of sport was a walk to the local chip shop.

Today, women participate at most levels in most sports, particularly in hockey, athletics, netball and tennis. Golf is also popular: there are approximately 100,000 female members of golf clubs in England. However, in many private clubs there is not full equality, as women are restricted to a 'ladies' section'. Women's football has also increased rapidly in popularity, and in 2001 there were around 4,500 clubs. Higher levels of participation are partly due to organisations such as the Women's Sport Foundation which promotes opportunities for women and girls in playing, coaching, managing and administering sport, and works together with the body Sport England.

Despite growing equality of access, general levels of participation remain low: today only one in ten women takes part in sport on a competitive basis, while three in ten men do the same. According to research carried out by the Women's Sport Foundation in 2004, by the age of 18 most women have dropped out of sport altogether. This appears to be because women have less free time due to the demands of work and family. Moreover, those in employment generally earn less money than men. Therefore, less competitive exercise forms are more common, such as cycling and swimming, and were practised by 15 per cent of adult women in 1990s. But keep-fit and yoga are also popular, and weight control is an important incentive for seven in ten women who exercise.

Sport and athleticism have become fashionable not only in the mainstream but also in gay subculture. But despite growing equality and acceptance of gay couples, very few gay sportspeople publicly declare their sexuality. Players fear abuse, ostracism and violence, as the attitude of sportsmen to gay team members is generally homophobic, and that of crowds hostile. A few gay teams do exist at amateur level, including the Kings Cross Steelers, a rugby union club based in London.

Sport and ethnicity

Just as women had to overcome prejudice and prohibitions on their participation, the children of post-war immigrants had to overcome racial prejudice in order to succeed in sports such as cricket, football and athletics. Until recently, black sportsmen were extremely rare in British sport. A notable, early example was in 1881 when the footballer Arthur Watson played for the Glasgow team Queens Park and also captained Scotland, before being invited to play for the leading English team Corinthian Casuals.

Black sportsmen have always been more numerous in boxing. Participation began when slaves were brought from America and other parts of the Empire in the late eighteenth century. Bill Richmond, Tom Molyneaux, Peter Jackson and Andrew Jeptha were well-known prize-fighters, with Jeptha being the first black boxer to hold a British title in 1907. Until 1948 non-white boxers could box, but were not allowed by the British Board of Boxing Control to compete for titles. However, when the ban was lifted black boxers began to compete successfully, most notably Dick Turpin, who the same year won the British Middleweight title. In 1950 his younger brother Randolph won the British and European Middleweight titles, and a year later became World Middleweight Champion, defeating the great American boxer Sugar Ray Robinson. Turpin had made his people proud, and he returned home to a hero's welcome in the genteel town of Leamington Spa, where thousands of cheering fans filled the streets.

Turpin's example was followed by many others in athletics, such as MacDonald Bailey and Arthur Wint from the British Caribbean. There were cricketers too, such as Learie Constantine from Trinidad, who played for Lancashire between the two world wars. But prejudice against black players was already present, and together with the Trinidadian writer C.L.R. James, Constantine wrote *Colour Bar* (1954), about racism in Britain, a theme which motivated James to explore further the interaction between cricket and Trinidadian society in *Beyond a Boundary* (1963).

After the immigration of the 1950s and 1960s a new generation drawn mainly from the West Indies, Pakistan and India grew up in Britain, and from the late 1960s and early 1970s black players began to feature more prominently in English football, such as Albert Johanneson at Leeds and Clyde Best at West Ham. In 1972 Clive Sullivan captained the Great Britain Rugby League side to victory in the World Cup, and in 1978 Viv Anderson became the first black footballer to represent England. But it was not until ten years later that a British-born black player played cricket for England – David Lawrence.

Despite their outstanding sporting achievements, many had to cope with racist chanting and abuse by opposing fans, as well as criticism and prejudice about laziness and a lack of commitment from ill-informed coaches, media and the general public. Consequently, some clubs were less willing to sign black players. Moreover, for many years the football authorities, commentators and journalists ignored prejudice and racism, until the early 1990s when the government and football authorities began working to introduce anti-racist legislation and anti-racist education campaigns. The Football (Offences) Act (1991) made racist chanting at football matches illegal, while the Professional Footballers Association campaigns 'Let's Kick Racism out of Football' in 1993 and later 'Show Racism the Red Card' were organised with the support of the Football Supporters Association, most league clubs, players, the Commission for

219

Racial Equality, local authorities, and the police. As a result, the incidence of overt racism at football matches has declined dramatically since the early 1980s, and offenders are frequently prosecuted.

The number of black players has steadily increased in the English football league since the 1980s. In 1990 approximately 12 per cent of players were black, and today the figure is around 25 per cent. This indicates a positive development, as talented players are able to develop their abilities and gain the recognition they deserve. However, although there is a high percentage of black athletes in sports that are cheap and accessible in an urban environment, the percentage is much lower in sports such as tennis, swimming and golf. This may be because black athletes feel excluded from sports that have a predominantly middle-class and public school composition, but it may also be due to the cost of joining a club with good equipment and facilities, which are important for younger players to develop good habits. A similar situation exists in country sports of hunting, shooting, fishing, horse riding and racing, where participation by black and Asian sportsmen is almost unknown.

Moreover, despite their reputation as football players, there are few black managers, coaches or referees, and there are few black spectators: black and Asian fans made up just 1 per cent of crowds at the top Premiership games in 2003–04. To remedy this, a government advisory body, the Football Task Force, aims to encourage more black and Asian players into the game, more minority ethnic representations at senior administration level, and more minority ethnic spectators at football matches.

Similarly, participation of black and Asian women in sport is still rare, although in recent years black athletes from the inner cities have triumphed in numerous international competitions, such as Fatima Whitbread, Denise Lewis and Kelly Holmes.

Although black competitors are now well represented in most levels of professional sport, Asians tend to be more represented in football and cricket at a local, amateur level. Commentators suggest this may be more to do with cultural attitudes, such as strong work and education ethics, which mean sport is not seen as a good career option, and is less important for social mobility. The poor attitudes of some coaches, and is lack of role models in sports like soccer, are also seen as influential. In recent years black sportsmen have also moved into areas such as sports presenting, punditry and advertising, as with ex-players such as John Barnes, Ian Wright and Garth Crooks.

Sport and disability

Women and black sportspeople have struggled to establish themselves in sport since the 1960s, and a similar struggle has taken place among the disabled. However, attempts to provide facilities originated much earlier.

After the First World War many soldiers returned suffering from head injuries which impaired their sight and hearing. The British Deaf Sports Association was later formed, and began organising a World Games for the Deaf. In the late 1940s war again provided the impetus to develop sports for the disabled after many soldiers returned from the Second World War with spinal injuries. Car and motorbike accidents in the 1950s increased the number of sufferers, but specialised treatment was developed at a dedicated unit in Stoke Mandeville Hospital. There, Dr Ludwig Guttman saw the potential of sport to raise morale and improve health, and introduced games such as wheelchair polo, archery and netball.

The Stoke Mandeville Games became international and went to Rome in 1960, taking part in a special tournament after the Olympic Games. In 1984 Stoke Mandeville held its first marathon, and in 1988 the first full tournament for disabled sportsmen and women – the Paralympic Games – was held in Seoul. Today, the British Paralympic Association comprises 26 national governing bodies and disability sport organisations. It ratifies funds from the government, organises donations and fund-raising activities, and manages the Great Britain Paralympic Team. They have been supported by the state policy 'Sport for All' which since the 1970s has stressed greater inclusivity. Today agencies exist to promote the sporting needs of all kinds of disability, such as British Blind Sport, and the British Wheelchair Sports Foundation. Parallel organisations co-ordinate the development of sport in Scotland, Wales and Northern Ireland, such as football, cricket, rugby and cycling, and the organisation SportsAid currently raises funds to help young people and the disabled. There are currently around 120,000 disabled sportsmen and women, and their enthusiasm and influence led to their participation in the Commonwealth Games in Manchester in 2002, the first major sports event in the world to include an integrated programme of events for disabled people.

Sport, commerce and popular culture

Until the 1960s there was a belief that sport was something to which a financial value should not be attached. Amateurism was seen as a virtue, and there was a traditional belief that sportspeople should compete for medals and trophies, rather than for prize money and salaries. It was an aristocratic, elitist attitude which showed a dislike of commerce, an attitude that had characterised British sport since Victorian times. But in 1961 the maximum wage for footballers was abolished, and wages quickly increased. Rather than staying in their local community, footballers now began to move around the country in search of the best deals and the best clubs. It also encouraged more players to stay in the sport, and younger ones to take it up as a career.

The victory of England at Wembley in the 1966 World Cup Final helped football to become culturally central, and it quickly replaced cricket as the most important national sport. This was aided by the growth of the new industries of popular culture, especially with the televising of matches and the marketing of magazines, posters and souvenirs. Meanwhile, leading footballers came to be idolised like pop stars. Some began making pop records, while a few professional singers and entertainers moved into the board rooms, such as Elton John who became chairman of Watford, and Eric Morecambe who became a director at Luton.

In the 1950s and early 1960s the press used to respect the privacy of top sportsmen and women. However, the tabloid papers were becoming less deferential and more keen to compete with television, which contributed to the creation of a sports press hungry for lurid stories of sex and drugs. Moreover, almost every household had a television, which allowed sportsmen and women to enter almost every home in Britain, and television appearances attracted advertisers and sponsors. Media attention became more intense, fuelled by the massive salaries which some footballers were earning.

The idolising of players was first epitomised by the legendary Manchester United striker George Best. On the field Best was fast, flamboyant and abundantly talented. His playful manner and natural style helped to make him a popular hero. But off the field his playboy lifestyle was new to football, and fascinated a hungry, popular press, who attempted to report his every move. At the time, Best received the kind of public adulation normally reserved for pop stars such as Jagger, Lennon and McCartney, and by the early 1970s his career was in decline, damaged by excess and an inability to cope with an intrusive, sensationalist press.

Public interest grew more acute in the 1980s, with the expansion of satellite broadcasting, as companies like Sky created global audiences for sport. Consequently, top footballers, managers and other sportspeople now had to deal not only with the press, but with a 24-hour media interest, as well as press agents and lifestyle magazines such as *Hello!* and *OK!*. This contributed in the 1990s to the creation of what is often called a 'celebrity culture', currently epitomised by the 'show-business' world surrounding former Manchester United player David Beckham, who began appearing on the front pages of the tabloid press shortly after he began playing in United's first team. His good looks, his selection for England and his marriage to the former Spice Girl, Victoria Adams, created a storm of media interest. Beckham began appearing at fashion parades, society events, galas and openings, and their wedding pictures were sold for millions of pounds to the celebrity magazine *OK!*, while the arrival of their baby was one of the biggest media stories of the time. The couple became worldwide celebrities, and their every move has since been reported, analysed and commented upon, and the conventions of privacy which characterised media reports until the 1970s have now disappeared.

Media interest has brought much needed finance into football, but it has also had some serious consequences. The football and cricket seasons have almost disappeared, as year-round coverage is shown of tours and tournaments around the world. Some critics say that attendances at live games have fallen because there is too much sport on television. Moreover, a small number of clubs receive most of the coverage and are getting richer, and in turn force up player transfer costs and salaries, but the vast majority are getting poorer, and today there is serious concern about the declining popularity of the Premiership, with falling crowds, higher seat prices and the dominance of a few rich clubs. Pressure to be successful has also led to some competitors attempting to gain unfair advantage through taking drugs, and therefore the need for regular tests and checks. In other sports, there are frequent complaints about a lack of professional coaches, a lack of investment, and poor quality facilities.

Faced with these problems, the search for funding has become particularly important in recent years. Sponsorship from large private companies has been a major source, along with funds from the National Lottery, introduced in 1994. For every ticket sold, 28 pence currently goes to sports and arts projects, and between 1994 and 2003, 23,175 grants were awarded, worth £1.9 billion pounds for sports projects, from small pieces of equipment to the building of major sports venues. One of the most visible benefits has been the renovation and replacement of sports and athletics stadiums around the country. Meanwhile, some football clubs in valuable central locations sold their grounds to property developers and moved to more modern stadiums in the outskirts of the city.

Until recently another major source of finance was the tobacco industry, with several tournaments and teams sponsored by companies such as Benson and Hedges, Marlboro and so on. However this has been banned in recent years under the European Commission's Tobacco Advertising Directive, and now other sponsors are being sought. The gambling industry has also provided large funds and prize money for horse and dog racing. Most newspapers carry information about the performances of horses and jockeys at races around the country, and bets can be placed on most sports in a betting shop or 'turf accountant'. But in recent years there have been a number of high-profile cases with allegations of corruption, drugs and race-fixing, which have cast doubt on the honesty of the racing industry. However, gambling remains popular in Britain, and at least once every two weeks 39 per cent of the population do the football pools, 20 per cent play on gaming and fruit machines, 18 per cent play bingo and 14 per cent bet on horses.

For many years amateurism represented the sporting ideal, but in Britain today it is rarely found in major sports events. A notable exception is the annual Boat Race between Oxford and Cambridge, which is watched by over 150 countries, and for the rights to broadcast this 'heritage' event the BBC pays hundreds of thousands of pounds. Interest in motor sport has also declined, especially in Formula One, in which races have become predictable, and the teams and drivers largely anonymous.

Cricket has also lost much of its former prestige. It is still played widely in English schools, colleges, and among county teams, but it has not become well established in Wales, Scotland or Northern Ireland. Meanwhile, the former colonies such as Australia, Pakistan, the West Indies and Zimbabwe continue to produce teams that dominate the sport. Moreover many West Indian and Asian immigrants still refuse to support the English national team, indicating that their identities and loyalties lie outside the UK.

In the past 50 years the country that wrote the rules of most popular sports has experienced much greater equality and cultural diversity, which has been reflected in sport as a whole. But as many branches of entertainment have become professional and commercial, market forces have made them more competitive and materialistic. The ethic of amateurism and the Corinthian spirit have almost disappeared, as a new vision emerges of what it means to be a British sportsperson.

Discussion topics and activities

1   Are there any types of sport which are unique to your region? What is their local/regional significance? Who plays them now, and who watches them? How do people feel about them? Are they important for a sense of local identity?

2   Think about the songs of your favourite club and the national anthem of your country. Who wrote them and who sings them? What is their purpose? Would you like to change them? If so, why, and what would you replace them with?

3   Discuss the view that sportsmen and women are entertainers who should earn whatever the market can bear.

4   A famous quotation attributed to the Duke of Wellington said the Battle of Waterloo was won on the playing fields of Eton school. This is probably untrue, as at the time of the battle in 1815, most popular games had not yet been invented. What do you think he meant? What are the benefits of doing games/sports at school? Should girls be encouraged to play football and other traditionally male sports?

5   Are there any foreign players in your local teams? Are they welcomed by the public? Do all members of your society get an equal chance to participate in sport? Give examples.

6   Think of possible reasons for racist chanting and incitement at football matches. What do campaigners in the UK do to combat racism? Is it the same in your country?

7   What kind of facilities exist for disabled people to play sports in your country? How could they be improved?

8   Due to public demand, some bloodsports, such as hunting with dogs, are now illegal in Britain. What are the arguments for and against their abolition? Do you agree with them?

9   Some argue that the seriousness of modern sport, the professional ethic and demands of commercialism have removed the element of fun, but there are still amateur activities which people practise to entertain themselves and others. One example is 'extreme ironing', organised through the Extreme Ironing Bureau, in which participants attempt to iron items of clothing, such as shirts and trousers, in 'extreme' locations, for instance on high mountains, on the wing of a plane or even underwater. Looking on the internet, can you find any other examples of unorthodox sports? What is their attraction? Would you want to take part in activities such as this?

Suggested further reading

Books

Birley, D. (1993) *Sport and the Making of Britain*, Manchester and New York: Manchester University Press.

Brander, M. (1992) *The Essential Guide to the Highland Games*, Edinburgh: Canongate.

Cashmore, E. (2003) *Beckham*, Cambridge: Polity Press.

Dunning, F. and Rojek, C. (eds) (1992) *Sport and Leisure in the Civilizing Process*, London: Macmillan.

Dunning, F., Murphy, P. and Williams, J. (1998) *The Roots of Football Hooliganism: A Historical and Sociological Study*, London: Routledge.

Elias, N. and Dunning, F. (1986) *Quest for Excitement: Sport and Leisure in the Civilizing Process*, Oxford: Blackwell.

Hargreaves, J.A. (1986) *Sport, Power and Culture*, Cambridge: Polity Press.

Hargreaves, J.A. (1994) *Sporting Females: Critical Issues in the History and Sociology of Women's Sports*, London and New York: Routledge.

Harris, H.A. (1975) *Sport in Britain: Its Origins and Development*, London: Stanley Paul.

Hill, J. (2002) *Sport, Leisure and Culture in Twentieth Century Britain*, Basingstoke: Palgrave.

Holt, R. (1989) *Sport and the British: A Modern History*, Oxford: Clarendon Press.

Holt, R. and Mason, T. (2000) *Sport in Britain 1945–2000*, Oxford: Blackwell.

Jarvie, G. (ed.) (1991) *Sport Racism and Ethnicity*, London: Farmer Press.

Mason, T. (1988) *Sport in Britain*, London: Faber & Faber.

Polley, M. (1998) *Moving the Goalposts: A History of Sport and Society Since 1945*, London: Routledge.

Townson, N. (1997) *The British at Play: A Social History of British Sport from 1600 to the Present*, Bucharest: Cavallioti Publishers.

Wisden Cricketer's Almanac, published annually for the past 133 years, is a mine of information about cricket and the most recent season. It also contains a summary of the rules of the game.

Journals

The International Journal of the History of Sport
The Sports Historian

Monographs published by the publishing houses of Leicester and Manchester Universities

Literature listed in specialised biographies and source lists, such as Seddon's *A Football Compendium* and Cox's *British Sports History Bibliographical Series*

10

Art and architecture

ART

Introduction

Contemporary British art has never enjoyed the same esteem as literature, drama or music, and public taste has frequently favoured the conventional more than the innovative and avant-garde. However, London is home to several fine collections of traditional and modern works. The principal one is held at the National Gallery, which opened in 1824 and currently holds over 2,000 works of Western painting from the thirteenth to the nineteenth century. British art and sculpture from 1500 to the present day is shown at the Tate Britain, while the new Tate Modern displays modern and contemporary art from 1900 to the present day. Tate galleries have also opened in Liverpool and St Ives. Portraits and photographs of distinguished figures from British history can be seen at the National Portrait Gallery, opened in 1856.

Numerous other collections are held in towns and cities around the country. In Scotland, the National Gallery of Modern Art, the Scottish National Portrait Gallery and the National Gallery of Scotland hold the three main collections, and all are situated in Edinburgh, while the National Museum and Gallery in Cardiff holds many works by Welsh artists.

Within Britain, London is the most vital and active city for the artistic avant-garde, and home of the most innovative and influential schools. The Royal College of Art (RCA), the Institute of Contemporary Arts (ICA), the Slade, St Martin's College, the Central School, the Euston Road School and

Goldsmiths College, among others, have helped to develop the work of many British artists, and in 2003 the University of the Arts was formed, Europe's largest centre for education in art and design.

The London location of the principal schools, together with opportunities to make contacts, show and sell work, promotes the highly centralised nature of the British art scene and the absence of almost any significant regional movements. However, the independent Arts Councils of England, Scotland, Wales and Northern Ireland subsidise a significant amount of the visual arts elsewhere in the UK. They also give financial support to young artists.

Exhibitions of more progressive and avant-garde art are often held at the Institute of Contemporary Arts (ICA), while the Royal Academy has a reputation as a more traditional centre. It was founded in 1768 to run the Academy Schools of painting, sculpture and print-making, and is the oldest art academy in Britain. Its well-known summer exhibition is held between May and August each year and comprises artworks submitted by members of the general public as well as professional artists.

Early influences and movements

Support and sponsorship have always been important for artistic development, and have often influenced the kinds of work created and shown. In earlier times art had an instructive role, and the Church, government and wealthy patrons strongly favoured works which carried a moral message. This was reflected in the work of eighteenth- and nineteenth-century landscape artists, such as Joseph Turner (1775–1851) and John Constable (1776–1837). Like the authors of Romantic literature and poetry of the time, they were inspired by the natural beauty of the countryside, which they saw as the source of spiritual and moral truths, and landscapes became one of the most traditional styles of painting, as well as Britain's major contribution to Western European art.

Faced with the horrors of industrialisation and increasing social disorder of the mid-nineteenth century, there was a return to the old certainties and reassurance offered by religion. This is amply reflected in the work of the Pre-Raphaelite Brotherhood. William Holman Hunt (1827–1910) and others often painted biblical scenes, which offered spiritual comfort and moral guidance. But simple, sentimental portraits of families and their animals were also popular, and are commonly found in the work of Sir Edwin Landseer (1802–73).

In many traditional works the subjects are clearly identifiable, but in the twentieth century British artists began to represent images in a more liberated and individual way. In the 1950s they were strongly influenced by movements taking place in America, where an avant-garde was established in New York, among European émigrés such as Max Ernst and Piet Mondrian, who had settled there and begun to teach. Under their tutelage, a new style emerged which excluded images of people or things. The work had no subject, apart from its own elements, for example a hard block of pure colour or simply the brush marks on the canvas were the 'theme'.

Meanwhile, the centre for bohemian and artistic activity in post-war Britain was the small fishing village of St Ives in south-west England, where a local community of artists such as Patrick Heron, Peter Lanyon, Roger Hilton and William Gear were known as the St Ives School. The group were influenced by the powerful cultural waves coming out of America and began representing the village and its landscapes in new, abstract forms. But their technique was less expressive or visually imaginative, consisting of the application of greens, greys and other dark tones. The group considered these honest and authentic colours, necessary for making faithful representations of the natural environment.

The abstraction and subjectivity of American art was free of tradition and ideology. In contrast, other British artists of the 1950s developed a realist style, which was closely associated with the rebellious ideas of the 'new wave' in writing. The aim was to reveal society and ordinary people – to represent them frankly and not deceive with fantasy and abstraction. Like many new movements in the arts of the 1950s and 1960s, it was focused outside London, in the industrial areas of northern England, such as Liverpool, Sheffield and Newcastle.

Realist subject matter often featured familiar, domestic environments, for example bed-sitting accommodation, with a bed, table, stove and sink, as exemplified in the work of John Bratby. In 1954 the art critic David Sylvester described the new genre as 'kitchen sink school', a term for a type of social realism which was subsequently used to describe films such as *Saturday Night and Sunday Morning*, plays such as *Look Back in Anger* and the new television soap operas such as *Coronation Street*. This was seen as a radical new departure in the arts, and received strong support from the political left, including the critic and author John Berger, who organised exhibitions to promote it.

Francis Bacon

Abstract painting and social realism were significant and contrasting tendencies in British art of the 1950s, the former from the USA, the latter home-grown. But two artists who would make highly significant, original contributions to British art were associated with neither. Francis Bacon (1909–92) was born in Dublin, but spent most of his life working in London. When his work was first shown in 1945, few imagined that later he would be acclaimed as one of the greatest artists of the late twentieth century. He was not formally trained and did not begin painting until his early 30s. His main influences were the horrors of the war years, such as the Holocaust and the atomic bomb. His early work *Three Studies for*

Figures at the Base of a Crucifixion (1944) depicts a crucifixion, but not a Christian one. It is the first of many disturbing works which suggest menace, hysteria and a darker side to human nature. It caused outrage when it was first shown in London in 1945.

His later work showed a fascination with the movement of the human body in paintings featuring friends, lovers and sometimes himself. There are frequent suggestions of inner torment and violence: men in suits sit formally, their blurred heads looking deformed and mutilated. Naked figures couple chaotically on beds. Popes are shown isolated and shouting madly. Other pictures use strong, emphatic brush-work to represent bottles, glasses, toilets and sinks, in a type of distorted realism, from which figures struggle to escape. Critical opinion frequently describes his works as disturbing, depraved, intense, cathartic, realistic, austere and occasionally ridiculous. He had several imitators, but no descendants or pupils. However, his originality and style have made his works some of the most highly praised in modern British art.

Lucian Freud

Many critics, public and collectors recognise Lucian Freud (b. 1922) as Britain's greatest living painter. The grandson of psychoanalyst Sigmund Freud, Lucian was born in Berlin, and as Jews his family fled to Britain in 1933 as refugees from Nazism. He studied briefly at the Central School of Art in London, then he served as a merchant seaman. Between 1948 and 1958 he taught at Slade School of Art, then was visiting assistant at Norwich School of Art in 1964–65.

In 1951 his *Interior at Paddington* won a prize at the Festival of Britain, but he became well known for his portraits and figure paintings, his subjects often being the people in his life: friends, lovers, children, family, and fellow painters such as Bacon, Hockney, Auerbach, and his assistant David Dawson. He is often described as a realist, making sharp, objective accounts of his subjects, which record every detail of their physical presence.

His paintings are often described as ugly, severe and unforgiving. In a world of 'kitchen sink' gloom, he is said to draw not only what he sees, but what he feels about his subjects. As he has said, 'I paint people not because of what they are like, but how they happen to be.' Colour is secondary to the mood of his paintings, which predominates. Key works include *Girl with Roses* (1948), *Girl with a White Dog* (1951), *Naked Girl Asleep* (1968), *Reflection* (a self portrait) (1985) and *Garden, Notting Hill Gate* (1997).

In recent years Freud's range of subject matter has become wider. In 2004 he turned his attention to the highly specialised area of horses' backsides with *Skewbald Mare*. Other new paintings ranged from a post-card-size picture of some eggs, to a giant canvas of his friend Andrew Parker-Bowles, resplendent in the uniform of the Queen's Household Cavalry. Two years earlier he painted a picture of the model Kate Moss pregnant and naked, which was sold for almost £4 million in 2005.

Although their art was often pessimistic, Freud and Bacon both enjoyed flamboyant bohemian lifestyles of heavy drinking and gambling, keeping company with aristocratic women and criminal gangs. Until they disagreed in the 1970s, the two were great friends and occasionally painted portraits of each other. Many critics believe Freud and Bacon to be among the greatest British painters, not only for their unusual abilities, but also because they have ignored dominant movements and influences. Instead, theirs are realistic, intense representations of the human figure in which subjects are shown as ultimately sad, alone and vulnerable.

Pop goes the easel: British pop art

America continued to have a powerful influence on cultural and artistic life in Britain of the mid-1950s. At the ICA in London, a number of writers and artists were inspired by the populist, commercial nature of American culture and mass media. They were known as the Independent Group and included the painter Richard Hamilton, the historian Reyner Banham, and the painter and sculptor Eduardo Paolozzi. In 1954 British art critic Lawrence Alloway used the term 'pop' (abbreviated from 'popular') to define the Independent Group's interests.

In an exhibition, *This is Tomorrow,* at London's Whitechapel Gallery in 1956, Hamilton showed his work *Just what is it that makes today's homes so different, so appealing?* It was an important moment in British art, when the first significant 'pop' picture received public exposure. Composed of a variety of images reflecting aspects of pop culture, the picture focuses on the fantastic images of the world of advertisements and mass communications, which are united in a satirical collage. Together they express leisure, pleasure, excitement and consumption, in an intoxicating distillation of American commercial culture, the very antithesis of rain, ration books and spam sandwiches of post-war Britain.

In 1957 Richard Hamilton defined pop as follows: 'Pop Art is: Popular (designed for a mass audience), Transient (short term solution), Expendable (easily forgotten), Low cost, Mass produced, Young (aimed at youth), Witty, Sexy, Gimmicky, Glamorous, Big Business.' Its influence grew quickly and soon afterwards many other artists began creating pop art, such as Peter Blake, Joe Tilson and Richard Smith. Pop imagery was loud, bright, vulgar and used clichés from the new mass media of advertising and television. They included stars of film and pop, for example 'pin-ups' such as Marilyn Monroe, advertisements for products such as Coca-Cola and design technology, expressed in the styling details of large American cars.

Pop art quickly became fashionable and popular at a time when pop music was becoming established. The tenor of the times was diverse, experimental, liberated and hedonistic, which seemed perfectly to match the spirit of pop art. The highly commercial nature of pop art soon took it into other formats such as record packaging. Pop artist Peter Blake designed the cover for the Beatles' album *Sergeant Pepper* (1967) and the Rolling Stones commissioned Andy Warhol to design several of their record sleeves. Colourful pop art posters became fashionable, and improvements in printing methods made them cheap and abundant. The extended use of pop art was helped by the development of photography as a new art form. Compact cameras and fast films allowed informal, natural photography which was more spontaneous and revealing than the traditional 'posed' styles. These were quickly put to use in fashion and advertising, where Anthony Armstrong-Jones, Patrick Lichfield, David Bailey, Terence Donovan and Terry Duffy developed innovative new styles, and showed their work in the new colour supplements of Sunday newspapers.

In the USA, pop art began to experiment with visual perception, producing exciting new styles of 'optical' or 'op art'. Bridget Riley became the best-known British exponent, whose geometrically precise black-and-white stripes seem to produce vibrations and rhythms across the canvas. The illusion of movement in op art became authentic movement in kinetic art, which featured suspended figures moving in currents of warm air, known as 'mobiles'. Others were motorised, or responded to the movement of water or the effects of gravity, for example elaborate fountains and other public sculptures.

By the mid-1960s a generation of pop artists had become established in Britain. But many critics argued that it was not a committed, serious art because it was superficial and apolitical, describing it as the 'disinterested presentation of trivia'. Despite their elitist arguments, it became internationally recognised as optimistic, vibrant, easy to enjoy, and much loved by many non-specialists.

David Hockney

Pop art was accessible and appealing, and some artists such as David Hockney (b. 1937) were attracting the attention of a wider, non-specialised public. Since his early success with a series of etchings, *The Rake's Progress*, completed while a student, he has become one of the most widely known and appreciated British artists. Hockney entered the Royal College of Art in 1959, but unlike many of his RCA contemporaries, he did not become closely associated with any particular school or movement. Instead, *Demonstrations of Versatility* (1962), an early piece, aptly describes his life and work.

During his career he has painted in a variety of styles. His eclectic influences have found expression in drawing, the design of opera sets,

Figure 10.1 David Hockney's *Mr and Mrs Clark and Percy* (1970–71)

photography, book illustration and fine portrait work, such as his detailed but economic study of the poet W.H. Auden (1968). Some of the most publicly admired works were completed in the late 1960s when he moved to California and developed an increasingly naturalistic style of painting. He depicted beach houses, swimming pools, grass and palm trees in elegant, spacious, scenes of pleasure and leisure, for example *A Bigger Splash* (1967), and used bright, sunny colours to create an atmosphere of comfort, well-being and hedonism. But he did not forget his friends and family in Yorkshire, and has painted them often, especially his mother Laura.

Many of his paintings have been based on photographic images, for example *Mr and Mrs Clarke and Percy* (1970–71). He seemed to paint to please, which made some critics comment that he was too light in attitude and subject matter. But his way of working has also been marked by innovation and interest in new technology. In the 1980s he was inspired to make art using the fax machine, inventing a photographic collage by mounting dozens of photographs to make compound, cubist-looking images of people and places, and staged a major exhibition in São Paulo, Brazil. Hockney is also passionate about painting and drawing, and has often spoken about the need to return to basics in order to see more.

In 1987 he established the 1853 Gallery, a converted textile factory in Saltaire, near his home town of Bradford in Yorkshire, which now holds the world's largest collection of his work and is open to the public. His mixture of styles, both traditional and innovative, has made him consistently popular with critics, collectors and the general public, and in recent years Hockney has been the subject of several major retrospectives.

Sculpture

British painting has been characterised by a number of different movements which sometimes occurred simultaneously, but sculpture has developed in a relatively linear way. During the 1930s and 1940s Henry Moore (1898–1986) provided the main influence with rounded hollows and smooth, tactile surfaces of forms in stone, bronze or wood. His larger, monumental works were often influenced by the landscape of his native Yorkshire, while smaller figures often incorporated influences from around the world, in particular those of pre-Columbian America. These were often inspired by shapes found in nature and are smooth, rounded and feminine in style.

Moore's sensuous style contrasted with 'geometry of fear' sculpture, which appeared after 1945. Its tormented mood was inspired by the horrors of war and particularly the destructive potential of nuclear weapons. The main exponents were Reg Butler and Lynne Chadwick, whose characteristic thin, angular, contorted, expressionist shapes suggest pain, suffering and torment of those affected by war.

Anthony Caro's abstract sculptures provided a major progression. Caro had worked as an assistant to Henry Moore, but in 1963 on returning from America, he began welding steel shapes together to make flat, abstract forms, imitating abstract paintings. These were then painted in bright, lively colours, to make the cold dark metal look animated, graceful and attractive. Brightly coloured works had not been seen before in sculpture and were referred to as New Generation work. Gradually, they developed into a style known as Heavy Metal, in which pieces were cut, twisted, combined into abstract shapes and then painted. This was a new development. It emphasised that instead of the traditional materials such as wood or stone, a sculpture could be made of anything. Today, Caro is known for his work using steel girders, tubing and steel sheeting in intriguing abstract works. In 2005 he held a major retrospective in London, and has been acknowledged as one of Britain's finest living sculptors.

In contrast to the twisted steel of Caro's work are the more traditional wood, stone and plaster works of Anish Kapoor (b. 1953). Although he was born into an Indian-Jewish family, he has lived and worked in Britain since the early 1970s, creating elegant, complex, sublime works which often suggest aspects of the human form. Many of Kapoor's sculptures are huge pieces of rough stone with smooth, highly polished cavities and interiors, such as *Void Field* (1989). In contrast, *Sky Mirror* (2001), a large reflective dish-like sculpture, is made from strips of stainless steel. *Ghost* (1997) is a huge black, rectangular block of granite. The outside has rough edges,

Figure 10.2 Sky Mirror by Anish Kapoor

and one face has been hollowed out and polished. Inside, a column of light hangs in the air like a flaming torch. *Holocaust Memorial* (1995) was created for a London synagogue in St John's Wood. It is a vast rectangular stone block. A doorway is carved out on one side; in the polished interior a hazy, inverted image of the viewer hangs in the air. Kapoor has been described as one of the most influential sculptors of his generation, and won the Turner Prize in 1991.

Rachel Whiteread (b. 1963) is another Turner Prize winner whose nostalgic, sentimental works have received international recognition. Her early pieces were plaster casts of bodies and personal mementos including childhood blankets. She once said that 'Many of life's key experiences happen in bed – being born, sleeping, dreaming, making love, giving birth, being ill and dying. These are times when we open up to others or are most alone or vulnerable.' In 1989 her first exhibition included several personal pieces such as *Shallow Breath*, a cast of the space under the bed in which she was born, which she made two months after her father died. She later developed interests in architecture, and combined them with sculpture. *Ghost* (1991) was a cast of the inside of a living room in a small Victorian house, while *House* (1993) was a cast of the interior of a complete terraced house which stood in east London. It was built by preparing a concrete

235

mould inside the house, and then stripping away the exterior walls. Recent work has included a Holocaust memorial in Vienna, and *Monument* for the 'empty' plinth in Trafalgar Square, London, one of Britain's most representative public spaces.

Trafalgar Square was designed in 1832 by Charles Barry 'to give scope and artistic character to sculptural work of a high class'. In the past, national heroes who distinguished themselves in the field of battle, such as Horatio Nelson at Trafalgar (whose column dominates the square), were given a statue on one of three plinths there. A fourth plinth remained empty, but today it is dedicated to different works of modern sculpture, which are changed every 12–18 months. Whiteread's *Monument* was one of the first to occupy the fourth plinth, and is a facsimile of the granite plinth on which it stands. It is made of clear resin, which she called 'a pause, a quiet moment for the space'. Most recently the plinth has been occupied by Marc Quinn's *Alison Lapper Pregnant*, a statue of a pregnant disabled woman. As he observes, 'in the past, heroes such as Nelson conquered the outside world. Now it seems to me that heroes are those (women and the disabled) who conquer the prejudices of others.'

Gilbert and George

In contrast to the inanimate sculptures of most British artists are the 'living sculptures' of the duo Gilbert and George. In the late 1960s they began posing as a quaint, formal, serious pair, dressed in collars, ties, old-fashioned grey suits, and with painted hands and faces. They appeared in strange and sometimes shocking contexts as performance artists. Rather than make art, they argued they *were* art. Their early pieces suggested an innocence and comical naivety: for example in the video-film *Gordon's Makes Us Drunk* (1972), Gilbert (b. 1942) and George (b. 1943) sit in the front room of their home, gradually getting drunk on gin. In another performance they became 'singing sculptures' repeatedly singing the old music hall song 'Underneath the Arches' until the words and music became meaningless.

In contrast to the light, comical nature of their earlier pieces, in the 1980s their works became darker and more challenging. Provocative works addressed themes of alienation and sexuality with titles such as *Prostitute Puff*, *Shag Stiff* and *Wanker*. These were composed of graffiti, photos and paint, and were collected together for their exhibition *Pictures 1982–86*. The pair were awarded the Turner Prize in 1986 for *Coming*, a colourful photo montage in which they are shown looking towards the sky in wonder, as suggestively shaped leaves fall all around. Later works included *The Naked Shit Pictures* (1995) in which Gilbert and George appear naked in large photo montages, surrounded by bodily fluids and substances, lost in a mixture of theatrical absurdity.

The couple have attracted controversy and censure. Critics accuse them of pushing their art to the edge, of using shock tactics, poor taste and pornography, and suggest that the titles of some of their works are their strongest elements. But others claim their art is progressive and multi-cultural, demonstrating the confused anger and alienation of the modern city, and the conservative nature of art criticism.

Bricks and nappies

The 1970s were marked by a fragmentation of styles and the appearance of experimental new works, often described under the general term of 'conceptual' art. Originating in America, its development in Britain was largely due to Victor Burgin, who used pictures taken from advertisements, texts from newspaper reports, maps and other material to create new associations, references and meanings. Others began to experiment in a similar style, creating adventurous new works with gases, liquids and even bodily substances. But their art could not be easily understood or evaluated by the public, the critics or potential buyers, who frequently described it as anarchic and self-indulgent. Similarly with performance art, which took the form of 'events' or 'happenings', where routines could be dull and repetitive, requiring considerable public patience.

Many artists became disillusioned, feeling that creative possibilities had become exhausted. Others felt the art world had become too commercialised, and that works lacked expression or content. In 1976 disillusionment turned to anger, when the Tate Gallery revealed it had bought *Equivalent VIII*, a minimalist work by the American sculptor Carl Andre, consisting of 120 fire bricks arranged on the floor to form a rectangle. At a time of inflation, high unemployment and strikes, there was shock and ridicule in the media that public money could be spent on something which, it was said, a labourer could have done. The press began a witch-hunt of modern artists. A pile of blankets by Barry Flanagan, Mary Kelly's dirty nappies exhibited in glass cases, and Michael Craig-Martin's glass of water called *Oak Tree* were all lampooned. Cartoonists, columnists and amateur art critics attacked modern art in general and the Tate in particular, alleging a shameful waste of public funds. The bricks seemed to touch a raw nerve of the nation. They entered the popular consciousness, remembered as a symbol of what modern art should not be.

But there was more to come. In October 1976 a show entitled 'Prostitution' was held at the ICA in London by a group of artists known as COUM Transmissions. The spirit of punk had been absorbed into art, and exhibits included pornographic magazines mounted and dated in glass display cabinets, a Venus de Milo plaster figure with a tampon hanging on each arm, and a box of live maggots which evolved into flies. Tabloid newspapers began a hysterical attack on the exhibition and its organisers, creating a sense of public shock and outrage. Questions were asked in Parliament and the Arts Council was forced publicly to deny any involvement or funding.

Art of the 1980s

After the fragmentation of the late 1970s, no particular style or school prevailed and art works became more personal and individual. Abstraction, figurative and portrait paintings, social satire, critical realism and feminist painting all found expression. In Scotland, there were attempts to develop the identity of Scottish art with several new exhibitions, such as *The Vigorous Imagination: New Scottish Art* at the Scottish National Gallery in 1987. The Expressionist tradition has always been strong there, and the work of John Bellany, Ken Currie and Adrian Viszniewski became more widely known. Working within an Expressionist style, they used dark, melancholic shades which reflected their pessimism over the industrial decline and effects of Thatcherism. The style became more prominent as Scotland began to gain more political autonomy in the 1990s. Scottish art is not a separate school, although certain styles such as Expressionism have consistently recurred throughout its history.

One of the most important Scottish artists of the post-war period is Eduardo Paolozzi. However, during his career he has worked mainly in London, where during the 1950s and 1960s he was closely associated with pop art. During the 1970s he was widely admired for his small, unusual works in bronze and wood. He later became Sculptor to the Queen in Scotland, and began creating much larger public works such as the giant bronze sculptures of hands and feet, which adorn the streets of his native Edinburgh. In London, his giant figure of Isaac Newton contemplating the universe sits outside the new British Library building in St Pancras. Many of his sculptures use recycled scrap metal, and he once described his work as 'the metamorphosis of rubbish'. However, earlier in his career he was well known for his dense collages which were often inspired by his interest in pop art, such as the brightly coloured kaleidoscopic figures set in a mosaic on the walls of Tottenham Court Road underground station in central London (1984).

The strong treatment of figures and images is also characteristic of Portuguese-born Paula Rego, who studied at the Slade art college and has lived in Britain for many years. Her work was almost non-existent between 1968 and 1988, but later in her career she began to produce highly praised paintings. She is widely acclaimed as a sharp observer whose characters often express clearly defined feminine qualities, such as *The Maids* (1987). Pictures are often set in familiar domestic contexts, but the family is presented as a mixture of both good and evil influences. Some of her pictures show women asserting themselves over men, such as her 'animal' paintings from the early 1980s, which often include bizarre sexual elements. *Going Out* (1995) is a milder, more humorous piece, which shows a girl putting on lipstick while her dog stares indignantly in the opposite direction, in anticipation of an evening alone. In 2004, aged 70, she had one of her most successful years, with a major retrospective in Porto, an altarpiece installed in Durham Cathedral and an exhibition of new work at Tate Britain.

The work of several other women artists began to receive recognition in the early 1980s. Mona Hatoum was born in Lebanon, but has lived in Britain since 1975. She has experimented with different formats including performance art, video and installations, which combine elements of sculpture, painting and other materials. Sonia Boyce is an Afro-Caribbean artist, who became well known for her *Lay Back, Keep Quiet, and Think What Made England Great* (1986), which consists of four panels in which a black female is presented as an English rose, said to be a metaphor of the black British woman who inherits a history of resistance and oppression. But female black or Asian artists are few. Critics argue this is because art institutions and artists are overwhelmingly white, middle-class and male, which dissuades those who do not fit the stereotype. Also, it is a very insecure world, and those from ethnic communities contemplating a career in art are often tempted to follow other more secure and lucrative professions.

The British art business

Exhibitions, galleries and their owners aim to draw attention to new artists, movements and ideas. The larger public galleries which hold regular exhibitions of new art include London's Tate Britain, the new Tate Modern, the Royal Academy, the Whitechapel Gallery, Camden Arts Centre and the Waterman Arts Centre. Of the private galleries, one of the largest in London is the Saatchi Gallery, which opened in 1985. Other commercial London galleries include the Marlborough, the Lisson, the Chisenhale, Sadie Coles, Victoria Miro, Flowers East, White Cube, White Cube2, Leslie Waddington and Anthony d'Offay, which all offer opportunities for new and more established artists to show and sell their work. Elsewhere in Britain, regular exhibitions are held in galleries of all the major cities, for example new work in video and digital media is shown at the Liverpool Biennial and Video Positive, while the National Review of Live Art in Glasgow shows new live performances.

Younger artists have traditionally depended on the patronage of gallery owners and powerful institutions to provide financial support and opportunities to show work. However, from the late 1980s many artists regained the initiative. Instead of waiting for the art establishment and gallery owners to recognise them as artists, they made this simple assumption themselves, and held improvised shows in basic, austere locations such as empty warehouses, starting with Damien Hirst's exhibition *Freeze* in a Docklands warehouse in 1988. In an extension of Thatcherism, self-help, independence and entrepreneurialism fused together to propel new artists into the public consciousness.

239

The introduction in 1984 of the Turner Prize also helped raise the profile of new artists. It publicises the work of the four shortlisted candidates who have most impressed the jury of art patrons, critics and the Tate director during the previous 12 months. In 1991 an upper age limit of 50 was introduced for candidates, while some critics cynically remarked that there should also be one for the judges. But critics complain that it has focused too much on the work of contemporary London artists, and that competitors are too concerned with winning the £25,000 prize money and attracting subsequent sponsorship, commissions and media exposure, rather than with the traditional concerns of social issues, artistic problems and solidarity among the artistic community.

Damien Hirst

The warehouse shows, the Turner Prize and the patronage of Charles Saatchi helped an exciting 'new wave' of young artists to develop, and one of the most successful is Damien Hirst (b. 1965). In 1988 he organised the first warehouse show, *Freeze*, in London's Docklands, together with 16 other students from Goldsmiths College. Since then he has produced unusual, memorable pieces which have attracted as much controversy as publicity.

Hirst uses theatrical installations featuring vitrines and surgical implements to disturb the public and create a reaction. In a warehouse show he exhibited *A Hundred Years* (1990), which represents the life cycle. It consists of two large vitrines connected by a tube, each measuring six feet square. In one is a dead cow's head, with flies, maggots and an insectocutor. The other remains empty, except for the flies. A larger version was subsequently made and renamed *A Thousand Years* (1990) and attracted huge publicity. Other works form a series of sculptures collectively known as *Internal Affairs*. One of these, *The Acquired Inability to Escape* (1991), again comprises two vitrines: one with a table, chair, cigarettes, a lighter and cigarette stubs, while the other remains empty.

The minimal style and attention to spatial relationships are also characteristic of his well-known *Natural History* series. The most dramatic work here is *The Physical Impossibility of Death in the Mind of Somebody Living* (1991), which is said to represent fear, death and the unknown. It comprises a 14-foot shark, suspended in a tank of formaldehyde solution. From the same series, *Mother and Child Divided* (1993) comprises a bisected cow and its calf. The four halves are displayed in two separate tanks side by side, allowing the viewer to pass between the divided animals.

Hirst is also well known for his 'dot' paintings, which resemble coloured pills or sweets on the white canvas and have names such as *Alphaprodine* (1993), and his more recent 'spin' paintings, produced by throwing paint onto a horizontal, revolving canvas. His work made him one of the best-known artists of his generation, and in 1995 he was awarded the Turner Prize for *Mother and Child Divided (ii)*.

Critics point out that animals have often been featured in British art, and a great theme of Western art is death. Both elements are central to many of Hirst's works, which illustrate the process of death in animals and its postponement in humans, for example his pharmaceutical cabinet *Pharmacy* (1998), which consists of an installation of shelves with packets of tablets and medicines for the head, stomach and feet on separate shelves. In 2005 he again expressed similar concerns with four large-scale paintings. These religious works are named after the evangelists from the four gospels of the Bible, and are set in large, vertical frames. Traditional Baroque imagery of blood, bright colours and heavy sentiment are complemented with the sinister, surreal presence of pills, pens and razor blades, which Hirst has embedded in the thick crusts of paint.

Through media coverage of his highly original and disturbing works and their black humour, Hirst has become one of the best known of contemporary artists, whose work is admired and appreciated – if not always understood – by collectors, investors, critics and the general public.

'BritArt'

In 1997 the varied and brave new works of young British artists captured the public imagination in the Royal Academy's summer exhibition *Sensation*. The title emphasised that exhibits were more about emotion than intellect and rational thought, and the traditional institution began promoting contemporary multimedia works and varied types of installations. The art on show reflected a variety of interests, which included abstraction, popular culture, feminism, racism and identity politics. But many members of the public found the works controversial and shocking. For example, Marcus Harvey's four metre high portrait of the child murderer Myra Hindley, created with a child's handprints, was attacked with ink and eggs by some protesters, while others angrily lobbied visitors to the exhibition.

Critics said the new work was so unconventional that there were no criteria for its evaluation, and therefore it did not deserve attention. Moreover, the art frequently exploited bad taste to gain publicity. For these critics, the only difference between known and unknown artists was in the marketing of the former. In contrast, those who liked the exhibition said most great works originally shocked the public, and that it is the purpose of art to provoke and probe the limits of acceptability. Instead, they spoke of the authority, intelligence and beauty of the work on show.

The 1,500 exhibits at *Sensation* were seen by over 300,000 members of the public, and excited so much interest and comment that some business people became major patrons of the artists. Charles Saatchi and his brother

Maurice are two of the best known. They were born in Iraq, but grew up in Britain where they created Saatchi and Saatchi, an advertising agency which became famous for creative advertising campaigns for the Thatcher government, and for Silk Cut cigarettes. Since then Charles Saatchi, or the 'artful adman' as he is sometimes known, has done much to raise public awareness of modern British art, providing the money, a gallery and patronage for many young artists.

In the 1990s following the success of so-called 'Britpop', the new art was quickly labelled 'BritArt' by the popular press. This was not a movement, but an expression used to refer to artists, who, at a time of cultural confidence and renewal were attracting attention, much as pop artists had done in the 1960s. Names often associated with 'BritArt' include Damien Hirst, Tracey Emin, Gillian Wearing, Jake and Dinos Chapman, Gavin Turk, Gary Hume, Fiona Rae, Mark Wallinger, as well as Helen Chadwick, Eileen Cooper, Amanda Faulkener and Gwen Hardie, Christine Borland and Sarah Lucas. A common theme connecting their work is the contemplation of life, death and bodily rhythms, documenting them using a variety of materials. Works are composed in a variety of ways, using video, sculpture, embroidery, machinery, everyday objects and other media to create collages and installations. One of the more unusual examples was in 2003 when Michael Landy's *Break Down* in Oxford Street, London, involved the public destruction of all 7,227 objects that he owned (valued at around £100,000, including a Chris Ofili print and a Gary Hume painting). Other recent works which received widespread publicity include Sam Taylor-Wood's 2004 video of the sleeping David Beckham, and Marc Quinn's *Self* (2003) in which he froze nine pints of his own blood into a cast of his head.

The popular interest in modern art which BritArt generated has been of clear commercial benefit to artists and gallery owners, but in 2005 critics hinted at BritArt's exhaustion, amid signs of a return to more conventional types of painting. These feature colourful, escapist, abstract works, for example, by Sacha Jaffri the young British Asian artist. Moreover, important patrons such as Charles Saatchi also appeared less interested in conceptual art and more interested in painting, as shown by the 2005 exhibition at the Saatchi Gallery entitled *The Triumph of Painting*.

But some things remained unchanged. The scene continues to be highly centralised in London, and many artists from outside England, as well as black and Asian artists, have yet to gain the recognition they deserve. Art in Britain continues to be overwhelmingly studied, practised, commented upon and commercialised by a predominantly white, English, middle-class community. Furthermore, public taste remains highly conservative, often seeing art as something to hang on the wall, depicting traditional portraits, still life or landscape scenes. As a consequence, many British artists have become better known abroad, where the public and media are often more receptive to new developments.

Tracey Emin

One of the most famous and controversial artists to emerge in the late 1990s is Tracey Emin (b. 1963) who uses intimate topics from childhood and adolescence to create compositions with confessional themes. She left school at 13 and later won a place at the RCA to study painting. In the 1990s she worked with Sarah Lucas, and later exhibited with the duo Gilbert and George.

Long before the popularity of TV reality shows, she appealed to public interest in other people's lives by using her own as the basis for her art, in which sex and drink feature prominently. One of her most famous was about the intimacy of sleep and relationships. *Everyone I've Ever Slept With* (1995) is a small tent with details of the suggestive title sewn inside; it attracted great publicity when shown at *Sensation*, before being destroyed in a fire in 2004.

My Bed is a more recent work, in which appears an unmade bed, surrounded by empty vodka bottles, KY jelly, soiled knickers and used condoms, in which the artist claims to have spent four days contemplating suicide. It was later bought by Charles Saatchi for £150,000. *Mine All Mine* (2000) is a photographic portrait of herself filling her knickers with money, a cynical comment perhaps on the nature of modern art, while *You Forgot to Kiss My Soul* was a solo exhibition in 2001, which included a range of work in drawings, installations, neon and videos. Hers is raw, confessional story-telling, a comment on the nature of a modern, confessional 'reality' culture, in which all must be revealed. However, critics often dismiss her work as original and highly personal, but lacking in variety.

ARCHITECTURE AND DESIGN

Introduction

Britain has been a heavily urbanised society since the late eighteenth century, and now more than 90 per cent of the population live in towns and cities. However, many people believe a superior quality of life exists in the countryside. Some of the most desirable and expensive styles of housing are farmhouses and rural cottages in villages whose architecture goes back several centuries.

In both the city and the countryside there is a strong preference for traditional styles of architecture, and conservation is a common practice. Historic and unusual buildings are protected by two public organisations: one is the National Trust (NT), the other is the English Heritage. The NT is a charity. It was created in 1895 to protect and preserve historic buildings and countryside areas of natural beauty, and its properties include hundreds of palaces, country houses, gardens and monuments which can be visited by the public.

English Heritage is a government agency, which advises and assists the government in matters of conservation. It currently 'lists' (protects) around 450,000 buildings and monuments, many of which are private houses. All relatively original buildings erected before 1700 and most others built before 1840 are automatically listed. Also included are buildings with special features, and recent works by influential architects. The owner of a listed building must obtain municipal permission for any alterations, but this is very difficult to obtain and severely restricts what the owner can do with the property. In Scotland, buildings are listed by Historic Scotland and in Wales by Cadw (Welsh Historic Monuments).

Movements and influences

During the industrial revolution of the eighteenth and nineteenth centuries Britain's cities quickly grew in size, and architectural styles such as Gothic and Georgian were common. The elegant, symmetrical Georgian style which originated during the reigns of King George I and his successors (1714–1830) is still one of the most popular with the public. Its main characteristics are uniformity and symmetry in relatively low, red-brick buildings with tall windows of many panes, which together project an air of dignity and calm.

Around 1850 architects began taking inspiration from earlier styles. Reinterpretations of the classical architecture of Greece and Rome were

Figure 10.3 Vermuyden School, Goole: a fine example of Georgian-style architecture, built much later in 1909

commonly used in the design of many civic and institutional buildings. To make them more individual, features from more recent styles were added, such as Georgian windows or Gothic arches, in a style known as neo-classical architecture. Its imposing appearance made many town halls, railway stations, courts, banks, stock exchanges, schools and hospitals a proud declaration of imperial, national and civic wealth, strength and pride, and today they are some of the most distinctive and admired buildings in towns and cities across Britain.

Although Britain is a heavily urbanised society, most people prefer to live not in the city centre, but in the suburbs, and in England in 2005 approximately two thirds of the population were living in suburban homes. The trend towards suburban living began after the First World War, when subsidies were provided to developers to build 'homes fit for heroes'. In London, the railway companies opened new lines from London to the surrounding home counties, where they also built inexpensive houses on cheap farmland, for instance, at Rayners Lane. In the green, leafy suburbs it was possible to live in a peaceful, detached way, far from the noise, dirt and squalor of the city. The characteristic style was a three-bedroom semi-detached house with curved 'bay' windows, steep roofs and tall chimneys. The building was often finished with a white or pebble-dash finish on the exterior walls, and had a garden at the front and rear. They were generally smaller than the older, more central houses occupied by middle-class families, as women were having fewer children and new household appliances reduced the need for servants. By 1939 some 16 million had been built, and today approximately one in four houses dates from that time.

Detached bungalows were also built in suburban areas. These single-storey houses were based on those found in the Indian province of Bengal (the name comes from the Hindi word *bangallo*, meaning 'of Bengal'). The first British examples appeared in 1869 in the county of Kent, where they were often built in coastal areas as a second home, and since then they have become one of the most desirable forms of housing.

The next major period of construction began in 1948, following the loss of many public buildings and some 2 million homes during the Second World War. One of the earliest major developments was on London's South Bank for the Festival of Britain in 1951. The focal point of the festival was the Royal Festival Hall, which was surrounded by pavilions containing exhibitions of colourful new designs in furniture, painting, pottery and sculpture. It was an exciting, romantic vision to a generation, many of whom had not eaten at outdoor coffee tables with umbrellas, had a foreign holiday or even seen any fresh, coloured paint.

Modernists

The Festival of Britain gave architecture and design a new vitality. Futuristic materials were introduced for furniture and decoration, such as nylon, plastic, formica and linoleum. But the most significant change was the new modernist styles, in which the design of a building reflected its purpose. Instead of symbolising power and prestige with imposing designs, functional buildings would be created to meet people's needs.

In the post-war period people demanded both social change and new buildings, and in a massive programme of reconstruction government offices, hospitals, schools and even entire new towns were built. But public housing was a priority. Many people could not afford to buy new houses, so cheap, rented local authority or 'council' housing was provided on a large scale. Tall, imposing, modernist apartment blocks were quickly erected in parks and gardens around Britain. Among the best known were the Alton Estate at Roehampton, London, and the Hyde Park Estate in Leeds. These were amazing structures compared with the small, old nineteenth-century houses nearby. They were heated and spacious. They had baths and indoor toilets. Outside they offered streets in the air, recreating the street life of children's games, gossip and community. Their modernist design aimed to promote physical health, and bright, airy flats were built with balconies for exercising and sunbathing. In their splendid isolation, these concrete-and-glass monuments looked down on the tiny terraced houses they were built to replace.

But the buildings quickly gained the new architecture a bad reputation. Residents complained about their cold atmosphere and the poor quality of the materials and finish. The plain, rough, concrete exteriors had no decoration or features and marked badly in the rain. They also required a lot of maintenance and repairs, which the municipal authorities could not always finance. But architects continued to design numerous public buildings in a similar style.

A variation of the modernist style was New Brutalism, which is attributed to the British couple Peter and Alison Smithson. In central London, municipal architects designed several Brutalist buildings as part of the South Bank arts complex, which continues to be Britain's premier arts venue. It comprises the Royal Festival Hall (1951), a multipurpose auditorium; the Hayward Art Gallery (1968); the Purcell Room and the Queen Elizabeth Hall (1967), which are both used as concert halls. The National Theatre (1976) completes the ensemble, to which were later added the National Film Theatre and the Museum of the Moving Image. However, the new buildings weren't popular with the public. Although they are dedicated to the visual and expressive arts, they are cold and serious. They have few windows, no clear entrance and the exposed concrete blocks of the exterior mark badly in the rain. The buildings have many critics, but they also have their fans: since the 1970s the complex has become a popular meeting place for young skateboard enthusiasts. In spite of public hostility, some large-scale works were successful. The 1960s were also a time of expansion for higher education, and many new colleges and universities were built with red brick, plate glass, ceramic tiling and concrete towers, such as the Universities of York and Warwick.

One of the most admired architects of the post-war period is James Stirling (1926–92), whose early work included several designs for higher education: the Engineering Faculty at Leicester University (1959), the History Faculty at Cambridge University (1964) and the Florey Building at Queen's College, Oxford (1966). These imaginative, unconventional buildings exhibit a variety of influences. But Stirling's work was appreciated less in Britain than abroad, where his three designs for museums in the German cities of Dusseldorf, Cologne and Stuttgart brought him international recognition. His works were not always expressed in the modernist style, but were often hybrid and highly individual, incorporating traditional and modern elements of design. The Neue Staatsgalerie (1984) in Stuttgart demonstrates his unique approach and became one of the most highly praised buildings of its time. In 1981 Stirling received architecture's most prestigious international award, the Pritzker Prize.

London remains a focal point for modernist design. The enormous residential complex of the Barbican Estate (Chamberlin, Powell and Bon, 1979) is well built outside and in, and its brutal exterior is softened with ornamental lakes, gardens and waterfalls, as well as numerous window boxes. It is also provided with local amenities such as bars and restaurants, and its major arts centre is a prime attraction for many visitors to the capital. Although it was initially disliked by many, it has since become a grade II listed building for the design integrity of the complex.

The striking central landmark of the Post Office Tower (now called the British Telecom Tower) in Cleveland Street, north London has also become a listed building, even though it has only been open since 1965. Designed by Eric Bedford when the Cold War was at its height, the 189 metre tall communications tower was planned as an important link between the government's bunker in the countryside and the rest of the world. The designers noted that the only buildings to survive nuclear bombs in Hiroshima and Nagasaki in the Second World War were round, and therefore built a cylindrical tower rather than a rectangular one. Fortunately it was never tested, and remains one of the most distinctive landmarks in central London.

Richard Seifert claimed he had changed the face of London more than any architect since Sir Christopher Wren in the seventeenth century. But unlike Wren's Baroque churches, such as St Paul's Cathedral, Seifert's designs were mainly temples to commerce, such as Centre Point, the tall imposing building which stands in central London by Tottenham Court Road underground station. Tower 42 (also known as Nat West Tower), built in 1981, is another of Seifert's London landmarks and is situated in the financial district known as the 'Square Mile' or 'City'. Its distinctive silhouette – which suggests a castle turret – remains a familiar feature of the city skyline.

247

New towns

To the overseas reader it may seem unusual that until recently there have been few attempts to create more desirable or convenient cities in Britain. The notion of a better quality of life has always been associated with the countryside, symbolised by public fondness for rural and pseudo-rural domestic architecture, decorations and furnishings. In the 1970s when more houses and better infrastructure were badly needed, the government encouraged migration to the countryside with the creation of several new towns there. This trend began in the nineteenth century, when several wealthy landowners and industrialists with strong religious convictions wanted to improve conditions for their workforce; they removed them from the horrors of the industrial cities and offered them education, health and work in newly built countryside communities, such as Milton Abbas in the English Midlands, Saltaire in West Yorkshire and New Lanark in Scotland.

The village of Bournville in the English Midlands is a good surviving example. It was built around 1900 by the chocolate-making Cadbury family. The Cadburys were Quakers, a Protestant denomination with a strong belief in social reform. They wanted to house their workers in an environment that would serve, not oppress its inhabitants, building a paternalist paradise of solid semi-detached houses with large gardens, each with a minimum of six fruit trees. Alcohol was seen by the reformers as the source of many social and domestic problems, and to the disappointment of some residents, the village was built without a pub.

In the twentieth century, more secular solutions to the problem of over-crowded cities resulted in the construction of Letchworth (1903) and Welwyn (1920), and between the early 1950s and mid-1970s the government financed 14 more new towns in attractive areas of green countryside. Milton Keynes is a recent example, built between 1976 and 1979. The architect Derek Walker took inspiration from 1960s Los Angeles, and designed low-rise buildings with easy traffic flow around them. Like many new towns, it has a low density of population and offered a high quality of life. It appears clean and classless, reflecting the architects' belief that they were creating a new social order. But it lacks the entertainments and facilities of a big city, as well as a sense of history and community, and critics originally described it as sterile, grey, bleak and empty, with neither charm nor character, an architectural esperanto.

Consequently, new towns have often become 'dormitory towns': places to sleep, but not to live and work. Gradually, enthusiasm for new towns declined, and towards the end of the twentieth century government policy began to focus on improving the quality of life in more established centres of population in programmes of regeneration.

Winds of change: architecture in the 1980s

Since the mid-1970s conservation has been a common practice in almost all areas of Britain, when the absence of finance and the fondness for older buildings created interest in their restoration and conversion, for example old factories and warehouses for use as flats, banks for use as bars and restaurants. It introduced a new way of thinking about the environment and soon there was a movement for the protection of historic and unusual buildings. Many old, unusual, historically interesting structures became 'listed', that is, protected by law from demolition, alteration or extension. Moreover, the owners have to maintain the buildings in their original condition. One of the first to be affected was the old fruit and vegetable market in London's Covent Garden, which in 1979 was saved from demolition. Soon afterwards there were outdoor cafés, boutiques, specialist food shops and street performers, which today make it one of the most popular areas of the city for entertainment, leisure and commerce.

Conservation has also been strongly supported by Prince Charles, who is a vocal critic of modern architecture. In 1988 he made the film *A Vision of Britain* for the BBC arts documentary series *Omnibus*, in which he attacked modernist architecture and its ugly urban offices and apartment blocks. In their place he advocated more programmes of Community Architecture, with their popular neo-classical and neo-vernacular styles which have been put into practice in the village of Poundbury, Dorset, where Charles maintains an active interest in the design of the buildings. The programme was seen by millions of viewers and a large majority agreed with his traditional, 'common-sense' opinions.

The quaint old-fashioned buildings of Poundbury present a sharp contrast to the urban architecture of the 1980s. The Conservative government elected in 1979 introduced severe cuts in public spending, and over the next 20 years architects' plans were influenced more by the private sector, unlike in the 1960s and 1970s when they were influenced more by pubic sector demands for arts, education and local government buildings. Demand was highest for high-tech buildings with communications cabling and air conditioning for energy-efficiency. These required deep floors and low ceilings, and structures only 20 years old, such as Seifert's Centre Point, could not be adapted economically.

In their place, new styles were developed using large, steel-framed structures of glass, steel, aluminium and chrome, and with the tubes, cables, nuts and bolts all openly exposed. Well-equipped buildings with all elements clearly visible were known as 'high-tech postmodern'. Inside, the best examples had dramatic visual contrasts of metal, glass and concrete which were made less harsh by soft lighting and a generous distribution of 'rainforestry' and modern sculpture. Many were designed around an atrium: a glass-covered central courtyard or interior patio, which brings light into the centre of the building. This is a practical feature in areas with a high density of office blocks where little light can enter through the side windows, and became a fashionable characteristic in designs of the mid-1980s.

One of the first buildings in this style was by Arup Associates in 1984, called simply 1 Finsbury Avenue. Its enormous, imposing, glass-covered courtyard won extensive critical praise and design awards. The style came to characterise offices in London's financial district – the City – where between 1985 and 1993 the number of commercial premises doubled. In the past, some of the most visually impressive and innovative buildings were built as religious monuments. In the nineteenth century they expressed civic grandeur. In the 1960s and 1970s they were built as tributes to the arts. But in the 1980s it was the commercial spirit which was embodied in futuristic, high-tech cathedrals to capitalism.

Not only individual buildings and factories but whole areas of the country were being rapidly redeveloped. The most spectacular of these is Docklands, an area of two square miles in the east of London on the River Thames, where low-rise offices, leisure buildings and luxury houses and flats were built in the high-tech postmodern style. Many exteriors are colourful and angular, and often finished with darkened glass. Access to the heart of London is by a driverless light railway and the whole area is punctuated by the massive, square, thick Canary Wharf Tower (Cesar Pelli, 1991). Inside this palace of business is an atmosphere of muted corporate luxury, with a reception area made of Italian and Guatemalan marble. Some 13,000 people work there, and it has its own train station, police station and shopping centre. It is the tallest building in Britain at around 800 feet, and the second tallest in Europe. Put up in just three years this striking temple to power and commerce was the ultimate Docklands development and epitomised the business values of the Tory government.

Richard Rogers

Richard Rogers (b. 1933) was born in Florence, Italy. He works using advanced building technology and several of his designs have become some of the most highly praised in modern British architecture. He began his career at Yale University in the USA, together with the British architect Norman Foster. Foster and Rogers subsequently became partners in a practice known as Team 4, which specialised in adventurous, stylish designs. Many were for houses and industrial buildings, but Rogers later worked with the Italian architect Renzo Piano to design the Centre Georges Pompidou, a futuristic arts building in central Paris. The exterior is one of several impressive aspects of the building. The escalators are carried in transparent tubes on the outside. Other tubes are colour-coded and carry water, air and electricity. The design allows convenient access for maintenance, repairs and improvements of service equipment. These are practical features, which mean it can be adapted quickly and easily to technical change. When it opened in 1977, it soon became the most talked about building in Britain and France, and began to rival the Eiffel Tower for attention.

The heart of London's financial district is home to another of Rogers and Partners' most celebrated works. The Lloyd's Building was conceived in the 1970s and completed in 1986. The building introduced high-tech postmodern architecture to London's financial district, and established Rogers as a leading British architect. It is a tall, impressive, machine-like edifice and became an icon of the advanced 'high-tech' style. It has a stainless steel exterior, supported by a web of tubes. The lifts and service equipment, such as air-conditioning units, are kept on the exterior. They provide a highly distinctive visual display and, as technology evolves improvements can be made quickly and easily. The location makes it difficult to appreciate the whole building, which fits tightly into central London's medieval street pattern. But inside there is a sense of space, where open floors are designed around a central interior patio surrounded by escalators. The design produces a dramatic effect, in which the building's occupants become actors. At the centre is the symbol of the Lloyd's insurance market, the Lutine bell, recovered from HMS *Lutine* which sank in 1799.

Sometimes Rogers has been involved with large-scale projects which have aroused controversy, for example his extension to the National Gallery in London was described by the Prince of Wales as 'a monstrous carbuncle'. In the late 1990s he collaborated on several architectural matters with the newly elected Labour government, for example the Dome covering the Millennium Exhibition site at Greenwich in London, which quickly became a national landmark, but was severely criticised for its allegedly poor content and level of organisation. He was also unable to see the Welsh Assembly building through to completion after costs escalated. However, among his colleagues and architecture critics he has received acclaim for his bold, eye-catching designs, and in 1996 he became Lord Rogers of Riverside.

Norman Foster

Innovative, high-tech projects have made Norman Foster (b. 1935) one of Britain's most distinguished architects. After studying in Manchester and the USA he worked with Richard Rogers in the innovative practice of Team 4. But his independent designs during the mid-1970s for an arts centre at the University of East Anglia and the Willis Faber office building in Ipswich quickly brought him to public attention. These are light, elegant, minimal structures inspired by his interest in aviation. They are visually distinctive and technically advanced buildings, which are well integrated into their environment. The Willis Faber building was so highly praised that it became a listed building within 30 years of its completion.

As Foster's reputation grew, he received a growing number of commissions from abroad. One of the most notable was for the Hong Kong and Shanghai Bank (1986). The floors of this high-rise building hang from eight towers, and make the building one of the most spectacular in the former colony, its success confirming him as a major architect of world renown.

His most recent commissions in Britain have been mostly in or near London, where he has designed more buildings (approximately 35) than Christopher Wren. Some of his recent works include 30 St Mary Axe (the 'Gherkin'), the new Wembley Stadium, Trafalgar Square and the Millennium Bridge, plus new galleries for the Royal Academy, a passenger terminal under an umbrella roof at Stansted Airport and the redevelopment of Parliament Square. Other projects include the Jubilee Line underground extension (1999) and Canary Wharf Station, arguably London Underground's best station since the 1930s, which resembles a subterranean cathedral.

Foster has also designed numerous buildings elsewhere in Britain, and on several continents overseas, from the Sage Music Centre in Gateshead (2004), to Beijing Airport, an 80-storey tower in Dubai and a 62-metre high glass pyramid in Astana, Kazakhstan. Together with Rogers, he is one of the few British architects well known to the British public, and was awarded the Pritzker Prize in 1999.

The High Street

One of the biggest visible transformations in recent years has been in the main street or 'High Street' of many provincial towns and cities. The name originates with the Romans, who built elevated roads to allow water to drain and to deter thieves. As the road passed through local communities, commerce grew up on either side.

Only 30 years ago the High Street still attracted a variety of small shops and businesses. However, the appearance is today much more uniform from city to city, with the same types of shops often owned by the same companies. Corporate businesses like the major banks, Boots, W.H. Smith, Carphone Warehouse and McDonalds have taken central sites in most of the main towns, while the smaller, family owned shops have closed or moved. For example, in 1988 there were approximately 18,000 butchers' shops in Britain, yet there were only 8,100 in 2001, due mainly to the arrival of new supermarkets and shopping centres on the outskirts of most towns, which have also helped destroy other traders on the High Street.

The pub is one of the most emblematic places in any High Street, and like many other buildings it has also undergone a transformation in recent times. Until the 1980s most were traditional in design and decor. They were generally quiet comfortable places, with rooms often resembling the lounges of people's homes. Seating was designed to promote privacy, and there were often several smaller rooms where meetings could be held.

252

But during the 1980s the credit boom and economic confidence created strong competition among shops and leisure services for a new generation of consumers who had more money available for pleasure and recreation. New styles appeared which sometimes seemed more like stages, as the emphasis changed from privacy to public display. They were often given long curved bars which allowed customers to see and be seen, with loud music and few seats to encourage faster drinking. The colours, materials and styles of lights, tables, chairs and other furnishings were integrated into their surroundings. Theme pubs became common, such as the 'Irish' pub or the 'sports' bar, with games, television, videos and music, with cavernous interiors to cater for large crowds of young drinkers.

A similar trend could be observed with restaurants, which started competing with design and decor, rather than with food and prices. Interiors often reminded diners of the owners' origins: the dim lights and 'flock' wallpaper of a colonial British officers' club in Indian curry houses; the paper lanterns and murals of the Great Wall of China in Chinese eateries; the crab pots and fishing nets of numerous Greek tavernas. But they were popular, especially with a young generation of consumers who revelled in their novelty.

In the mid-1980s house prices rose sharply, property renovation grew in popularity, and 'do-it-yourself' (DIY) became the nation's most popular hobby. Some commented that the possibilities for renovation and person-alisation of the home allowed it to become an extension of identity, and consequently many stores such as B & Q, Ikea and Habitat flourished, selling modern and traditional materials, accessories, furniture and fabrics, to those who wanted to express themselves through the home. House prices and DIY became a frequent topic of conversation, and today around £8.5 billion per year is currently spent on what has become one of the most important leisure activities in Britain, practised by almost as many women as men. Those who are unable, or do not want to, can commission the services of a newly arrived expert: the professional interior designer.

Building new Britain: architecture since the 1990s

In 1996 Britain had the oldest housing stock in Europe, with some 25 per cent built before 1914. However, attitude surveys repeatedly showed that the British prefer older houses to new ones. A view persists that they have more character, more individuality and are better built. Responding to public demand, some of the most modern and desirable small houses built in the 1990s were designed in a neo-vernacular style, but with modern heating, insulation and security features. This extended to the conversion of many centrally located warehouses and factories into flats, which from the late 1990s became some of the most fashionable kinds of accom-modation in British cities. Modern interior designs are easy to clean, well-insulated, energy efficient and fitted with alarms and security features. Only 40 years earlier 27 per cent of houses shared or lacked a bath or shower, but newly built accommodation often had two or more bathrooms.

Changes in society in recent years had resulted in an acute need to adapt buildings and the urban environment to meet people's needs. It was argued that women use the city environment more than men, spending more time walking and interacting there, and so understand its problems better. Furthermore, it is said that female architects are better able to communicate with clients and have a better understanding of their needs.

One of the most highly regarded female architects is Eva Jiricna. Born in Prague, she has worked in London since 1969. Her stylish monochrome interiors of shops, bars and restaurants have been widely imitated. Some of her most notable work has been in Mayfair's Le Caprice restaurant (1981) and the interior of the Lloyd's Building (1985–86). Zaha Hadid from Iraq is also widely respected for her designs which included the 'Mind Zone' of the Millennium Dome with Gavin Turk, while in Tyneside, north-east England, Jane Darbyshire has designed a number of popular projects including schools, council houses and hospices.

Today, many women are involved in a range of projects, such as designing interiors for fashionable restaurants, bars, city-centre apartments, and working with local communities to improve some of the less attractive boroughs of Britain. At the same time, designs have become less brash and imposing, and more subtle. Minimal decoration, pale colours and natural materials are preferred, in a style which has become increasingly common in a variety of establishments, from Indian restaurants to insurance offices.

But the profession of architecture remains a traditional, male-dominated one. The Royal Institute of British Architects (RIBA) exists to advance architecture and validates courses in architecture in Britain. All its past presidents were male, as are over 90 per cent of current practising architects. The related professions of engineering and building are also male-dominated, and some critics argue this tendency creates 'masculine' architecture: monuments of strength that reflect power and prestige, and in which power is exercised predominantly by men.

Towards the new millennium economic confidence was high, the economy strong, and to celebrate the end-of-century a series of new projects was planned for London and other regions of Britain, in arts, sport, transport and culture. Some were projects built to mark the moment, but the majority were built in areas which badly needed improvement or 'regeneration' as was the case in east Manchester prior to the Commonwealth Games in 2002, and prior to the Olympic Games in Barcelona in 1992 and Athens in 2004, where new stadia, galleries, theatres, restaurants and shops have all been built both to attract people into the city for business and leisure, as well as to improve the quality of life for those already there.

254

The north and south bank 'show'

In the new millennium London has become one of the most exciting cities in the world for art and architecture, especially on the south bank of the Thames. Although development there was slower than on its north bank, the riverbank area on both sides is now full of high-profile old and new cultural sites. One of the most iconic monuments of the new century is the Millennium Dome, built in 1999 to the east of London at Greenwich. Designed by Richard Rogers and Partners, it recalls the 'Dome of Discovery', the centrepiece of the Festival of Britain in 1951. The huge 50-metre-high structure has a diameter of 320 metres and a circumference of one kilometre. A dozen 100-metre steel masts fastened by cables support a glass-fibre roof. Nearby is the Millennium Village at Greenwich, designed by Erskine and Thompson, a futuristic housing complex incorporating energy-efficient buildings built around communal gardens, with a recycling of water and other waste materials.

Heading west and closer to central London is a reconstruction of Shakespeare's Globe theatre, built near to the site of the original. The open-air stage presents a variety of traditional and modern works in surroundings which resemble a film set. Further along the same bank is the Tate Modern art gallery. This was originally Bankside Power Station (1947) designed by Sir Giles Gilbert Scott, who also designed the familiar red telephone box, as well as the Foreign Office building in central London and the mod-gothic Liverpool Cathedral. Bankside is a striking building of red brick, but its adaptation to a gallery has made it airy and light inside, with several floors, comprising galleries, cafés, education centres and a large bookshop of the arts. Opened in May 2000, it now exhibits the best of modern art from around the world, with works by Rodin, Dali, Picasso, Hirst, Hockney and others. But instead of exhibiting art by time periods, the work is themed, allowing the observer to compare the styles of different landscapes, still lifes, portraits and so on.

Outside the gallery is a slim, elegant footbridge by Norman Foster and Anthony Caro (2000), which connects the south bank to St Paul's Cathedral and the wealthiest square mile in Europe, the City. The bridge is 320 metres long and 4 metres wide, and offers spectacular views of the new architecture up and down the Thames. Passing further along the riverbank past the South Bank arts complex, the observer reaches the London Eye. The renowned riverside erection by David Marks and Julia Barfield consists of a large revolving wheel, which takes 30 minutes to make a full turn. From 135 metres up there is a view over 42 kilometres, from 32 capsules, each holding 25 people. It opened in 2000 and has been highly appreciated by people of all ages.

A few metres away on the south bank is the imposing neo-classical building of County Hall, which until the 1980s was the headquarters of the Greater London Council. It currently houses the Saatchi Gallery, which hosts various exhibitions of contemporary art, as well as Charles Saatchi's own collection. Nearby is Vauxhall Cross, the home of MI6, Britain's secret intelligence service. This striking, resolute building was designed by Terry Farrell, and opened in 1995 with several floors built below street level, and bomb-proof walls to protect the most sensitive areas. It is sometimes called 'Legoland' after its resemblance to the children's building bricks, and attracted almost as much public attention as the Saatchi Gallery when filming took place there for the James Bond film *The World is Not Enough*.

Across the river in Millbank is Tate Britain, and a short walk inland to the north is the British Museum, where the Great Court has been restored by Foster and Partners to make a large, two-acre plaza which is covered by an intricate glass roof. At its heart is the famous Reading Room, which has been used by authors such as Virginia Woolfe, Thomas Hardy, Rudyard Kipling, Oscar Wilde and Karl Marx. Adorning it is a polished stainless steel sculpture by Anish Kapoor. But one of the newest, striking and most talked about buildings north of the river is 30 St Mary Axe, which is better known as the 'Gherkin' for its unusual, vegetable-like shape. Distinctive and playful, the 590-metre-high building was designed by Foster and Partners for the Swiss insurance company Swiss Re, and won the Stirling Prize in 2004 for its innovative design.

North by north-east

Outside London, the north-east of England has become a centre for world-class architecture to rival that of the capital, with several distinctive new buildings. Some of the most impressive are in Newcastle and Gateshead, which have recently experienced immense and traumatic economic changes. In the early 1980s, 50 per cent of all men were employed in shipbuilding, mining, steel and engineering. In 2004 the figure was just 3 per cent. The region was depressed, stripped of its identity and pride, but a series of new projects aimed at cultural regeneration has helped to restore its vitality. One of the most distinctive is the *Angel of the North*, a tall, imposing figure whose arms are held horizontally in the shape of a cross, standing at the side of the A1 road near Gateshead. Made in bronze and measuring 20 metres high, the *Angel* is a public sculpture designed by Anthony Gormley and built in the Tyneside steelyards in 1998. Many thought it bold and confident, but others found it sinister and Germanic, and local opponents argued the money could have been used for schools and hospitals. But it has since become a popular and successful symbol of the region in particular, and the north-east as a whole.

Nearby, Gateshead is an area not traditionally associated with modern art and architecture, but since the late 1990s the region has been trans-formed by a series of new projects, the most spectacular being around the waterfront of the River Tyne. Chief among these is the Baltic Exchange, which in 2002 was converted by Dominic Williams from a 1950s flour mill

Figure 10.4 Anthony Gormley's *Angel of the North*, Gateshead

into an art workshop and gallery, the largest contemporary art space outside London.

Nearby is the visually spectacular, shining, bulbous armadillo which is officially known as the Sage Music Centre (2004), designed by Foster and Partners with two concert halls, a rehearsal space and 25 music rooms, which together make it the biggest music resource in Britain. The Sage takes its name from its biggest corporate sponsor, a local company. At its heart is a 1,700-seat hall, which is intended to be one of the world's greatest concert venues. To achieve this, it has been built around the acoustics, with ceiling and wall inserts which can be adjusted according to the size of the audience, type of concert, instruments and so on. It stands near the Gateshead Millennium Bridge, built by Wilkinson-Eyre in 2001 to link the city to Newcastle. The spectacular new footbridge and cycle path is the first bridge across the River Tyne for 100 years, and opens using an ingenious tilting mechanism which makes the bridge pivot upwards to allow ships to pass underneath.

In Liverpool, Manchester and Birmingham, the architecture of manufacturing and heavy industry has been replaced by that of new service industries, reflecting wider trends around Britain. These now involve knowledge, commercial, cultural, sports and leisure sectors, which in recent years have played a steadily more important role in sustaining local communities. In Liverpool, the iconic Pierhead area on the waterfront of the River Mersey is the centre of regeneration plans, ahead of the city's role as European Capital of Culture in 2008, in which there will be a year-long festival of arts. The existing three Edwardian 'graces' or buildings which dominate the waterfront are complemented by architect Will Alsop's 'Fourth Grace', a spiral-shaped building on thin spindly legs, with a circular top floor which resembles a squashed doughnut, where shops, flats, bars, a hotel and a museum are all planned, to develop the area.

In nearby Manchester much has been done to help the city lose its 'Madchester' epithet of the 1990s. Buildings such as the Imperial War Museum North by Daniel Libeskind (2002), which resembles a shattered globe, Ian Simpson's icy, sea green 'mint lollipop' – the Urbis Centre for Urban Culture (2002) – and Arup Associates' City of Manchester stadium, built in 2002 for the Commonwealth Games and now the home of Manchester City FC, have all helped the city energise its cultural and knowledge sectors, as well as enhance the urban landscape.

In Scotland, the 'sails' of Edinburgh's Dynamic Earth Centre, an avant-garde construction, built on the site of an old brewery, tell the story of the Earth, using a mixture of real exhibits and virtual reality. In Glasgow, the Science Centre (2001) features interactive and multi-media exhibits, showing visitors how people and plants use their senses. In Edinburgh the Scottish Parliament building, designed by Enric Miralles in 2004 and featuring a distinctive roof like an upturned boat, opened three years late and massively over budget, making it, for all the wrong reasons, the most controversial building in Britain. A similar controversy surrounded the Welsh Assembly building in Cardiff by Richard Rogers, which opened in 2004 after Rogers had been dismissed from the project following escalating costs. The building is complemented by Jonathan Adams's Wales Millennium Centre (2004), a widely admired building made of stone and slate from quarries around Wales. Inside are auditoriums for music, theatre, opera, dance and ballet from around the world, which incorporate the latest high-tech acoustic and lighting systems. Above the foyer, an inscription reads 'Creu Gwir Fel Gwydr O Ffwrnais Awen' (In these stones horizons sing), a line by Gwyneth Lewis, a popular Welsh poet.

Around Britain, recreational facilities such as sports centres have also helped regenerate areas, often with funds provided by the National Lottery. Many football clubs have moved from their old, centrally located grounds to modern new ones, often on the edge of the city where land is cheap and access good. In London, the historic 'twin towers' of Wembley Stadium fell victim to the demolishers, as the ground which was built for the British Empire Exhibition in 1924 was completely redeveloped into a national 'superstadium'.

Despite the trend to modernity in the new millennium, architectural societies have demanded the preservation of early and unusual modernist buildings as part of Britain's architectural heritage, for example Cluster Block (Denys Lasdun, 1955), a modest but unusual early apartment tower in Bethnal Green, east London, and Trellick Tower (Erno Goldfinger, 1973) in west London, which have both been restored to create fashionable, high-quality accommodation.

But the conservation movement has to fight against opposition such as *Demolition*, a new programme on Channel 4 in 2005, which invited the public to nominate buildings it would like to see destroyed. However, many have objected, arguing it is a dangerous practice because public taste changes. Some buildings, once despised as ugly, are now highly regarded, for example the Midland Hotel next to St Pancras station in London, which has almost been demolished several times. Bankside Power Station also would have been demolished if such a list had existed in the past, not to mention the Brutalist enclave of the South Bank arts complex. The finality of demolition mirrors the finality of a death sentence; once demolished the building can never return. But times change and so do public taste and the kinds of buildings people want to see, live, work and play in. Public taste is fickle, and not to be trusted.

Discussion topics and activities

1   What differences do you see between modern architecture in Britain and that of your country? Think about residential accommodation, public buildings, and cultural/leisure facilities, their size, age and style.

259

2 Choose either an individual artwork, an art exhibition or a building with which you are familiar, and write a review of it for a magazine. Say what you like/dislike about it and why.

3 How has architecture changed in your town/country in recent years? What changes and influences can you identify? Are they similar to those in Britain. Do architects build what people want and like? Are people too concerned with protecting the architectural past?

4 How do you think environmental design can affect people's behaviour?

5 What pictures did your parents have on the wall when you were a child? What did they represent? Would you have them in your home now? Why/why not?

6 Which buildings that you know in your town/city would you like to demolish, and why?

7 Do you think art should confront and shock, or should it comfort and reassure?

Suggested further reading

Books

Biggs, L. and Elliot, D. (1987) *Current Affairs: British Painting and Sculpture in the Eighties*, Oxford: Museum of Modern Art.

British Art in the Twentieth Century: The Modernist Movement (1987) London: The Royal Academy of Arts.

Cocroft, W. and Thomas, R. (2005) *Cold War: Building for Nuclear Confrontation 1946–89*, London: English Heritage Pubications

Collings, M. (1997) *Blimey*, Cambridge: 21.

Durant, D. (1992) *Handbook of British Architectural Styles*, London: Barrie & Jenkins.

Gardiner, J. *From the Bomb to the Beatles: The Changing Face of Postwar Britain 1945–65*, London: Collins and Brown.

Glancey, J. (1991) *New British Architecture*, London: Thames & Hudson.

HRH, The Prince of Wales (1989) *A Vision of Britain: A Personal View of Architecture*, London: Doubleday.

Hayes, J. (1991) *The Portrait in British Art*, London: National Portrait Gallery.

Hughes, R. (1991) *The Shock of the New: Art and the Century of Change*, London: Thames & Hudson.

Hutchinson, M. (1989) *The Prince of Wales: Right or Wrong? An Architect Replies*, London: Faber & Faber.

Jencks, C. (1988) *The Prince, the Architects and New Wave Architecture*, London: Rizzoli International.

Kent, S. (2003) *Shark Infested Waters: The Saatchi Collection of British Art in the 90s*, London: Philip Wilson Publishers.

Long, K. (2004) *New London Interiors*, London: Merrell Publishers

Lucie-Smith, E. (1988) *The New British Painting*, Oxford: Phaidon.

Moffat, N. (1995) *The Best of British Architecture 1980–2000*, London: E & FN Spon.

Powell, K. (2004) *New London Architecture*, London: Merrell.

Rosenthal, N. (1998) *Sensation: Young British Artists from the Saatchi Collection*, London: Thames & Hudson.

Russell, J. (1993) *Francis Bacon*, London: Thames & Hudson.

Silverstone, R. (ed.) (1996) *Visions of Suburbia*, London: Routledge

Spalding, F. (1986) *British Art Since 1900*, London: Thames & Hudson.

The Vigorous Imagination: New Scottish Art (1987) Edinburgh: The Scottish Gallery of Modern Art.

Walker, D. (1982) *The Architecture and Planning of Milton Keynes*, London: Architectural Press.

Journals

Of several journals dedicated to modern British art, *Art Monthly* is the oldest surviving periodical. It is particularly strong on young British art and is intelligent, witty and up to date. The *Art Review* also provides commentary on contemporary art.

The *Architectural Review* was started in 1896 and is the leading British architecture magazine. It appears monthly and has contributions by prominent British architects.

The *Architects' Journal* covers topics of current importance, carries news and reviews, and pays attention to conservation issues. It appears weekly.

Details of each building listed by English Heritage can be found in some 2,000 volumes. They are now available on a computerised database and can be consulted at the offices of the Royal Commission on the Historical Monuments of England, in Swindon and London.

Glossary

accent

Accent refers to the type of pronunciation a person speaks with. In contrast, *dialect* refers to differences in grammar and vocabulary. In Britain, both accent and dialect may give clues about not only the person's background but also their general level of education. Those who use them most are generally NORMS (non-mobile, rural, male speakers).

Establishment, the

In the 1960s it was widely believed that Britain was controlled by a small number of wealthy individuals who had been to elite public schools and universities. They included the royal family and others who held key positions in the Church, government and armed forces. However, the concept has little use today when new types of unelected bodies such as the World Bank, the IMF and powerful media figures also hold great power and are able to influence official policy.

Ealing comedies

A distinctive range of comedy films produced at the Ealing Studios in London especially between 1948 and 1955, which typically featured the main group subverting authority or rebelling against the ruling class.

heritage films

The term is often used to describe a genre of films which strongly reflect conservative values of nationalism, patriotism and nostalgia for the days of British imperial greatness. The style has been frequently represented by the team of Merchant–Ivory in the 1980s, whose *A Room with a View* exemplifies the trend. However, another view claims the glorious, romantic past is fundamentally false, as the British Empire was a façade for an exploitative and sometimes cruel occupation. A stronger view argues it is a flawed attempt to represent a British cultural identity, one which is maintained because it consistently sells well with audiences at home and abroad.

hi-tech

A style in design and architecture which uses advanced technology and lightweight, flexible materials, such as steel, glass, aluminium. Unlike in earlier styles, the mechanical aspects of the building, such as pipes, lifts and air-conditioning systems, are sometimes displayed on the outside. The style has been exploited by Richard Rogers and Norman Foster among others.

IRA

The Irish Republican Army (IRA) is an organisation of Irish Nationalists dedicated to the establishment of a United Ireland, which was increasingly active in Britain from the late 1960s when British troops patrolled the streets of many Northern Irish cities.

'kitchen sink' drama

A style of play popular in the 1950s, a time when there was a new spirit of openness in society, and a desire in the arts to offer authentic representations of it. The 'kitchen sink' style put the lives of the poor and ordinary to the forefront, in drama as well as in television, film and art, before becoming absorbed into the mainstream of the 1960s, along with other elements of social realism.

Macpherson Report

This was a report in 1999 on the racist murder in 1993 of Stephen Lawrence, who was stabbed by a group of white youths in south London. The initial investigation was held to be inadequate, and following a judicial enquiry announced by the Labour government, the former High Court judge Sir William Macpherson found the police investigation showed professional incompetence, failed leadership and a catalogue of errors due to 'institutional racism' within the force. The report severely damaged race relations in Britain.

magic realism

Magic realism is a genre of writing which originated in South America, especially in the works of Gabriel Garcia Márquez, whose novel *One Hundred Years of Solitude* mixes extravagant fantasy with factual reality, partly in a playful way, but also in response to the manipulation of fact and fiction in South American politics by totalitarian regimes. It is probably not coincidental that in Britain the style was exploited in the 1980s

264

and early 1990s – notably by Salman Rushdie, Angela Carter, Graham Swift and Peter Carey – when for many people, what the Thatcher government said about society was very different from the reality of living in it.

moral panics

From time to time a particular kind of behaviour suddenly is treated as sensational and problematic by the government and the mass media, even though it has been present all along. In Britain, moral panics have often been encouraged by the political right, in order to criticise the left for its alleged incompetence. Some of the best-documented examples include studies of Teds, mods and rockers, muggers, New Age travellers and asylum seekers.

National Front

A small, far-right political organisation founded in 1966 and dedicated to the expulsion of non-white immigrants from the UK, as well as the reintroduction of capital punishment for certain offences.

neo-classical

This describes buildings from the early nineteenth to early twentieth century in the classical styles of ancient Greece and Rome. These included many civic and commercial buildings, such as town halls, banks and train stations which emphasised civic power and pride, as well as reaffirming the kind of society that the local government wanted to create.

neo-vernacular

Since the late 1980s there has been a trend in architecture to design types of houses which are traditional in appearance, having the 'look' of houses from perhaps 50–100 years earlier, but are modern in features and comforts. These are sensitive to their (often rural) environment, and popular with house-buyers, who generally prefer the look of older houses.

New Brutalism

A severely functional style of architecture, characterised by smooth, stark surfaces and sharp angles, which imposes itself on the environment and observer in a kind of architectural anti-aesthetic. In Britain the style was commonly found in local authority housing blocks of the 1950s and 1960s and the National Theatre complex, designed by Denys Lasdun. However, the reputation of such buildings suffered as they were often built quickly and cheaply, and concrete as a building material soon went out of fashion.

outing

During the 1980s and 1990s there was a reaction against what many saw as the hypocrisy of undeclared homosexuals in positions of power, who had spoken out against gay equality in the Church and elsewhere.

'Outing' them involved publicly declaring that the person in question was in fact gay.

pirate radio
Pirate radio refers to radio stations broadcasting illegally. In the mid-1960s many broadcast rock music from ships in the Thames estuary and in the North Sea, exploiting a legal loophole, which left them in international waters outside British legal jurisdiction. Today, pirate radio stations are more likely to be found in apartment blocks in urban areas.

political correctness
Many linguists believe that language shapes attitudes and behaviour, and during the 1980s there was a move to change language use in order to promote equality and avoid giving offence to groups such as women, gays, the disabled and ethnic minorities. Local authorities and other official bodies have attempted to promote political correctness by avoiding the use of language which could reinforce stereotyped thinking or cause offence, for example words with the suffix 'man' were altered to person, thus 'chairman' became chairperson, and some female forms such as actress, air hostess and spinster fell out of use.

political left/left wing
Since the nineteenth century British politics has been divided into two main groups, the left and the right, which have their roots in philosophies of the eighteenth and nineteenth centuries. The basic premise of the 'left' was that a better, fairer society could be achieved through the redistribution of wealth from rich to poor, and that social problems were largely attributable to social inequality. A more extreme view wanted to see the imposition of a communist society, in which, theoretically at least, everyone would be equal and nobody exploited; there would be no private business or private property; and elections would be unnecessary. This was largely the belief of Karl Marx (1818–83) and Marxist ideology, which divided the world until the 1990s. Although Marx lived and worked in Britain for some years, his works found little favour. The Labour Party was committed to some Marxist principles until the 1990s, such as the nationalisation of major industries, for example, coal, steel and transport.

political right/right wing
In contrast to the political left, the right was an early political view based on philosophies of the eighteenth and nineteenth centuries, which believed that a better society could be created with small government, strong law, low taxes and free enterprise. This found its maximum expression in recent times with 'Thatcherism' (see below).

soap opera
The term 'soap opera' was imported from America in the 1950s where mini-series with lots of drama, domestic conflict and crises were sponsored

by detergent manufacturers who used the commercial breaks to advertise their products, primarily to housewives watching daytime television.

social realism
Social realism emerged in the 1950s, with new works of theatre, literature, poetry and art, television plays and soap operas aiming to represent society in a more realistic way. It marked the beginning of the British 'new wave' in a movement which was influenced by the 'documentary' style developed in Britain in the late 1930s.

spin/spin doctors
Spin and spin doctors were a new aspect of 1990s media and public relations. The act of preparing and managing political or corporate information in the best possible light is known as 'spin'. The mass media frequently spin news to make it eye-catching, controversial or sensational; political parties spin news so as to avoid damage and present themselves in the most acceptable way. Those who 'spin' the news are known as 'spin doctors'.

suburbia
Suburbia is a generic name for areas of the city between the centre and the countryside. Most people in Britain live in the suburbs, and increasingly work there too. In recent years suburban life has been the subject of study, as an area once known for its limited interest and the narrow-mindedness of its conformist inhabitants is recognised as one far more varied and liberal than researchers initially suspected.

tabloid
This is a print industry term meaning 'compressed'. For many years it referred to smaller sized newspapers which were generally more sensational press with a wide appeal. They had shorter articles and sentences and often used informal vocabulary and slang. However, from around 2000, several of the larger, 'broadsheet' newspapers began to appear in a smaller, tabloid size, in the belief that many readers found the format practical and preferable. Papers such as the *Independent*, *The Times* and the *Guardian* now appear in smaller formats, and the term is no longer synonymous with 'low quality' press.

Thatcherism
Thatcherism refers to the ideology and practices of the Tory government under Margaret Thatcher between 1979 and 1990. It involved cutting public spending on social welfare and arts projects, a vast programme of privatisation of almost all state-controlled industries, and liberating market forces, together with a strong police force to keep in check the inevitable social consequences. Abroad, Thatcher's foreign policy included a tough anti-communist/socialist stance and much closer ties with the USA.

Thatcher frequently expressed her personal belief in the need to return to values of thrift, enterprise and the family, often referred to as 'Victorian values'. Her autocratic style and strength were enough to carry forward her programmes until she was finally dislodged by her own party following economic recession, the introduction of the poll tax and internal divisions over closer ties with Europe.

Thatcherism profoundly affected British society not only in the 1980s, but also through into the twenty-first century, as business values in the arts and society have since become mainstream. On the other hand, so-called 'Victorian' values have been largely ignored as society has become more tolerant, plural and liberal.

Tory
The Conservative Party is often referred to as the Tory Party.

youth culture
In the post-war period British youth culture has frequently been characterised by gangs and groups with specific values, attitudes, beliefs, behaviour, clothes, language, drugs, music and so on. Essentially youth culture refers to a *style* which is distinct from that of the dominant culture. Since the 1950s many youth cultures have been related to youth and deviancy, for example 'Teddy Boys', 'mods', 'rockers', 'punks' and 'yardies'. Their existence mainly among the working class is said to have provided a solution to their failure to adjust to mainstream society, or a rejection/ contempt for the values of the dominant class.

However, since the 1990s the 'tribalism' of British youth appears to have declined. According to some theories, this reflects the disappearance of labour-intensive manual industries and a decline in oppositional politics of left and right, as well as the development of a multiracial society, which together have contributed to a breakdown of traditional class divisions. At the same time, the public has become both more tolerant and increasingly familiar with the tendency of the mass media to exaggerate events, resulting in lower levels of interest and the removal of the media's role as an 'amplifier' of youth culture.

Index

Routledge History

British Civilization
6th edition
John Oakland

The sixth edition of this highly praised textbook has been rigorously updated and revised.

British Civilization provides a comprehensive introduction to a wide range of aspects of today's Britain, including its country and people, politics and government, education, the economy, the media, arts and religion.

It includes:

- discussion of recent developments and topics of specific interest in British society at the moment such as GM foods, immigration and Britain's relationship with the US and the EU and the war against terror
- new illustrations, cartoons, diagrams and graphs and tables
- expanded chapters
- a companion website.

British Civilization is a vital introduction to the crucial and complex identities of Britain.

For supplementary exercises, questions and tutor guidance, go to www.routledge.com/textbooks/0415365228.

Hb: 0–415–36521–X/978–0–415–36521-5
Pb: 0–415–36522–8/978–0–415–36522-2

Available at all good bookshops
For ordering and further information please visit:
www.routledge.com

Routledge History

British Cultural Studies
3rd Edition
Graeme Turner

British Cultural Studies

AN INTRODUCTION | GRAEME TURNER | THIRD EDITION

British Cultural Studies is a comprehensive introduction to
the British tradition of cultural studies. Turner offers an
accessible overview of the central themes that have
informed British cultural studies: language, semiotics,
Marxism and ideology, individualism, subjectivity and
discourse. Beginning with a history of cultural studies,
Turner discusses the work of such pioneers as Raymond
Williams, Richard Hoggart, E.P. Thompson, Stuart Hall and
the Birmingham Centre for Contemporary Cultural Studies.
He then explores the central theorists and categories of
British cultural studies: texts and contexts; audience;
everyday life; ideology; politics, gender and race.

The third edition of this successful text has been fully revised and updated to
include:

- How to apply the principles of cultural studies and how to read a text
- An overview of recent ethnographic studies
- Discussion of anthropological theories of consumption
- Questions of identity and new ethnicities
- How to do cultural studies, and an evaluation of recent research
  methodologies
- A fully updated and comprehensive bibliography.

Hb: 0–415–25227–X / 978–0–415–25227–0
Pb: 0–415–25228–8 / 978–0–415–25228–7

Available at all good bookshops
For ordering and further information please visit:
www.routledge.com